Blazing the Trail

Blazing the Trail

Way Marks in the Exploration of Symbols

Victor Turner

Edited by Edith Turner

THE UNIVERSITY OF ARIZONA PRESS

Tucson & London

The University of Arizona Press
Copyright © 1992
The Arizona Board of Regents
All rights reserved
⊚ This book is printed on acid-free, archival-quality paper.
Manufactured in the United States of America

97 96 95 94 93 92   6 5 4 3 2 1

Library of Congress Cataloging-in-Publication Data

Turner, Victor Witter.
    Blazing the trail : way marks in the exploration of symbols /
Victor Turner : edited by Edith Turner.
        p.   cm.—(The Anthropology of form and meaning)
    Includes bibliographical references and index.
    ISBN 0-8165-1291-4 (cloth : acid-free paper)
    1. Ethnology. 2. Symbolism.   I. Turner, Edith L. B., 1921–
II. Title. III. Series.
    GN452.T85   1992
    306.4—dc20   91-42776
                                                                 CIP

British Cataloguing-in-Publication Data
A catalogue record for this book is available from the British Library.

The Ndembu term for a ritual symbol is *chinjikijilu*, a landmark or blaze (derived from *kujikijila*, to blaze a trail by cutting marks on trees)—that is, a means of connecting known with unknown territory. The Ndembu compare the ritual symbol to the trail the hunter blazes in order to find his way back from unexplored bush to his village.

Contents

Prologue: Exploring the Trail

In this second volume of collected papers by Victor Turner published by the University of Arizona Press the theme is symbolism and ritual, in the setting of a variety of cultures and a variety of genres of ritual. To understand what is behind the variety, I will sketch something of the braided form of Turner's widely ranging search for anthropological understanding. As I wrote in the prologue to *On the Edge of the Bush* (1985:8), Turner often approached what he felt was his main goal obliquely, tacking like a sailboat (or in a knight's move in chess, as he would have said), first in one direction, then another.

The essays in this volume start with a key article on symbolism, "Encounter with Freud," in which Turner applies Freud's analysis to African ritual. Here we can trace how Turner's reading of Freud's *The Interpretation of Dreams* in 1953 provided much of the vocabulary needed for a breakthrough in the analysis of symbols (embodiment, affective meaning, bipolarity and multivocality of symbols). The next essay is "Death and the Dead in the Pilgrimage Process," written in 1973. By this time Turner had gone through several changes in his thinking. In 1957 he began his anthropological writing by putting together the social structuralist *Schism and Continuity*; in *Chihamba the White Spirit* (1962) his outlook changed to that of a mystic. He was already developing as a symbologist in "Ritual Symbolism, Morality, and Social Structure" (1961) and "Symbols in Ndembu Ritual" (1964a). In 1963 he turned to an interest in rites of passage with the path-breaking article "Betwixt and Between" (1964b); he subsequently wrote as a strong processualist in "Ritual Aspects of Conflict Control" (1966). From structuralist to mystic to symbologist to liminality theorist to political anthropologist, there were many changes; all, it should be noted, were within the bounds of African or tribal material.

In *The Ritual Process* (1969) Turner reached a new turning point, an attention to the ways of the West; he began to braid into his work some of his research on Western culture, Western history. It is that development which the articles in this book document—essays in which he relates his theories to culture in the historic period. In Chapter 1 Turner freely uses Freud's analysis in African ritual, showing how structuralism is not enough. In Chapter 2 he examines pilgrimage as a symbolic ritual. In Chapter 3 he lays out a theoretic framework for the genre that he terms the "liminoid," which describes the arts of the posttribal era, leisure pursuits, play—no longer in the matrix of religion. His further explorations enable him to compare African ritual to Dante's symbolism (Chapter 4). Next he compares African sacrifice to ancient Roman sacrifice (Chapter 5); then he branches out to an entirely different culture and lays bare the symbolism of a Japanese fire ritual (Chapter 6). Finally, in Chapter 7 he discusses the modern individual as a liminal being, often with play as his or her ritual.

The book represents an intellectual quest. Its place in contemporary anthropology is well indicated by John MacAloon (see also Babcock and MacAloon 1987), who discusses

> the lively intellectual and professional risks entailed by Turner's abandonment of the extended case study method in order to pursue the "liminoid genres" of pilgrimage and literature and to glean insights from all-too-brief field stays in various parts of the world. (This, after all, is the organizing theme of the volume: the possibilities and limits of comparative symbology.) Turner anguished over this himself and it brought him great criticism. . . . Turner suggests these problems openly in the texts herein, particularly in "Kannokura" [Chapter 6], and he struggles repeatedly to generate a language of contrasts between tribal and modern contexts. . . . [These issues] are more central and productive in anthropology today than in the 1970s; and Turner deserves more recognition for the distinctive contribution he made to constructing the problem of the Other as a compelling intellectual *conflict.*
>
>   . . . . When the current excesses of postmodernism, deconstructive ethnography, and other forms of anthropological navel-gazing have run their course, Turner's important rejection of subtler and more politically correct forms of exoticism will be rediscovered in the collective reorientation that must one day ensue. His genius resided precisely in his refusal to abandon the empiricist creed while contributing mightily to the hermeneutic turn. When we are done with neo-positivist nativisms on the

one side ("rational choice") and symbolic studies in which the subject
replaces the object ("critical cultural studies") on the other side, we are
going to have need of Turner again. I think this volume should serve to
prepare the way for this rediscovery, as much or more than it serves to
reassert the indubitable, namely Turner's "avant-gardism." (personal
communication)

These comments throw light on our explorations of the essays in this
volume. The book starts with an older strand in Turner's thinking: "Encounter with Freud: The Making of a Comparative Symbologist" (Chapter 1). At the outset Turner announces what has become the main theme
of this volume:

> It was no use ignoring this aggregate of individual symbols [in the
> Ndembu rituals he observed] and declaring that at any rate the "implicit
> aim" or "latent function" of ritual was "to promote or restore social
> cohesion" and "to reanimate the sentiments of solidarity on which the
> collective life depends". . . . The specificity of each symbol and their
> shifting combinations and permutations in performative ensembles pre-
> sented a challenge I could scarcely avoid. (pp. 3–4)

Turner then describes a simple episode of an Ndembu hunter praying to
his spirit; first he treats the episode in the Durkheimian fashion, in the
manner of the social structuralists, and then shows how this analysis is
insufficient for most of the symbolism. Therefore he turns to Freudian
analysis. Turner goes into detail: he uses the ideas of multivocality, projection, and cultural sublimation to explain the symbols "blood tree,"
"white clay," and others that find their place in the rite. These are symbols that possess not only social referents but also psychological ones,
and in some respects simply stand for themselves. Also, Turner defends
the whole episode from an overtight Freudian explanation, leaving the
matter open-ended for the possibility of religious explanations. Immediately the question of the limits of anthropology comes into focus.
Could there really be certain domains of humanity that are not material
for anthropologists? As an anthropologist, Turner believed, like the
Ndembu and Freud, that "the living truth . . . should be manifested"—
whatever the conclusions that truth may lead us to.

Turner ranged among different classes of facts: social facts with respect
to Durkheim, psychological facts with respect to Freud, nonrational facts
encompassing the paradox with respect to Kierkegaard (Turner taught
the works of all three at the Committee on Social Thought, Chicago). He
first read Kierkegaard on paradox in 1944, but his consciousness of the
implications of paradox was subsequently overlaid by the positivism of

his training in anthropology at University College, London. It surfaced later briefly in *Chihamba the White Spirit: A Ritual Drama of the Ndembu* (1962; reprinted in *Revelation and Divination* 1975a)—rather like the subject of that "revelation," the white hump of Kavula, the Ndembu thunder god, that surfaced from the earth in the forest at the climax of the major healing ritual of Chihamba. The god Kavula was both good and savage; his image was constructed by adepts, yet this *was* the thunder god; the neophytes "killed" him in an act of sacrifice with their rattles, yet they were "innocent" of murder.

The nature of the godhead is pure paradox, said Kierkegaard; these paradoxes had to remain in their strength as paradoxes and were not analyzable according to social-structural principles. It is a difficult question whether, as Jung asked, when one "reaches the bounds of scientific understanding, [crossing over into] the transcendental . . . no further scientific statements can be made" (Jung 1963:221). Jung was determined to include as scientific facts much that we would call occult, but he had trouble with his own resolve; although he said in one passage (1963:194) that the contents of psychic experience were real, in another he said, "The great advantage of the concepts 'daimon' and 'God' lies in making possible a much better objectification of the *vis-à-vis*, namely, a personification of it" (1963:337).

Are experiences of God real or invented in the mind or by society, clothed in personifications? One can trace in Victor Turner the same ambivalence, the mark of a searching mind. It can be seen how in an early essay, "Symbols in Ndembu Ritual" (written in 1957 and published in *Closed Systems and Open Minds*, 1964a) he created a self-denying ordinance (which he later broke through): that of relinquishing any anthropological rights to psychologistic interpretations of ritual, in order to deal only with social facts. Turner broke his rule, however, in *Chihamba the White Spirit* (1962); his self-enforced restrictions opened up at the same time that he became Catholic, and he interpreted the unnamed Ndembu demigod as an appearance of the divine unknowable.

It was at this time that Turner began to develop the concept of liminality. More closed areas of thought gave way once the process had started. "Liminality" arose out of his ponderings on Van Gennep's *The Rites of Passage* when he applied passage theory to the antistructural rituals and symbols of the circumcision camps among the Ndembu. The anomalous spirit dancer from ancient times that appeared in the seclusion period was liminal; the collectivity of men in a matrilineal society was antistructural. Liminality was also present in Turner's own rite of passage from England to America in 1964. He realized he had stumbled upon an anomaly in Durkheim's theory—it was that very betwixt-and-between liminal phase within rites of passage and its antistructure that had bothered him. Liminality was a social fact that was not a social fact. Turner discusses the difficulties in Chapter 7 of this volume.

Meanwhile our joint pilgrimage research began—a scheme that was originally designed as an investigation of the Mexican calendrical festival system, to be focused on an isolated northern mining city, Zacatecas. It was to be a single-city study with the aim of first mastering local social structures and tracing factions and social drama patterns as a foundation for later ritual studies. However, as among the Ndembu, the character of the field locale laid its own demands upon the character of the fieldwork. When we arrived in Mexico, it was the pilgrimage system that one noticed; it filled our eyes from horizon to horizon. It would have been pigheaded to deny it and stick to the Zacatecas scheme. So we went with the people down the pilgrimage routes, first to the Villa de Guadalupe in Mexico City, then exploring many other shrines and their ritual workings in Mexico for two seasons, then for two seasons more to the shrines of Ireland and Europe—in all, from 1969 to 1972. A popular ritual genre had captured us.

I have included in this volume (Chapter 2) an early result of this research, "Death and the Dead in the Pilgrimage Process," a paper given as the plenary address at the Annual Meetings of the American Academy of Religion in 1973 (first published in 1975)—in which Turner connects western European folk beliefs with views of the spirit world among pagan peoples. It was one of the first times Turner compared primitive and modern cultures, tracing in pilgrimage devotions many links with old pagan fertility customs. It is the dead—the saints, the Holy Souls, and other spirits—who can provide fertility and health for the living, just as ancestor spirits at one time did for the Ndembu. Here Turner uses fieldwork from Knock, Ireland, that consists of additional material over and above what went into the later book we produced on pilgrimage (Turner and Turner 1978).

In this essay Turner also deals with structure and antistructure in modern society, pointing out how in the modern world, churchgoers often find regular services more concerned with structure than with liminality, so that they welcome the antistructural trip to a faraway pilgrimage shrine. It is interesting to note that anthropologists studying tourism have seen the vacation tour as a quest for antistructure—in their terms, "the Other"—in the form of faraway places inhabited by exotic people apparently free of the tourists' own metropolitan structural difficulties (Cohen 1982).

"Death and the Dead in the Pilgrimage Process" contains one of Turner's earliest uses of the concept "liminoid," referring to those liminal-like genres carried out in the modern world in leisure time, genres no longer associated with the liminal betwixt-and-between phases of rites of passage. Examples of the old liminal genres are the parading of monsters in initiation rites, ritual and temple drama, secret symbols of the society's religion, accounts of supernatural events, ritual inversion, music, and religious graphic arts. The new genres, deriving from the old ones but now freed from the integument of religion, consist of carnivals, spectacles, major sports events, folk drama, national theater, the novel, poetry, the fine arts, and—because they are leisure-time activities—pilgrimages. The difference between these two types of genre, liminal and liminoid, is further discussed in Chapter 3, a study of the liminoid.

In Chapter 3, "Variations on a Theme of Liminality" (first given at the Wenner-Gren Conference on Secular Ritual in 1974), Turner reveals his explorations into the liminoid and adds another strand to the ever-crossing braid of his thought: that of play, to which he often returned. First he shows how in preindustrial societies ritual was regarded as a special kind of work. He demonstrates that play (also dance, drama, what we call entertainment) was often part of this ritual work, and then proceeds to discuss leisure, a quite different mode, existing in industrial societies. His interest in sport as part of the leisure mode was first spurred by John MacAloon's study of the Olympic Games; his interest in theater pursuits was rekindled by the Japanese scholar Araki Michio and later by the Western theater scholar Richard Schechner; and his interest in carnival was stimulated by Roberto da Matta. In this liminal/liminoid distinction he now possessed a theoretical base for understanding the nonstructural, often metacritical activities of our age.

At this point Turner was granted a liminal phase of peace and communitas at the Institute for Advanced Studies at Princeton, where he produced the papers on Dante and on sacrifice. Both included his Ndembu fieldwork on the ritual of Chihamba as comparative material. The first was entitled "African Ritual and Western Literature: Is a Comparative Symbology Possible?" (Chapter 4 in this book) and was delivered as the Spencer Trask Lecture at Princeton University in 1975. The second was "Sacrifice as Quintessential Process: Prophylaxis or Abandonment?" (Chapter 5 in this book), read at the Meetings of the American Society for the Study of Religion at Princeton University in 1976. Both these titles were in the form of a question. The first asked if symbolic universals exist; the second suggested two kinds of universals in sacrifice: prophylaxis—sacrifice as a kind of insurance against misfortune—and abandoning oneself and all one has to the divine. This latter theme was largely overlooked by Henri Hubert and Marcel Mauss, whose *Essay on Sacrifice* has been the starting point of anthropological discussion on the subject.

The subject of comparison in the first essay, Dante's *Divine Comedy*, was the topic of a course that Turner gave in the Committee on Social Thought at the University of Chicago in 1974. He had previously discussed Dante with John Freccero, a Dante scholar with whom he became friends when he was at Cornell. Why Dante? I believe that Dante underwent the supreme near-death experience and returned to tell the tale— like Bunyan and St. John of Patmos. Dante's journey, Turner realized, was an initiation and a pilgrimage. Turner compares the initiation ritual of Chihamba with Dante's initiation in purgatory aided by Virgil, his guide in that liminal realm. Throughout the essay Turner uses anthropological concepts to understand Dante's words—those words of poetry that emerge in a peculiarly musical tranced beat, a music we can hear even through Turner's analysis giving us a feeling of fresh air on that Resurrection morning on the shores of Mount Purgatory.

Turner points to the universal types of workings in the symbols of the African and Renaissance Italian cultures: multivocality, the unification of disparate significata, condensation, and polarization, within symbols themselves. He also finds in both many Lévi-Straussian binary oppositions and, deeper still, the general theme of the slain and resurrected deity. The fundamental difference between Chihamba and Dante's *Purgatorio*, he points out, was that Chihamba was a ritual and that it consisted of work for the Ndembu—both oral and kinetic—while Dante's production was written poetry—a voluntary solitary undertaking, one might say "liminoid," basically an art production, with not even an imprimatur by the church to prove that it was religious. Nevertheless, universals are clearly traceable in both genres.

Turner undertook the second Princeton essay, on sacrifice (Chapter 5), with some hesitation. He did not want to write on sacrifice; he had never been particularly taken with the self-sacrificial life, being gregarious, fond of parties, and built on a generous scale. "Sacrifice? A sour subject," he said to me. But he made the sacrifice and buckled down, and came up with the original primitive form of sacrifice, whereby the slaying of the god (illogically) gives increase and healing, and results in that extraordinary unity of the spirit being, society, and nature that I myself experienced when I underwent Chihamba. After discussion of the Chihamba sacrifice, Turner deals with some contrasting examples: the prophylactic sacrifices of the Roman era, particularly one at Iguvium; a classic "obsessive ritual," performed for insurance against misfortune, on behalf of what we now call frame maintenance or, as religion itself has been scornfully termed, as "all-purpose social glue." The rites verged upon the ludicrous. This bloodthirsty, highly choreographed performance, featuring dozens of oxen, scores of pregnant sows, and other animals going to their deaths in neat rows, ought to appear in the movies as a costume drama complete with wicked priests and ending with the rescue of the beautiful girl by the enlightened hero. Read it and judge. You will prefer the sacrifice of abandonment.

"The Kannokura Festival at Shingu: The Symbolism of Sun, Fire, and Light" (Chapter 6, first published in 1983) is an example of careful scholarship written in a light tone of enjoyment. Turner's original subtitle was "Some Fieldnotes and Bookish Gleanings." He obviously pictured himself as one of those Japanese folklorists whom I met later in Japan, soaked with old lore and seeming to have personally known the first emperor. This paper is symbology pure and simple. Turner participated in the festival, limping arthritically up the mountain in the wake of excited white-garbed men and boys carrying torches. He analyzed the color symbolism and other symbolic aspects using his own method, exploring the positional and operational levels for the meanings, as in the case of "redness" and "whiteness." He found himself investigating a world of ancient myth, for he saw that the fire ritual was stratified—that is, it revealed various levels of ancient connotations. But he found that "if we are to use the geological metaphor of 'stratification,' it is that of mobile 'plates' rather than of static 'layers.' The past is never quiet or frozen in the form of major rituals." The fire ritual in fact broke through its "strata" year after year.

The paper "Morality and Liminality" (Chapter 7 in this book) was written in response to a request. The department of religious studies at the University of Southern California wanted Turner to try out his anti-structuralism on the subject of "morality," and arranged for him to deliver the Firestone Lecture of 1980 on the topic "Morality and Liminality." He took the assignment very seriously and produced a commentary that plumbs the foundation of anthropological thought. In addition to the critique of Durkheim's concept of society mentioned above, he asked *whose* society was the one Durkheim called "God." One's own nation? If so, is that not chauvinistic? And if not one's own nation, and instead the whole of humanity is "God," what about the orthodoxy of one's own nation that Durkheim's "society" was supposed to defend? Turner also wrote on Burridge's distinction (1979) between "person" and "individual," upholding Burridge's term "person" to imply a "someone," an occupant of roles and statuses, while the individual is a "'no one'—who may hold particular nonconformist perceptions of truth that result in conscious and independent moral discrimination and innovation." Does that kind of "individual" end up lonely and under stress, or is she or he a creative hero or heroine? We tend to like this "individual" better than the "person."

Turner quotes Durkheim in this essay, showing that in Durkheim's ideal "religion of humanity" the individual would be more a product of society than its cause. No, said Turner, the individual is a source—and I myself comment that even a look at a tiny baby will tell you that. Anthropologists do not go all the way with Durkheim. Clearly there are passages in his writings that they do not take too seriously. For instance, Durkheim wanted to eliminate symbols, rites, temples, and priests from his "religion," which would be one of authority, not of culture. But anthropologists grant him the achievement of revealing the multiplex social bonds we all have with one another—created, Durkheim implies, in that very sacred realm which society has nurtured.

Turner's essay on morality and liminality is exploratory and free in tone. It roves into the field of play, with a discussion of the work of Evan Zuesse, turns to myth, swings suddenly back toward Durkheim, and moves on to a poem by Rainer Maria Rilke on Orpheus. Turner is chasing the vagrant buzzing "morality" into all its corners and out again— this is not the "morality" we get so tired of hearing about in church. He sums up thus: "Society, morality, and religion are bound up together as aspects of the Latin word *mores*, which maintains the contradictory notions of custom and habit based on group pressure, and the creative morality which may result from individual choice." Again, there are dark depths in this chapter as it swings back and forth. Toward the end Turner goes further still: "The 'deep ground' of the mystics must be sought forward, not backward." He continues, "And one suspects that the way forward is really quite simple. As simple as clowns"—and here at the end Turner indulges in play, quoting a delightful passage by Fellini about his clowns. So much for morality.

In an unpublished manuscript entitled "Sacrifice, Ritual, and Theater," written in 1982, Turner described the clown figure thus:

A kind of "mentifact" of popular creativeness in the public liminality of great cyclical rituals. In many rituals, the symbolic type Ritual-Clown may be the agent and vehicle of social self-criticism. In a recent article Don Handelman (1981:321–370) discusses the attributes and affinities of the clown whose role is confined to ritual contexts such as Pakistani wedding rites, Mayo Easter rites, Hopi rites of the summer solstice, and the Tewa Dance of Man. Handelman argues that this symbolic type is "clumsily integrated, but with strong connotations of movement, of motion, and of fertility. Internally, this type is composed of sets of contradictory attributes, among which it oscillates without stabilizing itself or making its composition homogeneous—as are, for example, the Hopi deity-types. In a sense, the clown-type straddles a boundary within itself, which it is dissolving continuously. So long as this figure is true to type, it evokes inconsistencies and ambiguities of meaning. The type is a mechanism of reflexivity, which exists in an on-going state of self-transformation. Hence it is a powerful solvent and a representation of 'process.' These attributes, and the affinity of the type to boundaries, enable it to shift ritual occasions through their sequential phases."

Turner claimed that play is a neurological process that plays inside the brain—constituting the most conscious, light-fingered, and somehow independently directed part of its workings. What is that "somehow"? A trick the human material has learned in order to liberate itself? Maybe an even more important matter than the liberation that is provided by our upright stature? With Turner it is clearly linked to antistructure. He included "symbolic types" among the sacred objects of the liminal phase of ritual, relating all such objects to the deepest processes of the brain: "The ritual clown has something of the numinosity, the *mysterium tremendum et fascinans* of true symbolic types" (Turner unpublished, 1982). Light-fingered yet numinous? The playful clown is a paradox. Turner went on to say in the same unpublished work:

> By scanning liminal processes and phenomena, we may, if we are lucky and percipient, obtain information, like the traces left by the movement of basic particles in a cloud chamber, about modalities of experience which normally escape the nets of cognitive theorizing and quotidian observation, valuable though these may be. Jakob Boehme, the Silesian mystic, once wrote: "In Yea and Nay all things consist"—and in centrally liminal ritual events we may sometimes glimpse the visible shadow of that invisible "Nay," counterstroke to all "positive" structural assertion. Roy Rappaport expresses a similar notion in *Ecology, Meaning and Religion* (1974:205): "In the liturgical sign, which is multivocalic and bipolar, which may be at once iconic, indexical, and denotative, and which is embodied in something substantial—a cross, a flag, a posture—there seems to be a union of a concatenated mass of simple significations into a single but complex representation. Once such representation is brought into being it may be treated as *being* what is symbolized." A symbol that stands for itself.

Turner continually prevents his discourse from expending itself on ideal forms or high religions. I give here a short piece from about 1980, which I wrote down as Turner said it. It throws light on all that he really thought about the common populace and the dead hand of the upper classes, whether neo-Marxists or theologians.

The partial, the limited, the incomplete is our subject matter—it includes subjective experience. Our aim isn't the absolute, the pure world mind. Anthropologists live in an immense arboretum of varying growths, all different, none complete and ideal, none to be cultivated above all else. When we try this kind of cultivation, we bind ourselves away from some part of life; it and we die to each other. Re-ligion [sic] has been operating like this up to now. World beliefs show they are aware of their mistake and are guilty about it. Tragic views of nature and culture are rife—the true simply being and the false expressed.

Structuralism clasps the tragedy to its breast and sets it in concrete—having an absolute eternal tendency toward entropy. But world rituals go the other way, they melt and melt that barrier down, they get back to the quick, they show the flash of the true, expressed. Anthropologists have been scared of these moments, and are happy to bewail their ephemerality and paucity of effectiveness to right the manifold sufferings of humankind. The fact remains that ritual techniques are used, indefatigably; the seed of the true touch appears to be necessary for each generation to be able to go forward at all. Maybe the neo-Marxist structuralists criticize the Romantics because they themselves are too greedy for these moments and see them as a fata morgana, a mere will-o'-the-wisp, wishful thinking, opium. They yearn toward perfection like the Kantians, and are never satisfied, fed, and delighted by mere flashes of truth in the welter of imperfect life, as the common populace is.

This common populace continually gives birth to belief and ritual out of itself. The people are warned by theologians of various religions that it isn't they who produce God, but that God comes in from without and dwells in them. Or that they have to forswear their limited, imperfect selves, lose their odd and evil and grotesque character and become pure. Still the people, in some marvelous instinctive way, contract their collective body and calve; by a wonderful means of creation they give birth to god. This is whipped away from them immediately by the transcendentalists as if it were a bastard, and produced again in the halls of the great as the sexless Son of God. Godfrey Lienhardt shows this calving process in Africa [on pp. 147–148 of Divinity and Experience, 1961]. Just as a single cell divides and produces its mirror image—seen on TV as a swelling, trembling object, pausing on the verge of self-birth, then performing the act unhesitatingly before your eyes—so the Dinka with trouble and pain treat a sick man, to "isolate a particular Power which can be regarded as a subject of activity within him, from the self which is its object" . . . "the process of making manifest an 'image.'"

Maybe this process of calving the gods has to be unconscious or it wouldn't happen properly. Maybe the theologians are right not to let us look too closely. We're not looking at anything ordinary. Because we refer all our experience to the world of the ordinary and use our Western analytic minds upon it in our inquisitive way, we have what we've got, a world without magic and practically without sex. There has to be a hiatus, a privacy within ourselves, so that we can say, "not I but Jesus Christ," or "not I but the wind that blows through me"; and it is not just "myself *remembering* Khartoum" in the Dinka example [in which a man had been in prison in Khartoum; this experience caused the city to become a "Power" inside of him, something that required explicit acknowledgment. He acknowledged it by naming his child Khartoum; Lienhardt 1961:150], but "Khartoum as a disturbing agent upon me, a subject that acts." This is fascinating. In the same way you get Umbanda trance and all the possession cults. These, though, are content to exist and flourish in that forest, that jungle in which no one religion is in fact stamping out all the rest. They may try, but anthropology shouldn't be taken in. The fertility's there, the competition's natural, not ultimately tragic, for what continually happens is the new sprouting of belief, ritual, and communitas.

There is a hiatus, a privacy still existing in non-Western or simpler people, into which the full Western drive for perfection and control does not reach.

In the spring of 1983 Turner was invited to Israel as an Einstein Visiting Fellow of the Israel Academy of Sciences and Humanities, which was to be his last major visit and research area. There he read with enthusiasm about the Jewish mystical tradition. Jewish Kabbalists such as Mordechai Rotenberg would appear at our apartment and be closeted with him for hours. We would attend Hasid synagogues at Purim and watch the figures in black suits and hats dancing shoulder to shoulder, almost seeming to levitate. Later, at the pilgrimage to the tomb of Bar Yohai, attended by nearly 300,000 people, 17 researchers assembled and made their way up the hill to Meron along with the crowd, Turner among them, grumbling because of his arthritis. When they arrived outside the tomb, they gave him a folding chair. He sat with the beggars, every now and then sticking out his hand and saying, "Pity the poor anthropologist." Afterward, in the Jewish Moroccans' tents, he ate sacrificial lamb in the form of kebabs and drank arrack, savoring most of all the palpable communitas spirit of the gathering (E. Turner 1992).

A month later Turner was listening earnestly to robed Sufi Arab divines at Baka el Gharbiyya near the old Jordan border, hearing words that recalled to him his early reading of the Sufi poet Rumi. He was present at the Samaritans' passover on Mount Gerusim at the sacrifice of lambs, and talked with the green-robed high priest. Many of these times I saw him only at a distance because of the separation of the sexes in Middle Eastern ritual. On a previous visit he was with me struggling up the gravelly Via Dolorosa in Jerusalem with the anthropologist Don Handelman to visit the Holy Sepulcher, bowing arthritically to enter its extremely low door.

Here was more of a jungle of symbols than one man could ever deal with. Victor Turner blazed the trail of his explorations into that forest, marking his path and showing the readers the way to his finds. Thus his writing was itself a symbolic enterprise, both in the Ndembu sense—where "a trail blaze" means "a symbol"—and in our own.

Edith Turner

Blazing the Trail

1 Encounter with Freud: The Making of a Comparative Symbologist

Problems in the Analysis of Ritual Symbols

Each human culture has its own form and style, and these insist upon being recognized by the anthropological fieldworker. The Ndembu of northwestern Zambia, among whom I did about two and one-half years' fieldwork, from 1950 to 1954, invested much time, energy, and wealth in the performance of various kinds of rituals. I had entered the field as an orthodox British structural-functionalist, motivated by my mentors to collect data on social and political organization. But the genius of the culture gently nudged me toward the description and analysis of ritual behavior. At first, of course, I thought that I had adequate conceptual instruments for this task in the repertoire inherited from Comte and Feuerbach via Durkheim, Radcliffe-Brown, and Malinowski: the rich legacy of confluent positivism, materialism, and rationalism. In effect, these scholars held that ritual symbols and processes "reflected" or "expressed" social structure with more or less ideological deformation or disguise, and that social structure was a more or less distinctive arrangement of mutually dependent institutions and the institutional organization of social positions and/or actors which they imply.

But I was immediately confronted with the difficulty that many of the hundreds, even thousands, of distinguishable symbolic objects and actions I found in ritual performances seemed on the face of it to have little, if anything, directly to do with components of social structure as defined above. And it was no use ignoring this aggregate of individual symbols and declaring that at any rate the "implicit aim" or "latent function" of ritual was "to promote or restore social cohesion" and "to reanimate the sentiments of solidarity on which the collective life depends"—to paraphrase and coalesce dicta on ritual by the distinguished predecessors I have just named. The specificity of each symbol and their shifting combinations and permutations in performative ensembles presented a challenge I could scarcely avoid. I knew nothing of French cognitive structuralism at the time. My notion of "positional meaning" came mainly from Gestalt psychology.

A Performance of Hunting Ritual

Let me give an example of an extremely simple Ndembu ritual performance. Without drumming and singing such a performance would be called *chidyika*; with them (synechdochically) it would be called "drum" (*ng'oma*). It is not uncommon to see an Ndembu hunter standing before a forked tree branch known as *chishing'a* (Turner 1967:285–298), peeled of bark, planted in the earth, its extremities sharpened, and adorned with small portions of meat (on the tips or in the crotches). If you listen you will hear him upbraiding a dead hunter kinsman whom he believes to be somehow present in the *chishing'a*, which we may perhaps translate as "shrine," for failing to bring him animals to kill, or even for driving them from his path. There is no question here of a public collective ceremony; it is just a private individual apparently talking to himself before a mutilated tree outside his village.

But when we begin to learn the cultural vocabulary and to grasp its syntactical rules, we find that we are in the presence of quite an elaborate system of beliefs and practices. Moreover, we discover that the curious monologue we have intruded upon is only a phase or episode in a sequence of ritual activities, some of which involve a few cocelebrants and fellow hunters of our irate friend, and others of which involve a large concourse of persons of both sexes and all ages, only a few of them hunters. Furthermore, we note that these ritual episodes are intermittent, broken by periods of nonritualized time in which a hunter goes into the uninhabited woodlands and plains in search of game, and his fellow villagers pursue their ordinary avocations.

But let us, for the sake of analytical parsimony, focus on the simple episode first. It is this kind of behavior which induced me in an earlier work (1967:19) to follow a well-worn anthropological tradition and define ritual as "prescribed formal behavior for occasions not given over to technological routine, having reference to mystical beings or powers." Prescription and formality are found in the manner in which the shrine is constructed and in the hortatory style of address to the shade of the deceased. The hunter is not employing the technological routine of his craft, and he is addressing an entity he believes to exist, although not as ordinary living men exist—for the addressee is dead though sentient, invisible though potent.

But my formulation, I have come to see, is anything but adequate. It is a flat description of ritual action as it appears to an alien observer and says nothing about what ritual means to a native actor. Nor does it capture the transformative capacity of ritual—its competence, from the actor's standpoint, to raise him from a lower to a higher level of knowledge, understanding, or social being. (There was at the time no "state/context dependency" hypothesis mooted in anthropology.) Nor does it correctly characterize the component of spontaneity present in much of the ritual, its responsiveness to present circumstance, and its competence to interpret the current situation and provide viable ways of coping with contemporary problems.

Probably our own culture has misconstrued the nature of ritual because it has been influenced, on the one hand, by the Protestant Reformation, which condemned Catholic ritual as mere empty "formalism," and, on the other, by cultural Darwinism, which regards ritual as a "survival" of formerly functional behavior patterns which have become irrelevant to present circumstances. If anthropology has taught us anything, it is to be wary of taking anything for granted, especially the axiomatic values of our own particular cultural heritage. If humanity is to make a metalanguage, we must have exhaustive knowledge of all the languages—and by "language" I mean nonverbal as well as verbal means of communication, for human beings everywhere exploit the total sensorium for their communicative codes. Sight, smell, touch, taste, and kinetic experience are exploited for their symbolic wealth, as is hearing (for speech demands an ear, without which tongue and palate would be "lodged with us useless").

This digression is necessary to prepare us for the particularities of the "simple" ritual act I described above, for we are dealing with a sequence of symbolic actions framed by a subsystem of symbols which is itself encompassed by a more inclusive system. In the first place, no Ndembu can lay claim to being a hunter outside a context of cult membership. Practical performance may be a necessary, but it is not a sufficient, condition of entry into "huntmanship." But an anthropologist cannot know this until he has achieved sufficient linguistic proficiency to ask members of the culture about the what, why, and wherefore of the witnessed ritual acts. This was my first "narcissistic wound" (to use Freud's telling phrase). For one of the implicit rules of my training had been that non-

Western behavior was to be explained by Western theory. The possibility that there were indigenous taxonomies and even "metalanguages" was not then taken very seriously.

But some anthropologists in Central Africa, notably Godfrey Wilson, Monica Wilson, and Audrey Richards, had strongly counseled anthropological neophytes to take seriously "the inside view" provided by native informants of their own culture. Even before I spent six months at the University of Cape Town, discussing my data with Monica Wilson, I had read articles urging ethnographers to collect native interpretations of the symbols in their own rituals. I therefore began to ask Ndembu who were patently interested in what they were doing in ritual situations and prepared to talk about it, how they interpreted the objects, gestures, actions, and relationships between persons and things manifested in ritual contexts. There was enough agreement between informants whom I considered intelligent to suggest that their explanations were not merely idiosyncratic (like responses to a Rorschach test) but were, within specifiable limits, collectively transmitted and held. I could now make much more sense out of the hunter's monologue before the shrine.

Explanations of Shrines and Cults

The shrines of the hunting cults were revealed to be of different kinds, and I came across them in different locales set in different types of terrain. Some were in the village at a little distance from the hunter's hut and were often elaborate and quasi-permanent ("quasi" because villages moved about every five years under the exigencies of slash-and-burn or swidden cultivation). Others were set on large termite hills (often fifteen feet high) or near crossroads. I found that these differences were associated with different types of ritual processes within the generic hunters' cult. This cult is divided into two main branches: the Bow-hunters' Cult (Wubinda) and the Gun-hunters' Cult (Wuyang'a). A bow is *wuta*; a gun is *wutawakesi* (bow of fire). The branch of bow-hunters has deep ancestry; the second, Ndembu say, was introduced in the latter half of the nineteenth century by Ovimbundu slave traders from the Angola coast, who brought muzzle-loading guns to trade for slaves (to be sold to the Portuguese, who used them as plantation laborers on São Tomé in the Gulf of Guinea, well after the international interdiction on this traffic).

The Bow-hunters' Cult was an assemblage of five rites: Mukaala, Chitampakasa, Kalombu, Mundeli, and Ntambu. The Gun-hunters' Cult was a graded series of four rites, each of which indicated the attainment of a certain degree of proficiency both in killing animals and in esoteric knowledge of the cult mysteries. The Bow-hunters' Cult was dominated by the idiom of affliction. It was concerned with the explanation of misfortune in the chase. Each of its named rites referred to a different kind of hunter's problem: the absence of game from part of the forest where they would normally be expected (Chitampakasa); the sudden bolting of a herd of antelope before the hunter could get within range (Mukaala); the mysterious missing of one's aim (Ntambu); and so on. Each connoted a different malignant manifestation of a deceased hunter ancestor: Mukaala appears in dreams, is short of stature, wears a dress of skins or leaves, manifests himself by whistling in the bush or as a marsh light misleading hunters into swamps, and rides the leading animal of a herd away from the hunters; Ntambu is a hunter-ancestor in the form of a lion (manifested in dreams). (I have discussed Mukaala extensively in "Ritual as Communication and Potency," 1975b.)

Here I wish to pay attention to a solitary hunter who is addressing a *mukishi*, a conscious, purposive, invisible being whom he believes to be afflicting him in the mode or form of Mundeli. I should mention that when I was in the field, the Bow-hunters' Cult and the Gun-hunters' Cult had become interdigitated in a single ritual subsystem of the total ritual system. The pervasive idiom of Ndembu rituals of affliction dominated this subsystem. A hunter advanced in prestige through the system not merely by slaying game but also by experiencing misfortune believed to have been brought on by a specific named ancestor. Between every stage of advancement in the Gun-hunters' Cult (*Wuyang'a*) lay a period of failure. The hunter went into the bush (*mwisang'a*) but was unsuccessful. Continued failure made him seek out a diviner. The diviner prescribed the performance of one of the five rites of the Bow-hunters' Cult, in no set order but dependent on the verdict of the diviner's apparatus. If the rite was successful, the hunter would kill again. If he killed well, he could proceed in the Gun-hunters' Cult—and every able hunter managed by hook or by crook, by purchase or inheritance, to acquire one of the ancient muzzle-loaders, often Tower muskets, which ranked as guns.

But progress in the dual system was an alternation of success and failure; the Gun-hunters' Cult registered success, the Bow-hunter's Cult mastered failure. The spirits of dead hunters were regarded as the dynamic of the Bow-hunters' Cult; they punished breach of taboos laid on hunters, they rewarded their recognition by the living in the form of ritual performance. The Gun-hunters' Cult was more a matter of moving from one stage of prowess to another.

Wubinda and Wuyang'a, though originating in different historical periods, thus came to be interlinked in a dialectic of ritual action, in which every positive advance was through the overcoming of a negative condition due to failure in contact or communication between living and dead members of the total binary cult. Misfortune followed by remedial action drew the hunter more deeply into communion not only with his deceased hunter kinsmen but also with his hunter fellows—who, incidentally, were scattered over a wide territory even beyond the limits of Ndembu land into Luvale, Kaonde, and Luchazi country. In other words, the hunters' cult had a pantribal, even an intertribal, character.

I found it necessary to know all this (and more) to make sense of a hunter's earnest address to an Invisible. In these frames the seemingly opaque utterance became a meaningful communication. Even if it was not overheard by anyone, it was meaningful at least for the hunter, for it related him in his own eyes to an ordered universe and explained his losses and gains in his chosen avocation. Two elements composed his performance: a harangue to the hunter-spirit and a sequence of symbolic acts. Let us examine the acts first, for they frame the speech, including it within the accepted system of Ndembu ritual.

The hunter I am discussing was not standing just anywhere. He was standing near a stream at some distance from his home village. Furthermore, he was standing in a cleared space. (For vividness, I will now use the ethnographic present.) A forked branch has been inserted in the ground; from its base two peeled wands of the *mukula* species are placed horizontally. Sometimes they merely reach the stream; sometimes, when they cross it, they are called "the bridge of the ancestral shade" (*chawu chamukishi*). During my fieldwork I came to understand that every detail in a ritual setting was important, everything "meant" something or, as Ndembu said, "went into" something. If you wanted to ask the "meaning" of an object or act, you usually asked, "*Chaya mudihi?*" "What does it go into?" We might say, "What is its place in the scheme of things?" In time I came to learn the significance of the cleared space, the forked branch, the *mukula* sticks, the stream, and other details.

In the first place, the clearing itself has symbolic value; it is not just what it seems to be, a site cleared with a hoe for convenience in performing ritual. As in many other instances in Ndembu culture, the name of the clearing is itself a symbol and can be connected by informants with other terms in a folk-etymological subsystem. Ndembu declare that *mukombela*, a "clearing for ritual purposes," is connected with (1) *kukomba*, "to sweep or clear dirt or rubbish away from a selected place"—all acts of prayer performed before a tree of any species planted in memory of an ancestral shade or some other type of spirit begin with "aspersion," the officiant using a broom made of the leaves of three species of trees to sweep the shrine tree's base; (2) one of the species so employed is *mukombukombu* which is said to be derived etymologically from *kukomba*; (3) *kukombela* (from *kukomba*) refers to the act of praying to or invoking ancestral shades—it is the verbal equivalent of the action of sweeping clean. Through prayer you "make your liver white" (*muchima to-o*), as Ndembu put it, indicating that there is no grudge, malice, or impediment, no *chitela*, in the relationship between the living and the dead, no remembered slight or injury, and that the living are in harmony with one another. The ideas of sweeping, confessing, cleansing, prayer, right relationship between living and dead and among the living, and whiteness are closely connected in Ndembu thought, as I have shown elsewhere (*The Drums of Affliction* 1968; *The Ritual Process* 1969).

The *mukombela* is, then, a cleared space for ritual activity, notably prayer and invocation. It is used in many kinds of ritual. In this case the behavior we are witnessing pertains to the earliest stages of Mundeli, one of the rites of the Bow-hunters' Cult. So what does the cleared space, *mukombela*, mean in Mundeli? Here let us pay attention to what Ndembu hunters have told me. One explains *mukombela* thus: "*Mukombela* is made to please the spirit of Mundeli, for Mundeli is of the water." I ask, "Why of the water?" The hunter answers, "Because Mundeli came with the Ovimbundu people from Angola. When these people first saw Europeans (*ayindeli*), they thought that they had come out of the water (the sea), for they were pale, like drowned persons with bleached skins. The Mbundu word for "ancestral shade" [*mukishi*] is *ondele*; they called Europeans by this word because they were white like spirits [*akishi*]." The Ndembu term for a living European is Chindeli, and the radical *-ndeli* is retained in the cult term Mundeli.

One of my informants told me what induces a hunter to begin the sequence of ritual phases making up Mundeli.

> The hunter has been unlucky and killed no animals for a long time. He then dreams he sees a European [Chindeli] near the water or sitting in a little ritual hut [*katala*—often made to serve as an intermittent residence for the shades of the dead]. The European tells him, "From now on I am not going to give you an animal because you have erred [*wunaluwi*] with regard to me."

My informant meant that the hunter had broken one of the taboos laid on initiated hunters. He continued:

> When the hunter wakes up, he goes to a diviner who shakes his basket [containing symbolic divinatory objects, including figurines] and says: "You erred. It was either because you let a woman eat some parts of the lungs and intestines of your kill [portions reserved for the hunter himself and forbidden to nonhunters], or you failed to give some portions to

your relatives. They complained about it. This Mundeli shade does not like people, especially a group of kinsfolk, quarreling and grumbling about meat. That is why he is denying you meat. What you must do is to cut two *mukula* branches and remove their outer bark coverings and put up a *muchanka* [one name for the forked-branch shrine] for Mundeli."

The same informant explained to me that in the pre-European past *mukombela* (the ritual clearing) also designated "a big path or road cleared with hoes." He said that the *mukula* sticks placed parallel to one another running from the stream to the *muchanka* also constituted a "path" (*njila*) from the watery abode of Mundeli to the forked-branch shrine, regarded as a temporary abode for hunters' shades. The whole clearing was described as "the eating place of the spirit." Offerings of meat are indeed made to hunter-shades on such shrines, impaled on their sharpened tips (which are compared by hunter-informants to the tines of antelopes' horns) or placed at the juncture of branches. Blood of a new kill may be poured out at their bases or over their branches as a libation. Honey beer (*kasolu*) is the sacramental drink of both hunting cults and is also poured before forked-branch shrines (*nyichanka* or *yishing'a*) as a libation to the hunter-shades. In the more complex public ceremonies of the cults, hunters and hunter-shades are believed to commune at meals of sacred innards (head, lungs, intestines, heart, liver, where blood is rich and plentiful) and honey beer. Ndembu hunters are associated with the richest, most nourishing, and most intoxicating viands and beverages—hence the most coveted and quarreled over. Correspondingly in Ndembu belief, hunter-shades are both the most beneficent and the most punitive super-superegos.

Mukula wood is used for the path from the watery habitat of the hunter-shade in Mundeli because *mukula* is a "symbol" (*chinjikijilu*—literally the blaze cut by a hunter with his ax or knife on trees to find his way home after pursuing an animal into unknown bush) for blood or meat (see Chapter 4 for other meanings). Ndembu explain this from the fact that *mukula* bark regularly cracks and exudes a red coagulative gum. This is declared to be (*diyi*) "blood" (*mashi*) or "meat" (*mbiji*, typically "bloody" meat).

Ndembu have many rites stressing blood (human and animal), and all represent blood by *mukula* symbolism (even when green leaves or brownish root scrapings of the "blood tree" are used, they have by metonymy the symbolic value "blood"). The rites range from boys' circumcision (Mukanda) to the Nkula rite for curing women's menstrual disorders (where both menstrual blood and "maternal blood" are represented by *mukula* symbols) and other gynecological rites, to antiwitchcraft rites (witches are necrophagous), to rites of the hunters' cults (where *mukula* dominantly represents the animals' flesh and blood, which nourish human beings and make for good "maternal blood," blood which in the pregnant woman coagulates around the fetus and makes a strong baby and a good placenta). By using *mukula* branches to frame a path, the hunter embodies in symbolic action his petition to the deceased hunter-ancestor to emerge from the water and bring meat along that path to his shrine and, more important, to the villagers dependent on him. Clearly these symbols embody a wish and are shorthand for a sequence of desired events.

The explanation given by my informant that the hunter was afflicted by a deceased kinsman who "came out in Mundeli," that is, manifested himself in the form of Mundeli as a European dream appearance and as an inimical influence on his hunting, because the shade was offended by the breaking of a taboo or the quarreling of kin, is far too abstract and stereotyped. Let me cite what I have actually overheard from a hunter addressing an afflicting shade. I checked over his harangue with him, and later invited my two best informants, Muchona and Windson Kashinakaji, to comment on it. We move, as you will see, from cultural generalities to particularities of social relationships.

Explanations of the Prayer

Praying is a complicated matter for Ndembu. Not only is there a verbal statement with set and free components, but there is also nonverbal behavior. The petitioner takes some powdered white clay (*mpemba*) from a pouch, moistens his right thumb, places it in the powder, then anoints his stomach just above the navel and his orbits just beside the eyes. Sometimes he may also anoint his arms and legs at the main joints. Whiteness, most fully expressed by white clay, represents the good things of life, both moral and pleasurable, ranging from piety to ancestors to milk and semen. Informants say, "*Mpemba* is placed above the navel [*mukovu*] because the stomach [*ivumu*, which also means 'womb' and 'matrilineage'] is where life [*wumi*] is, and where food goes.

"When it is put beside the eyes, it makes people see well, all things are clearly visible [*mwakumwena chachiwahi yuma yejima*]." As a general statement this means that a person thus anointed will see matters as they really are (*chalala*) and will not be deceived by appearances. When one seriously communes with the ancestors, one must be absolutely honest and pure, and then one will literally be given the gift of clarity of eye and heart. In the hunters' cults the use of *mpemba* has more professional benefits: "The shade gives him the good luck to see animals well, and to track them and shoot them properly." These desirable things are represented by the *mpemba* eye anointings. Seeing animals in the obscurity of the forest is a species of the thematic genus "revelation," which I learned was a pervasive theme of Ndembu ritual.

To bring matters into the open, either as nonverbal symbolic constructions or as explicit statements, is the way to undo the harm that concealment (*kusweka*), whether conscious and malicious or unconscious and thoughtless, is believed to cause to persons, to interpersonal relationships, and to entire social groups. Thus, when one prays to a shade, it is not enough to make a general confession or to admit inadvertent taboo-breaking. One must specify the secret grudge or problem in the relationship between the living and the dead. It is this covered-up matter which is believed to be affecting not only the quality of the social life but also the biological state of living members of the society, and their environmental conditions. Thus a plague may be affecting the health of the invoker's group, or the forest near his village may be mysteriously deprived of its usual number of game animals. Particulars must be stated if the general welfare, and not merely that of the person offering prayer, is to improve. This is my excuse for presenting the actual text of the prayer made at the beginning of the Mundeli ritual sequence by the hunter, Kusaloka. It also throws into relief my problems of how to define, describe, and then interpret Ndembu ritual action.

Kusaloka's name, "Sleeping Restlessly," is one of a limited set of names conferred on hunters initiated into the Gun-hunters' Cult, that is, on proven hunters. It is the first word in a sonorous phrase which it metonymously represents: *Kusaloka mutondu wakedilang'a mutondu wawanjing'a namayang'a-yang'a*, "Sleeping restlessly, a tree which produces fruits all the time, the tree of *njing'a* birds [which eat ripe fruit] and for trumpeter hornbills." Kills of game are often compared to fruits in the hunters' cults, and an active hunter will always be in the forest, "restless [*kusaloka*] until he produces through killing many carcasses, as a tree produces fruits for noisy birds" (representing Ndembu villagers). I heard Kusaloka pray to his deceased hunter-kinsman Sakateng'a as follows:

Sakateng'a twadisumbwili hamwaka ambanda.
Sakateng'a, we exchanged women in marriage long ago.

Ifuku dalelu mumbanda wanyinkeli wafwili Nyamukola.
Today [recently] the woman you gave me, Nyamukola, died.

Mwanyinkeli nyilong'a, ami nafweteli kud'enu.
You gave me cases at law, I paid you in full.

Mandume yenu nawa cheng'i wansema'mi.
Your mother's brother, moreover, begat me.

Ami Kusaloka nenzi dehi, kanda mutiya kutamaku.
I, Kusaloka, have come already. Do not feel ill disposed [toward me].

A Prayer in Its Social Context

The prayer goes on to detail how Kusaloka had married into the same village from which his father had acquired a wife. This was the village of the deceased hunter Sakateng'a, who was now afflicting Kusaloka with bad luck. Sakateng'a had been Kusaloka's cross-cousin, the child of Kusaloka's father's sister. Among Ndembu, cross-cousins of the same sex joke with one another and marriage between those of opposite sexes is encouraged. Particularly encouraged is the exchange of sisters between male cross-cousins. Normally this type of marriage does not entail the payment of bride wealth because reciprocity is built into the sister exchange. When a married person dies, the surviving spouse and his or her close kin are expected to pay the family and close matrilineal kin of the deceased a sum of money called *mpepi*. Quite often this is waived when there has been sister exchange, but sometimes the kin of the deceased put pressure on the widow's or widower's kin to pay up. (I have discussed *mpepi* technically in *Schism and Continuity in an African Society* [1957: 263–265, 267–274] and refer the reader to that account for further information.)

It is sufficient to mention here that Sakateng'a, when he lived, had demanded *mpepi* from Kusaloka when his sister, Kusaloka's wife, died. Kusaloka had refused to pay the large amount demanded. This was the origin of Sakateng'a's grudge (*chitela*) against Kusaloka, a grudge which survived death and induced him to "come out of the grave in Mundeli," as Ndembu put it, "to tie up Kusaloka's huntsmanship [*wubinda*]." The prayer by the stream concluded by Kusaloka's saying:

Lelu komana ching'a niyi mwisang'a nakuloza mbiji
Today indeed I must go into the bush to shoot meat

yatata yami adi atiyi kuwaha.
for my father, that he may eat and feel happy.

Eyi Sakateng'a walozeleng'a mbiji watwinkeleng'a ni Wuyang'a,
You, O Sakateng'a, used to shoot meat, you used to give us huntsmanship, too [that is, helped us to kill animals],

lelu wutwinki mbiji tutiyi kuwaha, ejima wetu tutiyi kuwaha.
today you must give us meat that we may feel good, all of us, that we may
feel good.

Kusaloka is referring to the fact that he is currently living with his
stepfather, the hunter Wamukewa, who married his widowed mother—
she, incidentally, also was raised in the aggrieved shade's matrilineal village, though she was not a close matrikinswoman of his. He is urging the
shade to relent and give him back his "huntsmanship," his power to slay
animals. He promises in his prayer to feed the shade, to put pieces of
meat on the forked-branch shrine and to sprinkle it with the blood of any
kill the offended shade may allow him to make.

How a Social-Structuralist Would Analyze the Ritual

A full contextualization of the prayer text, from which I have made ex-
cerpts, would entail writing a fair-sized monograph. When I was in the
field, given my British structural-functionalist orientation, I did indeed
try to work out the social-structural context of most rituals I observed. It
was much easier to do this with the help of clues provided in verbal behavior than by an examination of the rich arrays of nonverbal symbols.
At each ritual performance I attended, I made careful records of all the
prayers, invocations, harangues, addresses to the shades or to the congregation; they formed an inventory of the current state of relationships
between members of the group centrally concerned in the performance.
Some were torn with overt dissension and redolent with ill feeling (*kutiya
kutama*); others were reckoned to contain covertly disruptive tendencies,
secret grudges, hidden envy, concealed jealousy.

The principle that the hidden or the dark should be revealed (*kusolola*
or *kumwekesha*) to the ancestors, as betokened by the white clay used in
veneration, motivated people to confess their grudges in public—and
thus to render them accessible to remedial ritual action, to the beneficent
influences of the powers and virtues elicited from herbs and trees, from
slaughtered animals, from mimetic actions of various kinds. The long
cherishing of grudges was thought to lead to recourse to witchcraft; confession forestalled this deadly outcome.

Verbal behavior, then, revealed the seamy side of Ndembu social life
in its primary groups: its families, matrilineages, villages, and neighborhoods. But to understand the conflicts in the social system, one had
first to grasp it in its regular operation. As a structuralist in the tradition
of Radcliffe-Brown, Evans-Pritchard, Fortes, Gluckman, Colson, and

Mitchell, I conceived it to be my duty not only to collect full data on the abstract norms of kinship and local organization but also to take village censuses and genealogies and make plans of huts and gardens. From such information one could infer closeness or distance of current relationships between kin and neighbors.

Thus, to contextualize adequately the conflict-ridden relationship between Kusaloka and the late Sakateng'a I found it theoretically necessary to make a census of the villages in which they normally resided, to collect genealogies from all the village inhabitants, to trace the movements of each village over time (Ndembu practiced swidden agriculture and changed residential sites every few years) and of each of their members (since high spatial mobility of individuals, especially of hunters, and groups was a feature of Ndembu society). I further collected information about the gardens cultivated by village members, their acreage, distribution, type, time under cultivation, crops grown on them, and so on.

These data gave me information about the contemporary standing and wealth of protagonists in the ritual situation, which as Mundeli progressed through its public phases involved more and more of Kusaloka's kin and neighbors, as well as members of the Bow-hunters' and Gun-hunters' cults, unrelated political figures in the neighborhood, and a number of onlookers and bystanders attracted by the meat, beer, and cassava mush made available to them by Kusaloka and his wives, the fruits of his hunting and their gardening.

Such local data had then to be set in a context of information provided by my wider census and genealogical surveys in Mwinilunga District, the Ndembu and Lunda domain then under British overlordship. From statistics based on genealogies of seventy-seven villages and censuses of thirty, I discovered that Ndembu villages consisted sociologically of cores of closely related male matrilineal kin, their wives and their children, and their sisters who, as a result of widowhood and frequent divorce, had returned to their natal villages, bringing their young children with them.

Ndembu marry virilocally, that is, the wife resides in her husband's village. In a sense, village continuity depends on marital discontinuity, since one's right to reside in a given village is primarily determined by matrilineal affiliation, though one can reside in one's father's village while he is still alive. Villages persist by recruiting widows, divorcees, and their children. In *Schism and Continuity* (1957), *The Forest of Symbols* (1967), *The Drums of Affliction* (1968), and *The Ritual Process* (1969) I have tried to work out how stresses between matrilineal and patrilineal affiliation, between virilocal marriage and matrilineal succession and inheritance, and other processes and principles have affected various mundane and ritual processes and institutions in Ndembu society, such as village size, structure, mobility, and fissiveness; marital stability; relations between and within genealogical generations; the role of the many cult associations in counterbalancing cleavages in villages, lineages, and families; the strong masculine stress on complex circumcision and hunting rites in a system virtually dependent on women's agricultural and food-processing activities; and the patterning of witchcraft accusations.

Clearly, much of the content of Kusaloka's prayer can be demonstrably related to these and other social-structural factors. Thus the relationship between close male cross-cousins is always a tricky one, since the patrilateral and matrilineal affiliations involved in such a kin tie may tug against one another within a person in regard to the important matter of residence—with whom will one live, one's father's or one's mother's matrilineal kin? The fact that both father and mother are embedded in matrilineal groups emphasizes the ultimate triumph of the matrilineal principle and also explains the constant rearguard action of males to delay or deny that triumph through such devices as virilocal marriage and complex rituals celebrating male activities and attributes.

The conflict between cross-cousins of the same sex, especially if there has been sister exchange between them, is complicated by another Ndembu custom, that of positional inheritance. A man may inherit the social status, standing, and property of his mother's brother. Thus, if a man's mother's brother, an authority figure among the matrilineal Ndembu, dies and he inherits the dead man's "universe of law" and also his name, in a complex ceremony called *kuswanika ijina* he becomes "structurally" his cross-cousin's "father." That is, he ceases to be a joking partner of the same generation and becomes instead an authority figure of the generation immediately senior, since among the Ndembu fathers exert more authority than in matrilineal societies without virilocal marriage. When one resides in one's father's village, the father belongs to the first ascending genealogical generation and shares in the authority held by that set.

In the case before us, Sakateng'a had succeeded to the position of Kusaloka's father, and this had canceled out his previous institutionalized cross-cousin "joking" equality. I should feed into this information the further structural point that when Sakateng'a died, Kusaloka had formally inherited not only his muzzle-loader but also one of his upper incisors (known as *ihamba*), which he retained as a hunting "fetish," carefully concealed in a shoulder-slung cloth pouch when he hunted and hung on the forked-branch shrine before Kusaloka's hut when not in active employment. An *ihamba* concretely signifies, and actively demonstrates through its power to kill, that one has a deceased hunter-kinsman as one's guardian or tutelary shade to help in the chase. Thus Kusaloka was subordinate to Sakateng'a, both when Sakateng'a lived and after his death, in several asymmetrical dyadic relationships. When Kusaloka mysteriously lost his luck at hunting, it was perhaps only natural that the diviner, after eliciting enough information, should diagnose the afflicting agency as his aggrieved "structural father" and tutelary in the hunting cult. Diviners are always alert to stresses and strains in extant social relations and understand just where the major problem areas are located in the social field.

The Intractability of Key Symbols
to Structural-Functionalist Analysis

My own problem in the field was that while it was possible to make a perfectly satisfactory analysis of the verbal behavior even of a solitary individual in terms of the "surface structures" of Ndembu society, it was less easy to see how, if at all, the nonverbal symbols related to social structure at any level. The public, plural reflexivity shown in social conflict was all very illuminating—it revealed discrepancies between norms and principles of social organization and conflict between an individual's self-interest (refusal to pay *mpepi*) and his social obligations (piety to the dead, fair and customary division of slain animals among kin, and so on). But the problems and quarrels of these and similar kinds characterize all ritual performances, regardless of their stated purposes. They are the content, the business, if you like, transacted by the ritual actors; they do not constitute the ritual itself, the frames within which the verbal behavior is stimulated and encouraged to flow, the significant form of the ritual. Everyone has overt or hidden grudges, everyone quarrels, everyone is envious of others' success; and these propensities are framed in a specific social order, find their ends and means in its prizes, institutions, beliefs, favored goals of action, and so on. But each type of ritual has its own idiosyncratic clustering and series of symbolic forms and actions. These patterns cannot be directly explained either by abstract structural principles or by factional or personal conflicts conducted with cognizance of those principles. Even the individual symbolic objects and actions cannot be explained as epiphenomena of social-structural processes.

Thus, even in the simple performance of Mundeli's first phase, I found it hard to pinpoint social bases for such symbols as the clearing, the shrine tree, the "red" *mukula* road or bridge, the white clay smeared by the eyes and above the navel, the belief that hunter-ancestors would take the form of Europeans and emerge from water in dreams. And, in any case, why did the Ndembu make public their "structural" disputes with one another only at sacred times and in sacred spaces?

I followed the advice of other Central Africanists, notably Monica Wilson, and wherever possible obtained native explanations of the symbols. The outcome was that I had a heap of exegetic material to go with each set of observations I made. This only compounded the problem of how to analyze the specific symbols of each kind of ritual, and of each performance of that kind. Ultimately, I had something approaching a comprehensive account of all the kinds of rituals used by Ndembu (at least in the early 1950s, together with not a few elders' accounts of rituals no longer performed). I had, in addition, a set of observations and exegeses of variant forms of each ritual type. Scanning my field data, I find that arrays of nonverbal symbols exceed accounts of verbal behavior explicitly related to ritual occasions by about ten times. And only a limited number of nonverbal symbols can be directly connected with components and attributes of the "social structure" as this emerged from my analysis of both quantitative data and informants' accounts.

The Discovery of Freud

In the field, then, I was at a loss how to proceed further. I did not relish jettisoning so much painfully collected information (many sleepless nights I had, watching and recording ritual in action, even dancing ritual as best I could). It was at this point, about two years into my fieldwork (mid-1953) that I rediscovered (after about twenty years' latency period) Freud's *Interpretation of Dreams*. This great paradigmatic work is concerned in large measure with dream symbols and their interpretation. I was also concerned with symbols, but with cultural symbols, an aggregate transmitted from generation to generation by precept, teaching, and example, but not—at least for all practical purposes—psychogenic. They referred to the shared experiences of Ndembu and even, in numerous cases, of all West-Central Bantu-speaking peoples, to the activities of the family, the village, the gardens, and to the common stock of knowledge possessed by hunters as they tracked, snared, butchered, and divided up the game meat.

These sociocultural symbols had at least one important property in common with dream symbols as Freud conceptualized these. They were "multivocal," that is, susceptible of many meanings—or, to be more precise, a single sensorily perceptible vehicle (the outward form) can carry a whole range of significations. Thus, *mukula* wood (or leaves and roots) stands not only for the meat and blood of slaughtered game—its dominant signification in the hunting cults—but also for various categories of human blood. In the circumcision ritual, Mukanda informants declared that it represented the blood of the circumcised novices and its hoped-for coagulation after the operation; in the women's Nkula ritual it represented both menstrual blood and maternal blood (*mashi amama*) used to feed the fetus and "shown" during childbirth. It also stood for the coagulation of these kinds of blood, a coagulation which the ritual is expected to produce and thus prevent the blood "running away" uselessly in protracted menstruation or hemorrhage. In other ritual contexts *mukula*, often connected with other red symbols, such as powdered red clay (*mukundu* or *ng'ula*), stands for the patient's or novice's matrilineage.

Freud more than anyone else opened my eyes to the simple fact—monotonously confirmed by the explanations of my Ndembu informants— that multireferentiality was a central characteristic of certain kinds of symbols. I had hitherto regarded it as a blemish on my field technique or, at best, a freak of Ndembu culture that so many of the symbols given special attention in Ndembu ritual seemed to be polysemous or multivocal, susceptible of many meanings. Freud's analysis of dream symbols in his central European clinical experience gave me my first clue to the aggregative, even cathective, capacity of certain culturally crafted and sensorily defined perceptible forms (or, as one might now say, *signifiants* or vehicles). To them could be attached a large number of significations (denotations, *signifiés*, connotations, senses, meanings, designations, conceptions).

These vehicles, together with the significations given them by Ndembu, I called "dominant" symbols. "Dominance," however, was a relative quality; a symbol might be dominant in a single episode of complex ritual, in several episodes, in the whole symbolic sequence, in hunters' cults, in gynecological cults, in life-crisis rites, or in the entire field of Ndembu ritual—where it might be considered a "master" symbol. *Mukula*, the blood tree, was one such master symbol; *mudyi*, the milk tree, was another; *musoli*, the revelatory tree, yet another, as my various writings on Ndembu ritual abundantly document.

Multivocality, Polarity, and Sublimation

In my preliminary formulation I described a class of "instrumental" symbols which are univocal in representative capacity, having only one meaning, and largely employed to further the ritual action or reinforce the situationally dominant reference of a dominant symbol. At first, following Edward Sapir, I called these univocal or "single-sense" vehicles "signs" or "instrumentalities," reserving the term "symbols" for multi-vocal objects, activities, ritualized utterances, relationships, roles, and so on. I found, however, that the signata assigned by Ndembu to such multivocal symbols were often ordered into a system. Here Freud's notion of sublimation provided a useful theoretical aid. By it, Freud meant "an unconscious process by which a sexual impulse, or its energy, is deflected, so as to express itself in some non-sexual and socially acceptable activity" (Drever 1952:281).

When I set down the total array of information given me by informants about such dominant symbols as the blood tree, the milk tree, and the like, I found that it was possible to sort the signata into two contrasting clusters. *Mukula* the blood tree, as we have seen, represents various kinds of blood (blood of hunting, maternal blood, menstrual blood, blood of circumcision, and so forth). These I called the "physiological pole" of meaning. But *mukula* also represents "matriliny," a principle of social organization, and I found it also to be associated with sentiments of solidarity, reciprocity, and loyalty, together with the obligation to perpetuate the matrilineage and links entailed in the relationships between particular categories of matrilineal kin belonging to the *ivumu*, the "womb group," descended lineally from a specific woman through female links. This semantic "pole" I called the "normative" or "ideological pole" of meaning.

Here, of course, it was not a question of unconscious sexual impulses, since Ndembu were quite explicit about the sexual referent of the blood tree—they had hardly begun to experience the sexual repressions concomitant with the spread of the Protestant ethic. But the concept of sublimation enabled me to picture the process of Ndembu ritual as involving perhaps a deflection of impulses, of their energy. These impulses in a culture where ritual was a going concern were regularly aroused by the appearance of the blood tree under the stimulating circumstances of drumming, dancing, singing, wearing unusual dress and body painting, and so on, an appearance which reinforced previous similar experiences in other rituals. The impulses were deflected onto the abstract notions which formed the normative pole of the blood tree's "semantic field," as its total ambience of meaning may be termed. Thus the energy associated with blood images was deflected onto the ordering and maintenance of blood ties. (I may, of course, have been guilty here precisely of that Western Cartesian dualism which admits in any given domain two independent and mutually irreducible substances, like the Platonic sensible and intelligible worlds, and Descartes's thinking and intelligible substances.)

Where Freud is concerned, it should be stressed that a major difference exists between the sublimation process going on within an individual and this process of sociocultural sublimation. The latter is directed to a collectivity rather than arising within an unconscious psyche. Thus it is characterized by "average," generalized, typical, "habitual," universalized, "gross" features rather than possessing the uniqueness of an individual's development. One may then ask what happens within the individuals who participate wholeheartedly in an Ndembu ritual in which the blood tree plays a dominant symbolic role. (In my experience, in most societies only a few devotees do participate wholeheartedly.) It should first be noted that certain specific affects are attached to the ideas or idea complexes represented by the blood tree symbol, and these dynamize its physiological pole. They are the joys and hazards of hunting with its blood-spilling, red meat, and (afterward) rich feeding; the terror of polluting menstrual blood inimical to the "blood of hunting"; the triumph of giving birth with its attendant flow of blood; and the celebration of male initiation through the blood of circumcision.

It may be hypothesized that these mixed and often contradictory feelings of pleasure and nonpleasure, of happiness and anxiety, are, as it were, averaged out into a single ambiguous quantum of generalized affect, akin to Rudolf Otto's "numinous," the sense of awe, of the *mysterium tremendum et fascinans* (1957). This general, ambiguous potency, succinctly manifested as the blood tree, is then deflected to the more abstract values and norms of matriliny—the central articulating principle of residential and jural structures—making the obligatory desirable, inducing the individual to feel the awesome power of his social obligations instead of regarding them as either remote or a nuisance. (I have been criticized in *Current Anthropology* for postulating a generalized affectivity as ritually characteristic. The argument was, I believe, that ritual preserves specific emotions—fear, love, respect, and so on—"but distances" individuals from them, so that they no longer "invade" the individual but can be reflected on by him.)

I was not basing my analysis directly on Freud's system but, rather, using certain of his concepts analogously and metaphorically as a means of gaining some initial purchase on a set of data hitherto unanalyzed in any depth and detail by my structuralist-functionalist compatriots. One might say that what was required here was "something more like" Freud's approach than their approach. Freud's intellectual cutting tools were better honed to slice up the beast I was intent on carving—ritual seen as a sequence and field of symbol vehicles and their significations—than those bequeathed to me by the social anthropologists, who were concerned mainly with social and political control mechanisms. All symbols have something in common, and intrapsychic and interpsychic symbols, both formed in processes of human interaction and transaction, have a great deal in common. This, I imagine, was the general logic of my approach at the time. I am still Durkheimian enough to think that it is theoretically inadmissible to explain social facts, such as ritual symbols, directly by the concepts of depth psychology. But one can learn a great deal from the way a master thinker and craftsman works with data, especially when he is working in an adjacent field of problems.

Repression and Situational Suppression of Meaning

Freud of course opened up for me far more than multivocality and cultural sublimation. He showed me how to formulate the link between behavior manifesting actual, extant social relationships such as those mentioned in Kusaloka's prayer and the traditional forms and symbols of Ndembu religious culture, some of which framed that prayer. It was in the study of this link that I began to understand the connections between conscious and unconscious behavior in Ndembu culture. In a paper read to the Association of Social Anthropologists of the Commonwealth in London in March 1958 (published in *The Forest of Symbols* 1967: 19–47), I showed how in the girls' puberty ritual, Nkang'a, the dominant symbol, the milk tree, was the center for ritual and symbolic action throughout the first phase (the rite of separation) of this protracted performance, and how in each successive episode different facets of its total meaning were revealed.

What was more interesting, however, was that the behavior of the participants at each episode mimed conflict; that conflict contrasted with the native interpretation of the milk tree's meaning during that same episode. Thus, Ndembu stressed the harmonious, integrative aspects of the milk tree's meaning when talking about it in abstraction from ritual activity; but in that activity the tree could be seen as a catalyst of conflict. In exegesis, the milk tree, typically multivocal, at different times in the ritual stood for breasts, breast milk, the mother-child relationship, the novice's matrilineage, matriliny, womanhood in general, married womanhood, childbearing, and even for Ndembuhood, matriliny being the part taken for the whole metonymously.

Yet mimetic behavior of groups circling or confronting the milk tree clearly indicated hostility between men and women as categories; conflict between the novice's matrilineal kin and her husband's matrilineal kin, between the novice and her mother, between her mother and the adult women who are ritually incorporating her daughter into their married ranks and removing her from "mother's knee" (Ndembu use the same idiom as ourselves here), and between the novice's matrilineal village and all other villages—in effect, between matriliny and virilocality (the principle of removing a bride to her husband's village).

Thus, for every verbal statement of social solidarity there is, in effect, an action statement of social conflict. Tribal unity is contradicted by the female/male mimed opposition, lineage unity by the clash between novice's mother and other lineage women, family unity by the mother/ daughter opposition, marital unity by the contradiction between matriliny and virilocality—which we saw above was a prime source of turbulence in Ndembu culture.

Ritual Episodes as "Metasocial Commentary"

One must of course be wary of the use of "unconscious" here. Ndembu are perfectly aware, outside of the context of the girls' puberty ritual, that there are tensions between the categories and personas mentioned above. But one feature of ritual situations is that they "make visible" (to use terms employed by Ndembu themselves, *kusolola* or *kumwekesha*) only one aspect, norm, or principle of a cultural or social-structural schema at a time. There is, in fact, situational suppression (rather than repression, where painful emotions are thrust out of the consciousness) of all that may impugn the purity or legitimacy of the norm or principle currently being represented. To abstract is to suppress or at least to thrust from attention the other properties of the data from which certain common features are being abstracted. When such data make up the total load of rules governing social interaction in a given cultural milieu, it is impossible totally to exclude them in holding up a single rule or harmoniously interconnected set of rules for special ritual attention.

Thus women interconnected by matriliny find themselves divided by village affiliation or by loyalty to their husbands or by age group or some other recognized principle. Such division cannot be publicly admitted in ritual which expresses and extols matriliny, or even one of the dyadic relationships (mother's brother/sister's son, mother/daughter, mother's mother's brother/sister's daughter's daughter) composing a matrilineal lineage of restricted span. One might say that communitas based on one principle is constantly endangered by suppressed conflicts engendered by organization on other principles.

Another way of putting it would be to say that not only each kind of ritual but also each phase and episode of a ritual constitutes a discourse or "metasocial commentary" (Geertz 1972:26) on Ndembu culture as viewed from a given socioculture perspective, a particular corner of observation. Such a commentary may be explicit or implicit, verbal or non-verbal, direct or indirect. In the case of the girls' puberty ritual, its "discourse" reflects upon the full range of consequences of matrilineal organization for Ndembu social life. It is a reflection on matriliny itself, the story the Ndembu tell themselves about matriliny. Some consequences are harmonious, others disharmonious. Material symbols, objects such as the milk tree, postulate matriliny as a harmonious frame for social behavior; kinetic and mimetic behavior (actions) comment upon the struggles between social groups and roles which are the result of dissonance between matriliny and other principles, "commentary" here being in the sense of actions speaking louder than words.

Some of the notions I have just advanced have been influenced by the anthropological thought of Gregory Bateson, Clifford Geertz, Erving Goffman, Roberto da Matta, Barbara Babcock, Barbara Myerhoff, Terrence Turner, and others, stressing that ritual language is often a language "about" nonritual social and cultural processes rather than a direct expression or reflection of them, as the positivist functionalists supposed it to be. It is a metalanguage with its own special grammar and vocabulary for scrutinizing the assumptions and principles which in nonritual (mundane, secular, everyday, or profane) contexts are apparently axiomatic. This critical function of ritual is still incompletely recognized by investigators who continue to see ritual either as a distorted reflection of "reality" (that is, "empirical" or "pragmatic" reality) or as an obsessional defense mechanism of culture against culturally defined illicit impulses and emotions.

But the ritual "critique" is not, as in industrial societies, individualized; it is expressed, like proverbs, in formulas of collective wisdom, in this case, acted-out formulas. It is a genre of action, a performative, not oral, genre. From the point of view of those enacting a given ritual episode, implicit comment on conflict within supposed harmony may be, if not "unconscious" in the strict Freudian sense, at least temporarily thrust outside the field of individual attention or awareness (is this Freud's preconscious?); but from the pansocietal viewpoint its cultural embodiment in symbolic action indicates it to be part of a collective consciousness, known at least to the ancestors and handed down by tradition—a well from which groups and individuals may draw, if they so need or wish.

Metasocial commentary may be verbally quite explicit within the frame constructed by symbolic action and topographically laid out in patternings of symbolic objects on the ground. I have mentioned above how in the first phase of the Mundeli ritual of the Bow-hunters' Cult, the hunter's monologue or prayer to his deceased hunter-kinsman was rich with reference to personal conflicts between the two of them in the latter's lifetime, with the inference that Sakateng'a's grudge (*chitela*) continued beyond the grave. I mentioned how the fact that hunter and shade were cross-cousins made their relationship both more intimate and more fraught with conflict than the ordinary run of kin relationships, in view of the tension between matriliny and virilocality, as expressed in the metasocial commentary of such rituals as Nkang'a and Nkula (Turner 1968). The additional fact that they were fellows in the hunting cult further amplified both their comradeship and their competitiveness. In essaying to understand situations of this sort, Freud's view of ambivalence as the alternation, even at times coexistence, of the opposite feelings of love and hate was helpful.

Projection, Prayer, and the Ancestors

Still focusing on the framing of hunting ritual, Freud's notion of "projection" gave me clues to an understanding of the beliefs about ancestors' powers to harm the living if the latter transgressed social and cultural norms. In Mundeli specifically, ancestral shades, in the guise of aggressive and politically omnipotent Europeans—white, or even perhaps "anti-black" in color—deny Ndembu hunters the fruits of their skills because they or their close kin have transgressed values set on sharing meat, the most valuable food, or have broken the taboos of the hunting cults, those concerned with the procurement of this rich nourishment. Aliens here represent moral imperatives or, rather, are the sanctions against breaking such commands—and these are male aliens particularly.

For Freud, all this would be "suspicious." One would have to look, in his view, very much closer to home. Thus a theory that projects bad luck in the economic pursuit which produces the most happiness in the village and in its families and sibling groups onto the ultimate image of strangerhood, European ogres, must be taken with more than a grain of salt (to use one of our own culture's more "tasty" metaphors). For Freud, "projection" tends to mean the unconscious attribution to other people of thoughts, feelings, and acts of our own which would otherwise be felt as unpleasurable—perhaps feelings of guilt or inferiority. Projection is thus a defense against these feelings. We can see them thereafter as hostility directed from outside against ourselves, and thus can justify or legitimate ourselves in our own eyes.

What happens with the Ndembu is only one instance of the panhuman unconscious at work; in their case the other people are dead or ancient people, or at any rate, in principle if not in practice, not known, named, or intimately connected people. The feelings of inferiority and guilt in their case come in the form of the unsuccessful hunter's predicament. Thus, the hunter Kusaloka, in the case we have been considering, seems to have projected his own feelings of guilt at having distributed the meat of his kills inequitably onto the image of Mundeli, the deadly white European spirit, in which his own chronologically older cross-cousin was involved or "masked" (the shade "came out" in Mundeli form).

Several informants told me that Kusaloka, like most hunters, was "unfair" in his division of his kills. He kept much of the meat for himself, gave to his mistresses (*andowa*) more than their share of joints, and did not report his successes to those of his matrilineal and patrilateral kin who should have had good portions. But when he projected the responsibility for his temporary loss of success at hunting onto the figure of an intimately connected cross-cousin (his own father had also married into Sakateng'a's village) and viewed this cross-cousin as clothed in antique (Portuguese) European supernatural power (Mundeli), then he must have publicly cleared himself (in Ndembu evaluative terms) of guilt (*nshidi*). Moreover, he claimed merely that the shade had been affronted by the behavior of his (Kusaloka's) kin, particularly his female kin—who had probably broken a taboo laid on all who wish to eat a hunter's kill, by consuming portions reserved to members of the cult.

Thus Kusaloka's selfishness (in his own view) was not at issue, only the transgressions of others. In this way, too, the tensions that must have existed (and much other available evidence attests to this) between villages connected by a sequence of sister exchanges, producing complicated relations between cross-cousins (where mother's brothers become fathers-in-law and father's sisters become mothers-in-law, and joking cross-cousins become serious spouses), must have been ritually mitigated by similar processes of projection.

While I was in the field I was also struck by the congruence between the Ndembu theory of "revealing" or "producing to view" (*kusolola*), and the Freudian notion that cure of neurosis depends essentially upon educing from the patient a conscious understanding of the events and conditions which, too painful to endure in infancy and later replicated or revived in maturity, have been repressed into the unconscious, charging it with the affects of culturally defined "dangerous" wishes and impulses. Both Ndembu ritual and Freudian analysis rest upon the assumption that what is known, consciously articulated, and confessed before a legitimate public authority, individual or collective, has been defused of its inwardly believed power to harm. When the unknown, invisible, nameless agency has been "produced to view," the assumption is not only that it has now become aseptic, deprived of its capacity for ill, but also that the very energies which unconsciously debilitated the patient, when conscious actually empower him to help himself and his kin and friends.

What distinguishes the Freudian approach, based as it is on the western European scientific attitude (with its emphasis on controlled comparison, experiment, testing of hypotheses by rigorously controlled experimental data, and resting on materialist assumptions), from the Ndembu approach is that the latter rests on belief in the reality of invisible as well as visible beings (spirits, shades, witches' familiars, and the like), on the objective power of wishes and thoughts to bless and curse, and on the mystical efficacy of focused social intentions to benefit a patient's total "enterprise." Body and mind, soul and substance, are not distinguished in the same way that we post-Cartesians model humanity in the ghost-in-the-machine manner of Western cultures and their derivatives.

But the principle of "exposing to view" is the same, even if the exposure is in the one case to a legitimate collectivity and in the other to a certificated individual, the psychoanalyst. Confession in both cases cures, but confession in neither instance is an easy, spontaneous matter; rather, it is a complex process, with many stops and starts. In each case, the terms of confession which evaluate its honesty and depth are laid down in a cultural subsystem. Among the Ndembu an implicit *Weltbild* keys the confession to certain assumptions about the social, moral, and natural orders (to use terms familiar from our own cultural history). For psychoanalysis the metaphysical theory that matter is the only reality, and that "psychical" processes and phenomena are really epiphenomena of matter, holds sway.

Yet a curious complicity exists between these apparently disparate systems, even if Ndembu beliefs do not include psychoanalytical theories, and those very psychoanalytical theories were developed in the infancy of anthropological field investigations of tribal ritual. Both assume that the living truth of human social relationships should be manifested if the health of individuals or groups is to be sustained. Anything short of this internally divides the individual or the group. Where continuous self-revelation is viewed against the backdrop of a cosmology taken to be both an expression and an explanation of the nature of things sensibly apprehended, the rituals associated with this process may be termed "religious." Where self-revelation is confined to the individual psyche and its instrumentalities are claimed to have been derived by inference from clinically controlled data, the process of encouraging self-revelation may be called "psychotherapeutic." In practice, these distinctions tend to become blurred: Ndembu seek so to restore the morale of hunters that they recover their power to kill skillfully, and of women with reproductive ailments, including frigidity and propensity to miscarry, that they give birth easily to "live and lovely children."

And it is not altogether a libel to speak, as many have done, of a "religion" of psychoanalysis. For if religion means something like "ultimate concern," what ultimate concern is greater than full human capacity to function socially, sexually, and creatively? And if the capacity to relate to other human beings creatively and fully is the "ultimate concern" of a community of dedicated physicians, how can we deny such an intention the name of "religion"? Perhaps what is required is to impart a greater sense of communitas to psychoanalytical practices and a much richer knowledge of empirical cause-and-effect relations to "tribal" rituals. The results might be mutually fructifying, for human beings are relational creatures and cannot be validly studied apart from the network of love and interest in which they are incessantly involved. Each human being also possesses the dignity of his or her unique history and problems. If, then, we could give our therapies in the West a "religious" dimension and insist that these new "religions," as well as those in the Third World, take into full account the scientific aspects of therapy, we might learn something of practical consequence from the symbolic actions of the preindustrial peoples we have studied.

In conclusion, I consider my encounter with Freud's work, particularly *The Interpretation of Dreams*, to have been decisive in arriving at an independent theoretical position of my own. It was his style of thinking and working which gave me encouragement rather than his actual inventory of concepts and hypotheses. None of these could be applied mechanically or literally to the type of data I had collected. Social and cultural systems and fields are, at the level of observation, quite different from, though interdependent with, psychological relationships. They involve different kinds of sustentative processes, have different developmental cycles. But Freud's implicit emancipation from mechanistic approaches—despite his own attempts under the sway of the zeitgeist to employ "economic models" and the like—and his willingness to take into analytical account from the very outset the ambivalence, plurivalence, contradictoriness, and just plain cussedness of all human "constructions of reality" made it possible to see not only analogies but also homologies, correspondences in basic types of structures, between the cultural (especially ritual) symbols whose structures, properties, and relationships I was being forced by the data to explain, and the private dreams and symptoms of the European patients with which he, as soul doctor, dealt.

2 Death and the Dead in the Pilgrimage Process

It is appropriate to begin with three brief quotations directly connecting pilgrimage with death and salvation, three themes of this study. The first, from Leslie Farmer (1944:79), is on the Christian pilgrimage to Jerusalem: "It was a common custom to bring one's shroud to be cut to the size of the Stone of Unction" (in the Church of the Holy Sepulcher). The second is from Sir Richard Burton (1964, 2:183, n. 2): "Those who die on a pilgrimage become martyrs . . . the ghost departs to instant beatitude." And the last is from Romain Roussel (1954:240–241): "The pilgrim [to Mecca] knows that he will present himself at the Last Judgment covered with his ihram pilgrim's garb [two simple white pieces of cloth]. That is why many of those who fulfill the haj wish to be buried in the dress they wore at Mecca."

But it is only death on the way to or at the shrine that makes a pilgrimage a true rite of passage, as we shall see, though pilgrimages do share many features with initiation rites.

Pilgrimages in the salvation religions, like initiation rites in tribal religions, are full of symbols and metaphors for death, and also are directly concerned with the dead. The dead may include the founder of a religion; his kin, disciples, or companions; saints and martyrs of the faith; and the souls of the ordinary faithful. This is partly because both pilgrims and initiands are undergoing a separation from a relatively fixed state of life and social status, and are passing into a liminal or threshold phase and condition for which none of the rules and few of the experiences of their previous existence have prepared them. In this sense, they are "dying" from what was and passing into an equivocal domain occupied by those who are (in various ways) "dead" to quotidian existence in social systems. To use terminology favored by Radcliffe-Brown (1957:22), initiand and pilgrim cease to be members of a perduring system of social relations (family, lineage, village, neighborhood, town, state) and become members of a transient class of initiands and pilgrims, moving *per agros* (through the fields [or lands]).

This entails that the actors in ritual and pilgrimage processes leave a domain where relations are complex for one where they are simple. Their relations with others are, at least at first, no longer those of interconnectedness but of similarity. No longer do they occupy social positions in a hierarchical or segmentary structure of localized status roles; now they are assigned to a class of anonymous novices or plainly and uniformly garbed pilgrims, all torn or self-torn from their familiar systemic environment. Again, while a *system* has characteristic form and is governed by rules of social and cultural construction, a *class* of liminal initiands or pilgrims is without form, is a homogenized mass of like components—at least initially. While homesteaders are coordinated by interdependence, pilgrims and initiands are coordinated by similarity, by likeness or lot rather than interdependence of social position. And whereas members of an established social system play roles and occupy statuses that are functionally consistent, there may be no functional relationship among novices or pilgrims. Again, a stabilized social system has a structure, but novices and pilgrims confront one another at first as a mere aggregate, without organic unity.

In these respects, "system" may be symbolically equated in ritual with "life," and "extrusion from system"—as a phase of a ritual or pilgrimage process—with "death," since all that makes for interconnectedness, integration, coordination, form, structure, and functional consistency—all that constitutes the order of daily life in the lives of the actors—is annulled or abrogated. Metaphorically, the novice or pilgrim experiences "the pains of dissolution." This is one reason why symbols of death, dying, and catabolism proliferate in tribal initiation rites. For example, Monica Wilson writes on what I would call the "liminal" (threshold) phase of the rituals of birth, puberty, marriage, death, abnormal birth, and misfortune among the Nyakyusa:

> There can be no doubt that the induction [into the ritual situation] and seclusion represent death. Strewing leaves—or laying a litter—which is an essential act in every induction, is a sign of misfortune and death; and at the induction of a bride her "mothers" sing: "Go, go and never return," and "We wail a dirge." The mourners, the nubile girls, the mother of a new born child, and the parents of twins are all "filthy" and one with the dead; Kasitile [Wilson's best informant] said of mourners: "We have died, we are the corpse." (Wilson 1957:205)

In my book *The Forest of Symbols*, I give many further examples, drawn from tribal societies, of symbols and metaphors for death in initiation rites: "The initiand may be buried, forced to lie motionless in the posture and direction of customary burial, may be stained black, or may be forced to live for a while in the company of masked and monstrous mummers representing, inter alia, the dead" (1967:96).

Again, among the Ndembu of Zambia, in several types of ritual an officiant known as the "hyena" (*chimbu*), characteristically a snatcher both of carrion and of the young of other species, "snatches" the novices from their mothers to be circumcised in the Mukanda circumcision rites; the blood-soaked site of the operation is called *ifwilu* (the place of death or dying). Circumcision is partly a metaphor for killing, since it "kills" the novice's childhood state. Such instances could be greatly multiplied from ethnographic literature. Symbols and metaphors (and other tropes) for structural erasure, rendering the initiands faceless, "dark," "invisible," and anonymous, through disguise, body painting, and use of a generic term of address instead of a personal name ("novice," "neophyte," "initiand"), also abound.

The detachment of an initiand or novice from the system in which he has been embedded may also have a religiously positive aspect. It may be interpreted as rebirth and growth. From this perspective the abandoned system may be "death," and the new liminal state the germ of "life" or spiritual development. Thus, from one point of view the shift from complex interconnected relations to simple relations of likeness may be regarded not so much as a negative dissolution of an ordering articulating structure, the decay of a complex living organism, but as a positive release from the distancing between individuals which their membership in social positions in a system involves.

Structural distance may, then, be an apt symbol for death, the dissolution of distance, and rebirth into authentic social life. The initiands or novices may see the move away as an opportunity for a direct, immediate confrontation of others as total human beings, no longer as segments or facets of a structural system. Thus among many West Central Bantu peoples, the circumcised novices become fast friends during a long period of seclusion together, even though before the operation they lived in different villages and even chiefdoms, structured units normally in continuous low-key conflict with one another. Moreover, even the most harmoniously articulated structures in any culture produce some degree of alienation, for the fullness of an individual's being overflows the totality of his roles and statuses.

Structure, too, whether of small-scale or large-scale social systems, is provocative of competition and conflict. Social and political systems contain offices, high, medial, and low; chains of command; bureaucratic ladders. There are systems of promotion, rules, and criteria for status elevation and degradation; laws concerning the protection, disposal, transfer, and inheritance of property, and succession to high office. There are social controls over sexuality and reproductive capacity, rules governing marriage, and prohibitions on incest and adultery. In this many-leveled, ordered, and sanctioned field, individuals find it hard not to envy their neighbor's good fortune; covet his ox, ass, or lands; strive with him for office; compete with him on the promotion ladder; seek to commit adultery with his wife; become greedy or miserly; or fall into despair at their own lack of success.

But when they are lifted by initiation ritual or voluntarily elect to go on pilgrimage, they may see the metaphoric death mentioned earlier as a death to the negative alienating aspects of system and structure, as an opportunity to take stock of the lives from which they are now temporarily detached or, alternatively, to regain an innocence felt by them to have been lost. They may feel that a death from self—or in traditional Christian terms from the world, the flesh, and the devil—may be simultaneously a birth or rebirth of an identity splintered and crushed by social structure. Ordinary mundane life may be reinterpreted as the Terrene City; its abandonment, as a first glimpse of the Heavenly City. Therefore the move into liminality is here a death-birth or a birth-death. This is explicitly formulated by Monica Wilson in a continuation of the passage quoted previously. Furthermore, this quotation raises the problem of the second term in my title: What is the role of the dead in initiatory liminality? Later we shall examine this role in pilgrimage liminality; now we see it in tribal initiation, of which Wilson writes:

> The period of seclusion implies a *sojourn with the shades* [italics added],
> and our hypothesis is that it represents both death and gestation. The hut
> appears as a symbol of the womb in the pregnancy and "gasping cough"
> [a Nyakyusa category of illness] rituals, and the doorway which "belongs to the shades" is a symbol for the vagina. (Wilson 1957:205)

Wilson interprets certain symbolic actions, as when mourners or the girl novices in puberty rites run in and out of the doorway, to represent rebirth. I have noticed gateway symbols not only in African rituals but also as an outstanding feature of the precincts of Catholic pilgrimage shrines, as at Lourdes, Remedios in Mexico City, and Chalma in Mexico State.

Thus we have metaphorical death in tribal rituals, parallel perhaps with "mystical death" in the salvation religions of complex societies, and metaphorical rebirth, homologous to spiritual regeneration. Or perhaps we might speak of ritual liminality as an exteriorized mystical way, and the mystic's path as interiorized ritual liminality. We also have the involvement during liminality of the dead; in the Nyakyusa case, of the ancestral shades. The dead also partake of the ambiguous quality of liminality, the state of betwixt-and-betweenness, for they are associated with both positive and negative processes and objects, with life and death. "We have spoken," writes Wilson (1957:207), "of the Nyakyusa disgust for filth (*ubunyali*), which is associated with a corpse, menstruation, childbirth, intercourse, feces, and all these are identified in some fashion with the shades. Feces 'go below to the land of the shades.'" There is about all this the image of "dust to dust." But there is an opposite quality attached to the shades. Wilson writes:

> All through the rituals the connection of the shades with potency and fertility is emphasized . . . they are present in intercourse and ejected as semen; they control conception; they control fertility in the fields. "The shade and semen are brothers," said one informant. And another said: "When they shake the millet and pumpkin-seeds [after ritual connection] the seed is semen . . . and it is the shade" [quotations from various informants of the Wilsons]. (1957:205)

The shades therefore represent both the decay of the body and the spirit of fertility, reminding one of the biblical seed that must first die before it can yield much fruit. This metaphor has of course to be seen in the context of a religion of personal salvation and not, as in the Nyakyusa case, of a religion of community maintenance, where localized community has facets of system, class, and communitas. In the Christian case the death metaphor applies both to the "death" of the individual to the local structured community, and to the death of that organic group for the individual. Nevertheless, in both Nyakyusa pagan and Christian modes of liminality there are notions that initiands and pilgrims are simultaneously undergoing the death of social structure and regeneration in communitas, social antistructure.

First they must cease to be members of a system and become members of a class, then they must be reborn in that modality of social interrelatedness I have called, for want of a better term in English, existential communitas—which might be paraphrased as true fellowship, or agape, or spontaneous, altruistic love—if one also concedes that there is a well-defined cognitive or "intellectual" (in Blake's sense) component in the relationship. For it is not a merging of consciousness, nor an emotional melding, but a mutual recognition of "definite, determinate identities" (to cite Blake again), each with its wiry, unique, indefeasible outline. All are one because each is one. In this process of death and regeneration—at both social and individual levels—different types of religions assign a mediating function to the human dead, those who have already undergone the passage from visible and tangible to invisible and intangible states of being.

This function is on the one hand concerned with maintaining the social structure of the system in its characteristic form, with all its moral and jural rules, by acting as a punitive sanction against any major transgression of the basic legal, ethical, and commonsense principles determining the shape or profile of that system. On the other hand, the dead are concerned with two extrastructural, perhaps antistructural, modalities: biological (or natural) and spiritual. In the first modality, as in the Nyakyusa case—and quite typical of many parts of Africa (and elsewhere, as we shall see)—the dead are thought to mediate between the invisible ideal world of paradigms and archetypes and the sensorily perceptible world of sex and economics, begetting and food production, distribution and consumption. If the dead are honored, known, and recognized, they will differentially, and in terms of structural differences, bestow blessings.

Meyer Fortes's work on *pietas* is more pertinent here. But the dead, as we have seen in Wilson's work, are also regarded as powers, as themselves being the "force that through the green fuse thrusts the shoot" and through the loins and wombs of human beings thrusts progeny. In the Ndembu Chihamba ritual, a spirit or archancestor is "planted" in symbolic form, including the seeds and roots of food plants, in order that people and crops will multiply. And in salvation religions the dead are also regarded as possessing a mediating role in the drama of salvation, the freeing or binding of the immortal human soul, that invisible formative principle, which is believed to survive death but to undergo punishment or reward for its consciously willed acts during life.

The dead have influence over the living and are reciprocally influenced by their thoughts, words, and deeds. The dead can spiritually fructify the living, in Catholic theological thought at least; and it is not only in the folk dimension but also in theological terms that they are regarded as having an influence on the physical fertility, and certainly on the health, of the living. I quote from the *Knock Shrine Annual* for 1968, which records news of all group pilgrimages to the famous Irish shrine and publishes letters expressing gratitude to its mediating saints for favors believed to have been received through their intercession with God. One letter runs: "I wish to acknowledge my thanks to Our Lady of Knock, St. Joseph, and St. John for the gift of two little girls and also recovery from heart trouble, and for many other favors and graces over the years.

A client of Our Lady" (p. 119). This is typical of many hundreds of letters published by journals connected with pilgrimage shrines.

I am not competent to discuss the relationship between the living and the dead in such salvation religions (to use Weber's term) as Hinduism, Islam, Buddhism, Judaism, Taoism, and Jainism, to mention only a few of those which profess to offer permanent or temporary surcease or release from the "human condition" of what one might term structural morality and its behavioral consequences, either of "uptight" virtue or of the slavery of sin. But in the past few years I have gone, both as participant observer and as observing participant (the anthropologist's perennial human dilemma, which is resolved one way or the other, to his or her creative loss), on a number of pilgrimage journeys to Catholic shrines such as Guadalupe, Ocotlán, Remedios, Chalma, Izamal, Tizimín, Acámbaro, Amecameca, and others in Mexico; Knock, Croagh Patrick, Lough Dearg, Limerick, and Cork in Ireland; Walsingham, Glastonbury, Canterbury, and Aylesford in England; the catacombs, Santa Maria Maggiore, St. Peter's, Santa Maria d' Aracoeli, and other Roman churches of the pilgrimage path within Rome in Italy; Lourdes in France; and other pilgrimage centers in the Old and New Worlds. These travels in space led to travels in time, and I avidly read historical records of Christian pilgrimage through the ages in many places.

Personal needs as well as a theoretical and disciplinary interest led to my study of pilgrimages. I have always regarded anthropology as a process of *reculer pour mieux sauter*, which may be paraphrased as "going to a far place to understand a familiar place better," which in turn is a partial definition of the pilgrimage process. Pilgrimage is also a rehearsal of the pilgrim's own death. Sooner or later, we anthropologists have to come home having experienced a partial death of our home-born stereotypes and domestic values—a point outlined by Lévi-Strauss in his *Tristes tropiques*. "Home" for me is the tradition of western European culture, and since I have always defined ritual as "quintessential culture," to understand home therefore involves looking at domestic forms of the ritual process.

What I was looking for was, in fact, the characteristic cultural modality of liminality in the salvation religions, specifically that established in the formative period of Christianity—in other words, what was in Christian salvific belief and practice the homologue of the liminality of major initiations in tribal religions. I was looking for a substantial rather than a merely formal homology. Superficially, the Christian sacramental system, plus funerary purificatory rituals and some others, might seem to supply liminal phases equivalent to those in tribal and other rites of passage. But in terms of differences in scale and complexity between the societies practicing these religions, it seemed to me that pilgrimage was to complex salvation religion what the protracted seclusion periods of initiation rites were to tribal and archaic religions.

Christian pilgrimage, as an object of study, may have escaped Western intellectuals because it is too familiar to us, too close for comfort, whether we are scientists or theologians. I distinguish pilgrimage from initiation as a locus of liminality by saying that this, like many features of life in large-scale, complex societies, is rooted in optation, in voluntariness, whereas initiation is founded in obligatoriness, in duty. Initiations fit best in societies with ascribed status; pilgrimages, in those where status not only may be achieved but also rejected. In tribal societies men and women have to go through rites of passage which transfer them from one state and status to another, whereas in posttribal societies of varying complexity and degree of development of the social division of labor, people can choose to go on pilgrimage. This is true even when, as in medieval Islam and Temple Judaism, pilgrimage was held to be an obligation; a variety of mitigating circumstances and escape clauses made pilgrimage virtually a matter of optation.

Christian pilgrimage, though in the waning of the Middle Ages it became almost a matter of obligation—for those who had committed serious civil crimes as well as religious sins under the church's penitential system—remained in principle a matter for the individual conscience. In Catholic theology it was and remains an eminent "good work," of counsel, not precept, which may aid the individual's salvation by securing many "graces" but cannot guarantee it in the manner of an initiation—thus differing from the obligatory "recourse to the sacraments." This is the crucial difference between the two liminalities.

Initiation is an irreversible process, transforming the state and status of the initiand. Pilgrimage is part of a lifelong drama of salvation or damnation hinging on individual choice, which itself involves the individual's acceptance or rejection of "graces," freely volunteered gifts from God. In the case of initiation one is changed *ex opere operato* irrespective of one's intention. Moreover, initiation's primary referent is to the total social system. Individuals have meaning in this frame only insofar as it is necessary for the structured group to redefine them cognitively from time to time as members of a class other than that to which they belonged before—and, more than this, to alter them substantially to perform the duties and enjoy the rights of that class by means of symbolic action. Initiation rituals are, as Fernandez (1973:1366) would put it, "sets of enacted correspondences," metaphorical actions, which by virtue of novices' involvement in them, teach them, even nonverbally, how to comport themselves when they are inducted into their new station in life. They are to be returned, furthermore, to the same structural system, but to a higher level or position in that system.

In these societies life and death are often thought of as what the poet Rilke called the "great circulation." Rilke, like all poets, was nostalgic for societies where nature and culture were more directly conjoined in metaphor and metonymy than in our literate, industrial society—where, as Eliot maintains, "the shadow" (scientific objectification, making possible both the use and the misuse of nature by culture on a large scale, as well as "original sin") falls between them. In societies with initiation, organic processes and the seasonal round provide root metaphors for cultural processes that are perceived as cyclical, and proceed through the life and death of vegetation and the fertility and latency of animals, processes which mark the annual round. Thus, although initiations are irreversible, in their total sequence they convey the aging individual to the beginning again, to be reborn after the funeral—which is then an initiation—as an infant, perhaps descended from one of his own totemic clan members. In initiations, too, the fiat of the whole community, expressed through its representative elders, is crucial for inaugurating symbolic action.

Initiations also fairly regularly exhibit the rite-of-passage form discovered by Van Gennep with its three phases: separation, margin or limen, and reaggregation or reincorporation, conceived of as an irreversible sequence, like the human lives they service and mediate. But pilgrimages, though liminal (or, perhaps better, liminoid, since the liminoid resembles but does not coincide with the liminal), are in principle quite different from initiations. But as salvation religions become routinized, their pilgrimages tend to revert or regress to initiatory devices; they become, in Christian terms, the sacrament of penance writ large, though they never acquire a completely sacramental character. They are not, therefore, necessary for salvation, nor do they become a matter of ecclesiastical precepts. This makes pilgrimage a major expression of the "modern" spirit, the spirit expressed in the primacy, say, of contract over status (in Sir Henry Maine's terms), of ethics over magic, of personal responsibility over corporate affiliation.

Pilgrimage is to a voluntaristic system what initiation is to an obligatory system. That people opt to go on pilgrimage rather than have to be initiated, that they make a vow to a patron saint to be his or her client by making a pilgrimage to that saint's shrine, to my mind accounts for the pilgrimage's paradigmatic charm for such literary figures as Chaucer, Dante, and Bunyan. The plain truth is that pilgrimage does not ensure a major change in religious state—and seldom in secular status—though it may make one a better person, fortified by the graces merited by the hardships and self-sacrifice of the journey. Folk belief, in Christianity and

Islam, insists that if one dies at the holy places—Mecca, Jerusalem, or Compostela—one goes straight to Heaven or Paradise, a belief that lends support to the view that in salvation religions, of the Semitic type at least, stance is all-important for personal salvation. Death sums up and epitomizes the quality of an individual life. But even the best pilgrims may backslide. This is precisely because the will, the *voluntas,* of the individual is the fulcrum of the whole matter. Shift it a bit, and past achievement falls to the ground.

The role of the social in pilgrimage differs markedly from society's role in initiation. In pilgrimage the pilgrim divests himself of his structural incumbencies by personal choice; in initiation social pressures enforce symbolic, transformative action on the individual. In neither case is communitas ensured. The pilgrim may leave the familiar system and become a member of a class of pilgrims, but he does not necessarily enter a communitas of pilgrims, either in the easygoing Chaucerian fellowship of the road or in the Eucharistic communion at the shrine itself, mentioned by pilgrims such as Holy Paula and the Abbot Daniel, whose narratives are included in the volumes of the Palestine Pilgrims Text Society. In initiation the actor may enter the class of novices without helping to generate a communitas of novices. But the dying from system into class may, in each case, facilitate the communitas experience, the subjective sense of antistructure that has had so many important objective results in the history of religion.

Another difference is that initiation is often localized in a protected place—though its ordeals may be dangerous—while pilgrimage is often hazardous. Pilgrims are exposed to diverse geographical, climatic, and social conditions, sometimes traversing several national frontiers. Although at the end they perform formal rituals, on the way they are vulnerable to historical happenstance. This implication with history is, again, modern. I have recently been studying pilgrimage systems—processes focused on specific shrines—in their historical dimension, both from the perspective of their internal dynamics, their entelechy, and from that of the currents of thought, movements of political power, and shifts in popular opinion supporting or assailing them. Pilgrimages, though rooted in temporal paradigms, experience temporality in ways rather foreign to the protected milieus of initiation rituals.

All this is consistent with the emphasis on free will, personal experience, casting one's bread on the waters, the capacity to retract from commitment, and so on, characteristic of salvation religions arising in and helping to shape international fields of social relations that are ethnically plural, multilingual, and multicultural. It is worth mentioning that the limen of pilgrimage is, characteristically, motion, the movement of travel, while that of initiation is stasis, the seclusion of novices in a fixed, sacred space. The former liminalizes time; the latter, space. Time is here connected with voluntariness; space, with obligation.

One could ramify difference here, but I will return to the central themes of death and the dead. In the liminality of initiations, the dead often appear as near or remote ancestors, connected by putative ties of consanguinity or affinity with the living, part of a communion of kin beginning with the founding ancestors and, it is hoped, with due performance of ritual, continuing to the end of the world. The dead, as ancestral spirits, punish and sometimes reward the living. Kin are punished for quarreling or for having failed to remember the ancestors in their hearts or with offerings and sacrifices. Usually specific ancestors punish specific kin or groups of kin. Most misfortune, sickness, and reproductive trouble in Central African society, for example, is attributed to the morally punitive action of the "shades." Once recognized, named, and propitiated, however, they become benevolent guardians of their living kin, usually their lineal kin.

The dead are both the jural and the moral continuators of the society formed by their jural descendants and the procreative biology, the increase and multiplication, which ensures the continuation of the human matter on which that structural form is imprinted. When initiands become their companions in liminal seclusion, they, too, become moral and fertile. When I came to investigate Catholic pilgrimage processes, sensitized as I was to the role of the dead in African initiation and other passage ritual, I soon became aware that these, too, were pervaded by ideas about how the living and the dead were interconnected, but that these interconnections were consistent with voluntaristic religion and the total culture in which they were embedded.

In a crucial way, the Catholic faith hinges on the self-chosen, voluntary death of Christ for the sake both of those who would come after him, his spiritual posterity, and of the good pagan dead, neither in heaven nor in hell but in limbo, who had preceded him and whom he released by his descent into the nether regions during the three days between his death and resurrection in the body. This *via crucis*, death, and resurrection paradigm became the inspiration of the early martyrs whose "imitation of Christ" led to their death for the faith and for the future faithful at the hands of the pagan political authorities. Hence the well-known expression "the blood of the martyrs is the seed of the church," where blood equals spiritual semen.

Scholars generally hold that after the era of pilgrimage to the holy places of the Holy Land, the tombs of the martyrs, scattered throughout the Roman Empire but particularly numerous in Rome itself, became the first pilgrimage centers. They exemplified the supreme act of Christian free will, the choice of death for the salvific faith rather than life under the auspices of state religion. It was also believed by the masses that these places of redemptive self-sacrifice—since martyrdom was thought to be a projection into history of Christ's redeeming self-sacrifice—were places where heaven and earth came close, even communicated through prayers, miracles, and apparitions. Here there might be "gaps in the curtain."

A miracle, "an effect wrought in nature independently of natural powers and laws," the extreme expression of the rare, unprecedented, and idiosyncratic in experience, is counterposed to order and law, supreme symbols as well as agencies of social structuration, and exemplifies for the faithful the volitional character of faith as against the "necessary cause and effect" character of both natural and state law. Miracles might happen at martyrs' graves because martyrs gave up their lives for the belief that God alone is above and beyond nature and is the direct and immediate cause of salvation, defined as the "freeing of the soul from the bonds of sin and its consequences and the attainment of the everlasting vision of God in heaven." Miracles occur fitfully, not systematically or regularly, precisely because they are supreme acts in the drama of free will and grace, creative acts in the moral order.

From these beliefs and other sources, the development of the pilgrimage process became closely linked with the doctrine of the communion of saints. This postulates that under certain conditions the dead and the living can freely help one another to attain heaven, that is, the beatific vision of God in the company of all the other saints and angels. Roman legalism has worked on the notion of the communion of saints and has come to define it as "the unity under and in Christ of the faithful on earth (the Church Militant), the souls in purgatory (the Church Suffering), and the blessed in Heaven (the Church Triumphant)."

In principle, all these people—living and dead—are in the church in the first place through optation, for even if it was the parents' will that their child should be baptized, it is as the result of the child's own will that that child ultimately attains salvation. God plies the soul with graces, the devil plies it with temptations, the flesh is weak, and the world is full of occasions of sin. The drama goes on until the general judgment. But the different components of the church can help one another. In prayer, communication or fellowship is most active. The living pray to God and the saints on behalf of the suffering, and to God in honor of the saints. The saints intercede with God for the suffering and the living. The suffering, the souls in purgatory, pray to God and the saints for others. It is thought to be particularly efficacious if the living seek the intercession of the saints with God on behalf of the souls in purgatory. Here the system comes closest to tribal animism, for in practice, people pray most often for and to their own dead kinsfolk.

My own Catholic background and field research among Catholic country folk in Europe and Middle America have made me familiar with the doctrine of the *benditas ánimas* (in Mexico) or holy souls (in Ireland), that is, the members of the Church Suffering who are in purgatory. Purgatory, in Catholic thought, is the place and state in which souls suffer for a while and are purged after death, before they go to heaven, on account of their sins. Dante's Mount of Purgatory is the supreme literary expression of the doctrine. Most souls, it is thought, go to purgatory, if on the whole they have shown themselves to be reasonably moral, decent people, Walt Whitman's "divine average." These souls are there either because they have committed unrepented venial sins or, having in the sacrament of penance confessed their grave sins, they have been forgiven but still have to pay a "debt of temporal punishment." They are purged by the pain of intense longing for God, whose beatific vision is delayed, and by some pain of sense, popularly believed to be by material fire.

In this liminal period between earth and heaven, institutional faith is the means by which the souls in purgatory can be helped toward heaven or eased of pain by the prayers and sacrifices of the living, especially by the sacrament of the Eucharist; thus, virtually every mass is offered on behalf of a named relative of some parishioner. And although there has been no ecclesiastical decision on the matter, it is widely believed throughout the Catholic Church that one should pray not only for but also to the souls in purgatory, so that they will intercede for the living with God. In popular belief, the holy souls do not have immediate access to God as the saints in heaven do; that is part of their purgative suffering. But in a sense their prayers for the living, made while in purgatory, accumulate, and when a holy soul finally becomes a saint—and no one knows the hour of this—such prayers are considered to have surplus efficacy for having been so long pent-up. Therefore, argues the Catholic peasant in many lands, it is a pretty good bet to pray both for and to a holy soul, since if you pray for him, he will be grateful to you for speeding his release from purgatory, and if you pray to him, he will carry to heaven a great heap of your requests for God's immediate attention.

The holy souls—and it is fitting to discuss them in November, for the Catholic church dedicates this month to the beloved dead—resemble the Nyakyusa "shades." They are polluted and polluting, since they are not yet cleansed of adhering sins; but at the same time they are sacred and capable, if remembered and propitiated by sacrifices, of bringing such benefits to the living as fertility of people, animals, and crops, and of fending off or ameliorating afflictions, such as illness, accident, injury, famine, drought, blight, plague, or reproductive disorders. There may well be some delay here, but the outcome is virtually certain.

Neither holy souls nor shades are saints, for these two categories are liminally in between the *moyen sensuel* of the living and the ideal sphere of the perfectly moral dead. They need as well as bestow help. In practice, both holy souls and shades are one's kinsfolk, though in the tribal case kinship, particularly lineal kinship, may often be the very frame of institutionalized social life, whereas the Catholic prays for and to kin familiar to him owing to residential continuities based on feudal, postfeudal, and industrial-rural concrete circumstances rather than on societal axiomatic rule. But in both types of religion a normative communitas is postulated among the living and the dead. The dead need the sacrifices and prayers of the living; the living need the fructifying powers of the dead, either as mediators with divinity for the living or as a direct emission from the benevolent dead themselves.

Pilgrimage may be regarded as an accelerator of normal liturgical practice. It is popularly felt that the merits acquired by the saint or martyr lend power to masses said on the altar of a church dedicated to him. Also, popes and bishops grant indulgences to those receiving Communion there. When the pilgrim reaches his goal, priests at the target shrine are expected very speedily to perform two rituals of the sacramental liturgical set: penance and the Eucharist (confession and mass, as they are usually spoken of). Having made a pilgrimage amplifies these two sacraments in the pilgrim's eyes. These sacraments differ from the others— baptism, confirmation, marriage, ordination, and extreme unction—in not being life-crisis rituals (rites of passage properly speaking) but are what anthropologists might call contingent rituals, being concerned with the day-to-day maintenance of concrete individuals and groups in a state of moral, spiritual, and hence (in terms of medical theory, which regards body and informing soul as a dynamic continuum) physical health.

Thus, when a pilgrim asks for a mass to be said for his dead relatives in purgatory, this mass is thought to be more effective on account of the time, energy, and patience expended on the pilgrim's journey to the shrine and of his other sacrifices—exposure to danger and bad weather, loss of comfort, and his overcoming of temptations on the way. There is a general theory among pilgrims, however vague, that personal sacrifice can be the source of graces and blessings for others. Through the pilgrim's sacrifice these personal losses may be transmuted, like base metal, into the gold of graces and blessings, released from God's treasury, in which are also stored the merits of the faithful in all the ages, for the benefit of those whom the pilgrim specifically names as beneficiaries. In this specificity of benefaction, purgatorial notions most remind us of animistic religions.

It is almost a truism that Catholic ideas about the fate of the dead in purgatory have received most reinforcement from pre-Christian religious beliefs on the western fringes of Europe, in the surviving haunts of the Celtic peoples—Ireland, the western Highlands of Scotland (Barra, South Uist), Wales, Armorican Brittany, and Galicia in Spain. William A. Christian, Jr., has written an excellent account of Spanish folk Catholicism in the Nansa Valley of northern Spain. He writes: "Devotion for and worry about the dead is characteristic of the entire Atlantic fringe from Galicia, through Brittany, Ireland, and England" (1972:94). Similarly, Georgiana Goddard King (1920:235–249) and Walter Starkie (1965) have stressed connections in purgatorial beliefs between Galicia and Ireland, and Starkie has quoted from old traditions how spirits of the dead, temporarily released from purgatory, have begged mortals in the twilight to pray for them, that they might complete the pilgrimage to St. James's shrine at Compostela and so have their suffering remitted. If pilgrims are companions to the dead, it is to the dead of the Church Suffering; and if pilgrims are equivalent to the dead, it is to the dead in purgatory.

My own most vivid encounter with the continuity between Celtic animism and Catholic pilgrimage beliefs about the holy souls was in the west of Ireland—though Mexico, too, has its Christian cult of the dead uniting Galician and Asturian beliefs of this type to pre-Columbian Aztec traditions. An example is the "Day of the Dead" in Morelos, where on November 1, all household members make offerings in the house and cemetery (pantheon), not only for the direct ascendants of the family but also for all household residents, including women married into it.

My wife and I spent some months in the summer of 1972 going on pilgrimages in the west of Ireland and studying them. The most important contemporary pilgrim shrine in Ireland is that of Knock in County Mayo, where, it is credibly estimated, at least 700,000 people each year visit the shrine during the pilgrimage season, a substantial proportion of the total Catholic population of Ireland, north and south. This pilgrimage is of the type I have called "apparitional." The type became established in the post-Napoleonic, industrial era of Europe and includes such major shrines as La Salette, Lourdes, Pontmain, Pellevoisin, Fatima, Beauraing, and Banneux. The Latin countries of France, Portugal, and Belgium (though here Flemish speakers have also been involved) have been the main sites of apparitions of the Virgin Mary, usually to children alone or in groups. In most cases a message has been given by the Virgin;

at La Salette in France and at Fatima in Portugal especially, the message has been minatory and apocalyptic, prophesying disasters for men on earth and hell for them after death if they do not mend their ways.

Knock, though apparitional, contains no threatening figure portending disaster for overly technocratic, rationalistic people. The Knock apparition was peaceful and silent. Moreover, it was seen not by children alone but by at least fifteen people ranging in age from six to seventy-five. Nor was it the Virgin alone who was seen. A group of people saw a group of supernaturals, or so they believed and testified with convincing mutual consistency before a commission of three senior priests convoked by the archbishop of Tuam less than two months after the apparition. On the rainy night of 21 August 1879, at the beginning of one of Ireland's afflictions by potato famine and in the political context of Michael Davitt's and Parnell's struggles for land reform, Margaret, Mary, and Dominick Beirne, Mary McLoughlin, Catherine Murray, and eventually at least a dozen more villagers of the small hamlet of Knock, consisting of about twelve or so cottages, claimed that they saw "a sight such as was never before seen," near the gable of the village church, itself one of the first fruits of the Catholic emancipation of 1829.

What did they see? Let Michael Walsh take up the tale:

> They saw three figures standing at the gable wall of the church, about eighteen inches or two feet above the ground. The central figure was recognized as that of Our Lady. She was wearing a large white cloak fastened at the neck and on her head was a brilliant crown. . . . She was raised slightly above the other figures. . . . On her right was a figure recognized as that of St. Joseph. On her left was a figure considered by Mary Beirne (the chief informant) to be St. John the Evangelist . . . on the grounds that he resembles a statue of St. John which she had seen in the church at [the coastal Mayo town of] Lecanvy. He was dressed like a bishop . . . held an open book in his left hand . . . and appeared to be preaching. On his left was an altar, full-sized, and on it was a lamb . . . facing the figures. Just behind it was a cross. . . . The figures were full and round as if they had a body and life, but they spoke no words and no words were addressed to them. (1967:6–7)

One of the informants, Patrick Hill, thirteen years old, testified that he saw "wings fluttering" around the lamb. Those who relate the apparition to the holy souls often advert to this statement. Some regard the wings as signs of angels; others, as indications of the presence of the holy souls. The apparition began about seven o'clock in the evening (8 P.M. modern summer time) and lasted several hours before fading away.

Despite anticlerical criticisms of varying kinds—for example, that the apparitions had been produced by a concealed Jesuit with one of the primitive magic lanterns of that period, or that they were really a heap of holy statues ordered by the parish priest, Archdeacon Cavanagh, or that Mary McLoughlin, the priest's housekeeper, a well-known alcoholic, had stirred up the lively fancy of the villagers (none of which hypotheses stood up to the test of evidence)—the news of the apparitions spread, crowds soon collected at the gable, and miraculous cures were reported. The report of the Archbishop's Commission, though not positive, was not negative either, attesting to the honesty of the fifteen witnesses; a full-blown pilgrimage began, which, with ups and downs over the decades, finally succeeded in obtaining a papal coronation for the image of the Virgin of Knock, who is now known as the Queen of Ireland.

I first became aware of the intimate connection of Knock with the doctrine of purgatory when my wife went on pilgrimage to Knock from Castlebar, Mayo's county seat, twenty miles or so away. This day, 20 August 1972, was the Sunday nearest to the day of the apparition, a day on which many normally at work during the week could attend. She went with Bridgy Lydon, a pious old lady who spent much of her time traveling—a true palmer—from shrine to shrine. At the Knock Shrine Society Office, Bridgy, an old-age pensioner, gave a "widow's mite" of five pounds, more than a week's pension, for masses for the holy souls.

Later we learned that the people held a theory that the "wings" or indistinct "flames" seen by witnesses were not angels (that is, beings in heaven), as some supposed, but were souls in purgatory. As can well be imagined, the theological imagination of several generations of Irish clergy and laity has exercised itself most eloquently on the meaning of the "silent apparition." Most agree that the apparition was a reward to Ireland for keeping the faith through centuries of persecution and not a warning that divine retribution would follow loss of faith, as in some of the French and Portuguese apparitions, which manifested themselves in periods of antireligious and anticlerical ascendancy.

Many also agree that the holy souls believed to be present were those of the countless heroes and martyrs of the Irish struggle, which since the Reformation has also been a Catholic struggle against English overlordship. They argue that since for many years Catholic priests were forbidden under the penal laws to administer the sacraments, including the last sacrament, many souls, through no fault of their own, must have died unshriven, so that they would have to spend much more time in purgatory than they would otherwise have had to endure.

Clerical endorsement of the belief that the apparition was connected with the souls in purgatory is not lacking. For example, in 1962 a Franciscan Capuchin priest, Fr. Hubert, wrote "The Knock Apparition and Purgatory" for the *Knock Shrine Annual*, in which he comments on the fact that the apparition was seen just after the parish priest, Fr. Cavanagh, had offered his hundredth mass for the souls in purgatory. He therefore suggests that Our Lady of Knock should "very fitly be styled the helper of the Holy Souls and Mother of the Church Suffering" (p. 3). He then focuses on the composite figure of lamb, altar, and cross seen in the apparition, illustrates it with a drawing showing wings hovering above the altar, and suggests that this apocalyptic vision was a "showing forth of the glorious vision for which the souls in purgatory are continually yearning and to which many of them have already attained through the sacrifice of the Mass which had just been offered the hundredth time for them in church at Knock" (p. 7). From these and other signs Fr. Hubert concludes that the apparition "was due to the intervention of the holy souls" (p. 8).

Ordinary pilgrims, the kind who swarm at the shrine every day, have deduced that the apparition was a response to the prayers of the countless Irish martyred dead, and that it was somehow connected with the Book of Revelation (popularly supposed to have been written by St. John the Evangelist, one of the figures near the gable, during the persecution of the then scattered Christian communities by the Roman Emperor Domitian, identified by some of the Irish clergy with the English). Michael Walsh (1967: 57) has written: "It can reasonably be said that the immediate purpose of the apparition at Knock was to console the afflicted Irish community."

The cover picture of the *Knock Shrine Annual* for 1967 makes the purgatorial component quite clear. It purports to represent the apparition. But unlike earlier portrayals of this event, it quite frankly places to the left of the altar—now given a central position—and balancing the group of Mary, Joseph, and John to the right (that is, looking toward the people from the gable), a shadowy crowd of suffering souls in purgatory, regarded both as the initiators and as the benefactors (through the prayers of the faithful) of the apparition. The wings over the altar have now become explicit full-bodied angels, no longer regarded as suffering souls now that these have been openly portrayed. In this way iconography follows popular thought.

Irish pilgrims go to Knock to seek help from the supernatural power there for much the same problems and afflictions that send Africans to the ancestral shrines. The *Knock Shrine Annual*, like many Catholic journals associated with pilgrim shrines, publishes letters from pilgrims expressing gratitude for favors received after fulfilling their vows to visit the shrine. They refer mainly to the cure of illness, the gift of children, success in examinations, recovery from operations, the cure of sick farm animals, and similar matters. Often there is reference to the intercession of the holy souls. At Knock, the pilgrims feel that the whole church is present in a communitas of prayer. The living pray to Joseph, Mary, Jesus, John, and the angels (the Church Triumphant) for the holy souls (the Church Suffering), and to the saints and holy souls to intercede with God for themselves in their own troubles as members of the Church Militant. All this reinforces their faith that death is not extinction, and that the dead of all the ages are still in loving communion.

In the interstitial, interfacial realm of liminality, both in initiation rites and in the pilgrimage process, the dead are conceived of as transformative agencies and as mediating between various domains normally classified as distinct. These include the sensory as against the world of ideas: birth and death, structure and communitas, person and God, culture and nature, visibility and invisibility, past and present, human and animal, and many more fundamental dyads. It is important to note that the symbolic or metaphorical death undergone by initiands or pilgrims puts them in the in-between state of life-in-death, like the seed with rotting husk but thrusting cotyledon in the ground. Illness is one of the signs of this liminal condition, and it may be turned to fruitful account if, with the help of ritual, it can lead the initiand to open up to the communitas dimension outside of social structure.

In tribal society communitas is associated with physical fertility; in Christian pilgrimage, with spiritual fruitfulness. The seclusion camp and the pilgrim's road are also schools in which gnosis (liminal wisdom) is communicated to the individual in passage. Thus, when we are outside structure, in initiation or pilgrimage, whether literal or metaphorical, we are, in a sense, in communion with the dead, either the saints, prophets, philosophers, poets, or impeccable heroes of our own most cherished tradition, or the hosts of ordinary people, the "holy souls" who sinned, suffered, but loved enough to stay truly human, though now invisible to us.

In that we may fear destructuration, we may regard our dead as filthy and polluting, for they make themselves known in the liminal space that is betwixt and between all "pure" classifications and unambigious concepts. But if we regard them as part of a space-time communitas of humankind spanning the ages, may we not see them, on a wider scale than the world either of the Ndembu or of traditional pilgrimage, as a fructifying force, a tradition of grace rather than of blood?

3 Variations on a Theme of Liminality

Liminality is a concept, borrowed from the French folklorist Arnold Van Gennep (1960 [1908]), which, like a pebble, I tossed speculatively into the pool of my anthropological data in 1974, to try to make more sense than I had previously been able to do of ritual processes I had observed in Central Africa. Since then it has been spreading rings in my work and thought over wider ranges of data drawn not only from preindustrial societies but also from complex, large-scale civilizations. My theoretical focus has correlatively shifted from societies in which rituals involve practically everyone to societies in which, as Durkheim puts it, "the domain of religion," if not of ritual, has "contracted," become a matter of individual choice rather than universal corporate ascription, and where, with religious pluralism, there is sometimes a veritable supermarket of religious wares. In these societies, symbols once central to the mobilization of ritual action have tended to migrate directly or in disguise, through the cultural division of labor, into other domains: aesthetics, politics, law, popular culture, and the like.

We will briefly examine liminality, what Van Gennep meant by it, and how I have elaborated his formulation. Van Gennep examined rites of passage in many cultures, and found them to have basically a tripartite processual structure, even when they had many isolable episodes. He defined *rites de passage* as "rites which accompany every change of place, state, social position, and age." I will use "state" as a metonym for the other terms; it refers to any type of stable or recurrent condition that is culturally recognized. These rites of transition, says Van Gennep, are marked by three phases: separation; margin (or limen); and reaggregation. The first and last speak for themselves; they detach ritual subjects from their old places in society and return them, inwardly transformed and outwardly changed, to new places. A more interesting problem is provided by the middle (marginal) or liminal phase. It is interesting in itself, but more so perhaps on account of its implications for a general theory of sociocultural processes. The term "marginal" has been pre-empted by various sociologists (for example, Stonequist, Thomas, Zanieski, and Riesman) for their own purposes—so we are left with "liminal."

A limen is a threshold, but at least in the case of protracted initiation rites or major seasonal festivals it is a very long threshold, a corridor al-most, or a tunnel which may become a pilgrim's road, or, passing from dynamics to statics, may cease to be a mere transition and become a set way of life, a state, that of the anchorite or monk. Let us refer to the state and process of midtransition as "liminality" and consider a few of its very odd properties. Those undergoing it—call them "liminaries"—are be-twixt and between established states of politico-jural structure. They evade ordinary cognitive classification, too, for they are not this or that, here or there, one thing or the other.

Out of their mundane structure context, they are in a sense "dead" to the world—and liminality has many symbols of death. Novices may be classed with spirits or ancestors or painted black; in Central Africa the place of circumcision in the boys' initiation rites is called "the place of dying." They are also "polluting," as Mary Douglas might say, because they transgress classificatory boundaries. Sometimes they are identified with feces; usually they are allowed to revert to nature by letting their hair and nails grow and their bodies get covered with dust. Their struc-tural "invisibility" may be marked not only by their seclusion from men's eyes but also by the loss of their preliminal names, by the removal of clothes, insignia, and other indicators of preliminal status; they may be required to speak in whispers, if at all. They may have to learn a special liminal vocabulary; normal word order may be reversed or even ran-domly scrambled.

Against these emblems of death or limbo, other symbols and symbolic actions portray gestation, parturition, lactation, weaning. The novices at times may be treated as embryos in a womb, as infants being born, as sucklings, and as weanlings. Usually there are words and phrases which indicate that they are "being grown" into a new postliminal state of being.

But the most characteristic midliminal symbolism is that of paradox, of being *both* this *and* that. Novices are portrayed and act as androgynous, or as both living *and* dead, at once ghosts and babies, both cultural and natural creatures, human *and* animal. They may be said to be in a process of being ground down into a sort of homogeneous social matter, in which possibilities of differentiation may be still glimpsed, then later positively refashioned into specific shapes compatible with their new postliminal duties and rights as incumbents of a new status and state. The grinding-down process is accomplished by ordeals; circumcision, sub-incision, clitoridectomy, hazing, endurance of heat and cold, impossible physical tests in which failure is greeted by ridicule, unanswerable riddles which make even clever candidates look stupid, followed by physical punishment, and the like.

But reducing overlaps with reconstruction. The rebuilding process is by instruction, partly in practical skills, partly in tribal esoterica, and proceeds by both verbal and nonverbal symbolic means. Sacred objects may be shown, myths recited in conjunction with them, answers given to riddles earlier left unexplained. Very often, masked figures invade the liminal scene—usually framed in a sacred enclosure, cave, *temenos*, or other sequestered site—these masked figures being themselves liminal in their bizarre combinations of human, animal, vegetable, and mineral characteristics. Such maskers and monsters are often composites of factors drawn from the culture of mundane, quotidian experience, but split off from their normal, expectable contexts and recombined in grotesque, weird, even anatomically impossible configurations, which have as at least one of their functions that of provoking the novices or initiands, the "liminaries," into thinking hard about the elements and basic building blocks of symbolic complexes they had hitherto taken for granted as "natural" units.

Actuality, in the liminal state, gives way to possibility, and aberrant possibilities reveal once more to liminaries the value of what has hitherto been regarded as the somewhat tedious daily round. A man-headed lion, leaping into the firelight from the bush, may make one think about the abstract nature both of human heads and of feral bodies, or of the relationship between culture, which can *manufacture* monsters, and nature, which *generates* lions, or of the symbolism of social control (a chief has lionlike powers); each culture will stress its own salient dichotomies and draw its own lessons. And this is one of the simpler monsters; the Chinese dragon, a complex monster indeed, has been claimed by Elliot Smith to be a cultural construct in its entirety: Every part of its body has cosmological significance; the colors and shapes of its eyes, its limbs, its wings, its tail, its scales, its claws, its postures—all derive from the principles and symbolic lexicon of a cosmological system. Thus masks and monsters may be as much pedagogical devices as instruments of coercion through terror and awe; like other liminal things, they are probably both.

This is, of course, a synoptic account. Not all preindustrial societies have protracted rites of passage; some stress particular themes and symbolic processes, and play down others. Here I wish to show that where transition in space-time is ritualized, *how* it is ritualized, the nature and properties of the ritual symbols and of their interrelations, gives us clues not only to the cherished values of the society that performs the rituals but also to the nature of human sociality itself, transcending particular cultural forms.

This is not the place to discuss in any detail the distinction between sequestered and public liminality—which roughly corresponds to the difference between initiation rites and major seasonal feasts. In the former, the liminaries are humbled and leveled to make them fit for a higher status or state; in the latter, the liminaries are everybody in the community, and no one is elevated in status at the end of the rites. But by way of compensation, such major rites as sowing and harvest festivals, first-fruits festivals, change-of-season rites, or rites celebrating important points on the sun's ecliptic from northern to southern solstice very frequently involve symbolic status reversal or the creation of mock hierarchies for the mundanely poor and humble.

Humbling and submission to ordeal, whether inflicted by self or others, goes with preparation for elitehood—whether in this world or in the next; having an extremely good time, and playacting at having superior status, goes with a basic persisting secular egalitarianism among those who become liminaries for the occasion (see Turner 1969).

Here, another question must be raised: Whatever happened to liminality in *post*tribal societies? The answer will involve me in a brief discussion of a set of concepts which may help toward an explanation: work, leisure, play, the liminal and the liminoid, communitas, and flow. I am not, in this essay, going to use liminality in a metaphorical sense. I am going to look at cultural phenomena which may either be shown to have descended from earlier forms of ritual liminality or are, in some sense, their functional equivalents.

Work

In tribal and archaic societies, what people do in ritual is often described by terms which we might translate as "work." Raymond Firth speaks of the "work" of the gods in Tikopia as a native description of the annual ritual cycle of these Polynesians. Bantu-speaking peoples in Africa use the same term for a ritual specialist's activity as for what a hunter, a cultivator, a headman, or today a manual laborer does. Our own term "liturgy" is from the Greek *leos* or *laos* (the people) and *ergon* "work," cognate with Old English *weorc* and German *werk*, and ultimately derived from the Indo-European base *wergon*, "to do" or "to act." I could cite many other examples, but the point I wish to make is that the ritual round in tribal societies is embedded in the total round of activities and is part of the work of the people, which is *also* the work of the gods. We are dealing with a universe of work in which the whole community participates, through obligation, not optation. Furthermore, though there are special rites for special categories of persons, and for particular points in the culturally defined life cycle of each person, sooner or later no one is exempt from ritual duty, just as no one is exempt from economic, legal, or political obligations. Communal participation, obligation, the passage of the whole society through crises—communal or individual, directly or by proxy—these are the hallmarks of "the work of the gods" and sacred human work. Without sacred work, profane human work would be impossible for the community to conceive.

But, on the other hand, the ritual "work" to which I am referring is not quite what we, from our stance on the hither side of the industrial revolution and perhaps the Protestant ethic, might regard as "work." For it includes what we might think of as "play" or, more solemnly put since Huizinga, the "ludic." In many tribal rites, there is built into the liturgical structure a good deal of what we and they would think of as amusement, recreation, fun, and joking; furthermore, there is often the actual "playing" of games—ceremonial lacrosse among North American Indians, for example, the exhausting combined race and ball game of the Tarahumara of Mexico, or the "push-of-war" contests found among West-Central Bantu of Africa. Among the maskers are clowns; among the myths, Trickster stories.

Liminality is particularly conducive to play. Play is not to be restricted to games and jokes; it extends to the introduction of new forms of symbolic action, such as word games or masks. In short, parts of liminality may be given over to experimental behavior. Here I mean by "experiment" any action or process undertaken to discover something not yet known, *not* scientific experimentation nor what is based on experience rather than on theory or authority. In liminality, new ways of acting, new combinations of symbols, are tried out, to be discarded or accepted.

Ritual, and particularly liminality, should not be regarded as monolithic. A tribal ritual of any length and complexity is in fact an orchestration of many genres, styles, moods, atmospheres, tempi, and so on, ranging from prescribed, formal, stereotyped action to a free "play" of inventiveness, and including symbols in all the sensory codes mentioned by Lévi-Strauss: visual, auditory, olfactory, gustatory, tactile, kinesthetic, and so on. It has free and formulaic verbal behavior, and bodily acts of many kinds. The essence of ritual is its multidimensionality; of its symbols, their multivocality. Merely to equate such ritual with the obsessional "rituals" of Western neurotics, as Freud did, is to rob it of its creative potentials, and of its nuanced interplay of thought and mood. Ritual's multiplicity of elements allows for great flexibility and gives it an immense capacity to portray, interpret, and master radical novelty. This same complex flexibility makes it adaptable to change. I am referring here to tribal ritual, where ritual is the nerve center of cultural sensitivity.

But whatever happened to liminality, and to the richness, flexibility, and symbolic wealth of tribal ritual? As an adherent of one of the religions of the Book, I regret the deliminalization of Christian liturgy except on rare occasions, such as Christmas or Easter, where some liminal sonorities of song and language are allowed to linger. With deliminalization seems to have gone the powerful play component. Other religions of the Book, too, have regularly stressed the solemn at the expense of the festive. Fairs, fiestas, and carnivals exist, of course, but not liturgically. Other major historical religions have fared less badly. Thus, in Vedic India, according to Alain Daniélou, the "gods (the *sura* and *deva*, who are the objects of serious sacrificial ritual, which is the "work" of the householder *ashram*—*grihasta*—stage of life), the gods *play*. The rise, duration, and destruction of the world is their *game*." Creation is not only the "work of the gods" but also the "play of the gods." And human ritual is both earnest and playful. Modern Bhakti movements still have this spontaneous, "performative," ludic quality—where Eros sports with Thanatos, not in a grisly *danse macabre* but to symbolize a complete human reality.

Leisure

Now that we have spoken of "work" and "play," let us consider "work" and "leisure." In recent years much has been written of this pair of concepts. Joffre Dumazedier has argued strongly for the view that true leisure exists only when it complements or rewards work. Thus he refuses to classify the idle state of Greek philosophers and sixteenth-century gentry as "leisure," since this cannot be defined in relation to work but replaces work altogether, work being done by slaves, peasants, or servants. For Dumazedier, then, "leisure" presupposes "work." It is a nonwork, even an antiwork, phase in the life of a person who also works. Leisure, he holds, arises under two conditions. The first is that society ceases to govern its activities by means of common ritual obligations; some activities, including those of work and leisure, become, at least in theory, subject to individual choice. Second, the work by which a person earns his or her living is "set apart from his other activities; its limits are no longer natural but arbitrary"—indeed, work is organized in so definite a fashion that it can easily be separated, in both theory and practice, from his or her free time.

It is in industrial and industrializing societies that we mostly find these conditions. Here work is organized by industry, by clocking in and out, by office hours, and so on, so as to be separated from "free time," which includes, in addition to leisure, attendance to such personal needs as eating, sleeping, and caring for one's health and appearance, as well as familial, social, civic, political, and religious obligations. In tribal society all these would have been parts of the work-play sacred-profane continuum and would have been done with substantially the same group of people, and not, as in industrialized society, with different groups for each segmental activity spun off by the division of labor.

Leisure tends to be mainly an urban phenomenon—we see early forms of it perhaps in the fourteenth-century Italian city-state. When the concept of leisure begins to penetrate rural societies, it is because agricultural work is tending toward an industrial "rationalized" mode of organization, and because rural life is being penetrated by urban, industrial values. Dumazedier follows Isaiah Berlin in arguing that leisure has aspects both of "freedom *from*" and "freedom *to*." Leisure is *freedom from* a whole slew of institutional obligations prescribed by the basic forms of technological and bureaucratic organization in the work domain. It is also *freedom from* the forced, chronologically regulated rhythms of factory and office, and a chance to recuperate and enjoy natural, biological rhythms again, on the beaches and in the mountains, and in the parks and in the game reserves provided as liminoid retreats.

Play

More positively, leisure is *freedom to* enter, even for some to help generate, the symbolic worlds of entertainment, sports, games, diversions of all kinds. It is *freedom to* transcend social-structural normative limitations, the freedom to *play*—with ideas, with fantasies, with words (in literature, some of the "players" have been Rabelais, Joyce, and Samuel Beckett), with paint (think of the pointillists, surrealists, action painters, and so forth), and with social relationships (new forms of community, mating, sensitivity training, and so on).

And now we are getting closer to our lost liminality, for in this modern "leisure," far more even than in tribal and agrarian rituals, the experimental and the ludic are stressed. There are many more options in complex, industrial societies: games of skill, strength, and chance may serve (to use Geertz's terms) both as models *of* past work experience and models *for* future work behavior. Football, chess, and mountaineering are undoubtedly exacting and governed by rules and routines at least as stringent as those of the work situation but, being optional, they remain part of the individual's freedom, of his growing self-mastery, even self-transcendence, as we shall see when I discuss the notion of "flow." They are imbued more thoroughly with leisure than are those many types of industrial work in which men and women are alienated from the fruits and results of their labor. Leisure is thus potentially capable of releasing creative powers, individual and communal, either to criticize or to prop up dominant social-structural values.

This is not the place to discuss the effects of the Protestant ethic and bureaucratization, or even the entertainment genres of industrial leisure, making for professionalization of the arts and sports, and giving rise to the notion that art is a quasi-religious vocation with its own asceticism and total dedication—exemplified by Blake, Kierkegaard, Baudelaire, Proust, Rilke, Cézanne, Gauguin, Mahler, Sibelius, and so on. Here I wish to draw attention to some similarities between the leisure genres of art and entertainment in complex industrial societies and the rituals and myths of archaic, tribal, and early agrarian cultures. It is, I suppose, possible to conceive of leisure as a betwixt-and-between, neither-this-nor-that domain between two lodgements in the work domain, or between occupational and familial and civic activities. Leisure is derived from old French *leisir*, itself derived from Latin *licere*, "to be permitted." Interestingly, the Latin comes ultimately, according to Skeat, from the Indo-European base *leik*, "to offer for sale, bargain," referring to the liminal sphere of the market, with its implications of choice, variation, contract—a sphere that has connections in archaic and tribal religions with such Trickster deities as the Yoruba and Fon Elegba and Eshu, and the Greek Hermes. Exchange and marketing are more liminal than production—as focused fantasies of modern commercial advertising still attest.

The Liminal and the Liminoid

We have now seen how tribesmen play with the factors of liminality, with masks and monsters, symbolic inversions, parodies of profane reality, and so forth. So do the genres of industrial leisure: theater, ballet, film, the novel, poetry, classical music, rock music, art, pop art, and so on, pulling the elements of culture apart, putting them together again in often random, grotesque, improbable, surprising, shocking, sometimes deliberately experimental combinations. But there are certain important differences between the tribal genres, relatively few in number, of liminality, and the profusion of genres found in modern industrial leisure. I have called the latter "liminoid" by analogy with "ovoid" and "asteroid." I wish to convey by it something that is akin to the ritually liminal, or like it, but not identical with it. The "liminoid" represents, in a sense, the dismembering, the *sparagmos*, of the liminal; for various things that "hang together" in liminal situations split off to pursue separate destinies as specialized arts and sports and so on, as liminoid genres.

Furthermore, the liminoid is very often secularized. Many of the symbolic and ludic capacities of tribal religion have, with the advancing division of labor, with massive increase in the scale and complexity of political and economic units, migrated into nonreligious genres. Sometimes they have taken their sacred tone with them, and one speaks of "high priests" and "priestesses" of this or that art form or of criticism. Certainly, symbol and ritual have gotten into drama and poetry. On the one hand, literary critics speak of the nineteenth-century bildungsroman, the story of "our hero's" progress from poverty to glory, innocence to experience, as a "rite of passage" or "an initiation," with a linear, irreversible, monological, diachronic progression. Julia Kristeva, on the other hand, writes of the "carnivalization" of the novel—the kind of synchronic, dialogic, nonlinear, reversible, multigenre work that Rabelais, Cervantes, Lawrence Sterne, Joyce, Virginia Woolf, and others have produced, which may have its ultimate roots in seasonal rituals of reversal and celebration of fructifying chaos, rather than rituals of status elevation.

One striking piece of "secularization" seems to have occurred after the massive burning of images of the Virgin Mary by Thomas Cromwell at Chelsea in 1558. Devotion came by the end of the century to be addressed to a secular Virgin Queen, Floriana, or Oriana, Elizabeth I, to whom the liminoid humanists, the secular poets and dramatists, dedicated their rich symbolic offerings. Other arts have developed quasi-liturgical properties or have laid claim to the prophet's mantle. Music, for example, has often been called "the religion of the intellectuals," and poetry, as Blake and Rimbaud saw it, was the language of the prophet and *voyant*.

Continuing to contrast "liminal" and "liminoid," we may say that liminal phenomena tend to be collective, concerned with calendrical, meteorological, biological, or social-structural cycles and rhythms, or with crises in social processes, whether these result from internal adjustments, external adaptations, or unexpected disasters (earthquakes, invasions, plagues, and the like). Thus they appear at what may perhaps be called "natural breaks" in the flow of natural or sociocultural processes. Liminoid phenomena, on the other hand, may be collective (carnivals, spectacles, major sports events, folk drama, national theater, and so on), and when they are, are often directly derived from tribal liminal antecedents.

But they are more characteristically produced by known, named individuals, though they may have collective or "mass" effects. They are not cyclical but continuously generated, though in times and places sequestered from work settings in the leisure sphere.

Liminal phenomena are centrally integrated into the total social process, forming with all its other aspects a complete whole, and in its specific essence representing the "negativity" and "subjunctivity" of that total process, rather than its "positivity" and "indicativeness"; its possibility rather than its actuality, its "may be" and "might have been" rather than its "is," "was," and "will be"; or even a *via negativa* entered by everyone, not just by mystics. On the other hand, liminoid phenomena develop most characteristically outside the central economic and political processes, along their margins, on their interfaces, in their "tacit dimensions" (though liminoid ideas and images may later seep from these peripheries and corners into the center). They are also, in contrast with liminal phenomena, plural, fragmentary, and experimental—by "fragmentary" I mean the total inventory of liminoid thoughts, words, and deeds. Individual liminoid productions may, of course, be highly coherent because they have passed, as Ben Jonson said, through "the second fire on the Muse's anvil," craftsmanship.

Liminoid phenomena, being produced by specific named individuals or particular groups, schools, or coteries, tend to be more idiosyncratic and quirky than liminal phenomena, which are generalized and normative. They compete with one another in the cultural market and appeal to specific tastes; liminal phenomena tend to have a common intellectual and emotional meaning for all the members of the widest effective community. Liminal phenomena may, on occasion, portray the inversion or reversal of secular, mundane reality and social structure. But liminoid phenomena are not merely reversive, they are often subversive, representing radical critiques of the central structures and proposing utopian alternative models.

Another set of topics can be spun off this set of distinctions—for example, the ways in which both liminal and liminoid phenomena constitute metalanguages (including nonverbal ones) devised for the purpose of talking about the various languages of everyday, and in which mundane axioms become problematic, where the cherished symbols of the forum, agora, and stoa are reflected upon, rotated, and given new and unexpected valences. I see the germ of such metalanguages and reflexivity in certain of the phenomena of tribal liminality where we observe parodies of the sacred, and even playful mockery of the gods, as well as of chiefs, priests, and patriarchs.

Again, I can hardly do more here than touch upon the obvious fact that even in so-called tribal societies there is an easily recognized "liminoid zone" of culture. All anthropologists have encountered this: the great wood-carvers and painters who produce for delight as well as for ritual occasions, the singers of tales and composers of folklore, the manifold children's games, some of which comment ironically on the practices and beliefs of their elders, the satirists who employ keen, malicious wit to put down prigs and bosses and one another for the delectation of their mass audiences. On the other hand, there is a well-marked "liminal zone" in our own culture: in the liturgies and services of surviving religions; in the initiation rites of clubs, fraternities, the Masons, Elks, Lions, Knights of Columbus, secret societies both political and criminal; in the rites of passage of academe (anthropologists will recall Meyer Fortes's analysis of the Anglican rites by which the atheist Sir Edmund Leach was inducted into the office of provost of King's) or even more celebrated academies—some will have read Claude Lévi-Strauss's address after he had been formally and ceremonially admitted as fortieth "Immortal" into the Académie Française, in which he compared the rites, point by point, with those through which he had been given honorary tribal membership in a group of Northwest Coast Indians, thereby calling attention to certain universal, symbolic structures in liminal ritual.

Furthermore, there can be "reliminalization" of the liminoid. I think this is what may have happened to pilgrimages in the later Middle Ages. Formerly pilgrimage, like all liminoid phenomena, was an effect of multiple individual choices and arose spontaneously—in this case as a counterthrust to the corruption of ordinary life in manor and village and town. Later it became built into the structure of Christian culture as a "penitential system," as a rite of passage for readmitting criminous and reprobate individuals into the *Unam Ecclesiam* and, indeed, into civil society. Again, when a group of liminoid artists constitutes itself as a coterie, it tends to generate its own admission rites, providing a liminal portal to its liminoid precinct, a portal—to throw in a liminal monster or two— guarded by three-headed dogs and flaming-sword angels. Nevertheless, despite the coexistence of liminal and liminoid phenomena in all societies, it remains true that in complex societies, today's liminoid is yesterday's liminal.

Communitas

Here I will add a few comments on some social and psychological aspects of liminal and liminoid processes. I have often spoken of "communitas," or social antistructure, meaning by it a relational quality of full, unmediated communication, even communion, between definite and determinate identities, which arises spontaneously in all kinds of groups, situations, and circumstances. I distinguish three types of communitas: (1) the *spontaneous*, "existential" type I have just mentioned, the wind of which bloweth where it listeth, and which defies deliberate cognitive and volitional construction; (2) *normative* communitas, the attempt to capture and preserve spontaneous communitas in a system of ethical precepts and legal rules, something akin to Weber's "routinization of charisma"—though here the charisma is "pentecostal," something that descends on a group and is evanescent, rather than a constant personal attribute; and (3) *ideological* communitas, the formulation of remembered attributes of the communitas experience as a utopian blueprint for the reform of society—here we see that "ideological communitas" seems already to fall into the class of liminoid phenomena.

At the opposite pole to spontaneous, existential communitas is "social structure," in the sense of American and British structural-functionalist sociologists and anthropologists. Robert Merton puts it as well as any when he defines structure not as Lévi-Strauss would—as a system of unconscious categories—but as "the patterned arrangements of role-sets, status-sets, and status-sequences," on the whole consciously recognized and regularly operative in a given society. When we participate in social structure thus regarded, we gain through being presented with an orderly social world, with a recognized system of social control, with prescribed ways of acting toward people by virtue of our incumbency of status roles. But we lose immediacy, we are constrained by laws and conventions, and we are usually limited in the degree to which we can "play" with ideas or innovate behavior. Recognition should be given, if this view of the social is a valid one, to both key modalities of human relatedness—structure and communitas—if the social process and personal life are to develop fruitfully and usefully. Hypertrophy or atrophy of either may well produce social conflicts and psychological problems. Repressed communitas may be as warping as sexual repression.

One of the social aspects of liminality is probably to produce optimal conditions in small-scale, preindustrial societies for the emergence of communitas among liminaries, particularly among those jointly undergoing initiation. The leveling and stripping processes I mentioned earlier—the reduction of initiands to a sort of common human *prima materia*—may have the effect of strengthening the bonds of communitas even as it dissolves antecedent social-structural ties. Initiands frequently lose their very names and their previous kinship ties are situationally annulled, as are their former residential and political connections. But they are often allowed, even encouraged, to form small groups of friends in the seclusion camp—and such ties of friendship often endure, whether institutionalized or not, throughout life. Friends of this type, among Ndembu, may act as mediators if there is a blood feud between their respective lineages. Liminally originated friendship exists in our own society, of course. Members of the same class at Sandhurst or West Point, regardless of national, state, or class origin, continue to meet ceremonially, whenever possible, throughout life. The same is true of gatherings of alumni on American campuses in the summer, a liminoid time of leisure.

So I am speculating that certain kinds of liminality may be conducive to the emergence of communitas. Again, there is a difference between the tribal-liminal and the industrial-liminoid. In the former, the whole group is engaged in this process, directly or through its representatives. In our society, it seems that the small groups which nourish communitas do so by withdrawing voluntarily from the mainstream not only of economic but also of domestic familial life. The social category becomes the basis of recruitment. People who are similar in one important characteristic— sex, age, ethnicity, religion or some aspect of a religion, in the possession of a common physical or mental condition (often pathological), standing in a local community, trade, profession, and so forth—withdraw symbolically, even actually, from the total system, from which they may in various degrees feel themselves "alienated," to seek the glow of communitas among those with whom they share some cultural or biological feature they take to be their most signal mark of identity. Through the route of "social category" they escape the alienating structure of "social system" for communitas, or social antistructure.

This may well be "normative communitas" only, but there is no doubt, if one listens to enthusiastic members of street gangs, the Lions, the women's movement, Catholics for Peace, the New Minyan movement, rock climbers' clubs, or poetry reading and writing groups, that subjectively these people have a sense at times of being what Buber would call "an essential We," or what David Schneider would call "symbolically sharing common substance." Furthermore, in the retreats these groups make for themselves, they generate sensorily perceptible rituals and symbols which frame and consolidate their identity as a communitas. The paradox of such groups is that while existential communitas is in feeling tone a striving toward the universal, an open society, and an open morality, the normative communitas they achieve often separates them even more completely from the environing society as symbolically framed in-groups. The social-engineering trick, I suppose, is to keep the pipeline open between the society in general and each of its communitas groups, so that the former is seen as an amplification of the latter, and the latter is seen as an "organ" of the former. There are, however, dangers of total-ism in all this which are highly undesirable—the danger of the "corpo-rate state," for example.

Flow

Finally, I want to focus on a concept, "flow," which was the subject of some fascinating research by a Chicago colleague of mine, the social psy-chologist Mihaly Csikszentmihalyi. The precise nature of the connection between "flow" and "communitas" is in question: As we shall see, Csikszentmihalyi stresses the competitive, "agonistic" frames of "flow," while I see communitas as often arising out of the cessation of agonistic processes. In *Beyond Boredom and Anxiety* (1975) Csikszentmihalyi speaks of "flow" as "the holistic sensation present when we act with total in-volvement," and says that it is "a state in which action follows action ac-cording to an internal logic which seems to need no conscious interven-tion on our part." Csikszentmihalyi's earlier work was in the study of play and sport. He collected many responses from mountaineers, rock climbers, footballers, hockey players, and made his preliminary gener-alizations about the state of flow on the basis of these. Later he extended "flow" beyond sport to "the creative experience" in art and literature, and to religious experiences.

Tentatively, Csikszentmihalyi located six elements or qualities or dis-tinctive features of the "flow experience":

(1) *The experience of merging action and awareness.* There is no dualism in flow; while an actor may be aware of what he is doing, he cannot be aware that he is aware—if he should be, there is a rhythmic behavioral or cognitive break; self-consciousness makes him stumble. Pleasure gives way to problem, to worry, to anxiety. The player loses the point, the rock climber slips, the swordsman gets pinked. A personal cavil here: Is it not precisely through the effort to resolve such problems of reflexivity that knowledge advances?

(2) In Csikszentmihalyi's view, this merging of action and awareness is made possible by a *centering of attention on a limited stimulus field.* Con-sciousness must be narrowed, intensified, beamed in on a limited focus of attention. Past and future must be given up—only *now* matters. How is this to be done? Here conditions that normally prevail must be "sim-plified" by some definition of situational relevance. Bracketing and fram-ing are employed. Sometimes this is by physiological means—drugs (in-cluding alcohol) which do not so much "expand consciousness" as limit and intensify awareness. I can see some help from this for the study of

liminal and liminoid rituals, where social structure is simplified—elders and juniors, initiators and initiands, and action may be ritualized. But Csikszentmihalyi looks for his first model in Western games and sports. There intensification is brought about, on the one hand, by formal rules and, on the other, by motivational means, for example, competitiveness. A game's rules dismiss as irrelevant most of the "noise" which makes up uncontrolled, daily social reality, the multiform stimuli that impinge on our consciousness and sensorium. When we play football or chess, we have to abide by a limited set of norms. Then we are motivated to do well by the game's intrinsic structure, often to do better than others who subscribe to the same set of rules. Our minds and wills are thus focused sharply in certain known directions.

For Csikszentmihalyi, rewards for good knowledge and invincible will, when harnessed to tactical skill, complete the focusing. But he is much more interested in the flow induced by these means than in the rules, motivations, or rewards. He believes that the flow is what makes the participants accept the rules, for the sake of a flow experience. The participants should also have "inner resources," the "will to participate" (like other liminoid attributes, this goes back to voluntariness; one chooses to play), the capacity to shift emphases among the structural components of a game or to innovate by using the rules to generate unprecedented performances—the sort of thing a great coach can do, as can the players in team games.

(3) *Loss of ego* is another "flow" attribute. The self which is normally the broker between one person's actions and another's, becomes irrelevant when flow begins. Translating it into my terms, the "self" Csikszentmihalyi is talking about is the broker who functions in the field of social-structural relationships. The nonself or nonmind of flow awareness is highly characteristic of existential communitas, as well as of what Suzuki would call "Zen awareness." In Csikszentmihalyi's "games view" of flow, the actor is immersed in flow—he accepts the rules which are binding on the other actors—no "self," in the ordinary sense, is needed to bargain about what should or should not be done. Reality, says Csikszentmihalyi, tends thus to be "simplified to the point that is understandable, definable, and manageable." He insists that this also applies to "religious ritual and artistic performance" as well as to "games." Consensus about framing is a necessary if not a sufficient condition for flowing.

(4) An actor in flow, says Csikszentmihalyi, finds himself "*in control of his actions and of the environment.*" He may not know this at the instant of flow, but upon reflecting on it, he may realize that his skills were matched to the demands made on them by ritual, art, or sport. This helps him to

build up "a positive self-concept." Outside flow, such a subjective sense of control is difficult to achieve, due to the multiplicity of stimuli and cultural tasks—especially, I would hold, in industrial societies with their complex social and technical division of labor. Perhaps there is a similar motivation behind the withdrawal of persons into initially categorical groups based on selected characteristics that I mentioned earlier and participation in sport—each helps people to build up a positive self-concept, in the face of the many-selves "Protean man" of social structure, and by means of the no-self flow experience. Anyway, it is certain, Csikszentmihalyi argues, that with control in, say, the ritualized limits of a game or the form of a poem, a person may cope; worry goes, and so does fear. Even when, as in rock climbing or Formula One driving, the dangers are real, the moment flow is elicited and the activity is entered, the flow delights eliminate the consciousness of danger and other problems.

(5) *A fifth feature of flow is that it contains coherent, noncontradictory demands for action*, and provides clear, unambiguous feedback to a person's actions. This is entailed, Csikszentmihalyi says, by the limiting of awareness to a restricted field of possibilities. Culture reduces the flow possibility to defined channels—chess, polo, gambling, the stock market, liturgical action, miniature painting, yoga exercises, and the like. You can confidently "throw yourself" into the cultural design of the game of art, and know whether you have done well when you have completed the round of culturally prefigured acts. In the extreme case, as in completing the race at Le Mans, if you survive, you have performed adequately; in other cases the public, the crowd, the audience, or the professional critics have an important say, but if you are a real "pro," the final judge is yourself, looking back on your work or performance with established criteria in mind.

Csikszentmihalyi shows himself here as being in the classical rather than the romantic tradition, in his stress on self-imposed limitations or accepting the rules of the game. For him, "flooding" is not "flow." Flow is channeled and terminable by fiat. For the true romantic, the formal rules that center attention are only the beginning, discarded when the fancy starts to fly. Shelley, for example, in his "Lament for Adonais" after Keats's death, uses a conventional poetic form to get started, but finds himself—fairly quickly—"driven darkly and fearfully afar" to where "the soul of Adonais, like a star, beacons from the abode where the Eternals are." The same distinction would probably hold between priestly and shamanic ritual.

(6) Finally, *flow is autotelic*, in the sense that it seems to need no goals nor rewards outside itself. Cultural forms such as sports and art, according to this view, are set up for the sake of the flow they may induce, not

for the particular rewards they may appear to offer: the prizes, trophies, or fame.

Relating "flow" to "communitas," I would have to say that while I go along with Csikszentmihalyi's notion that flow involves a merging of action and awareness, an egoless state that is its own reward, and that communitas, too, has these attributes, as he writes in a recent monograph, I do not agree with him that flow requires "formal rules" and circumscription in space and time as preconditions. Communitas *is* a sort of shared flow—but it can and does occur both in structured and in unstructured situations. On the other hand, many games, sports, artistic performances, musical compositions, poems, and attempts at meditation are totally without flow, frustrating in the extreme to those who have recourse to them primarily for the "flow" experience. In protracted games, too, the moments of genuine flow are few and far between, even in some regarded as "classical" and "memorable." What the framing of sociocultural processes may do, however, is to call attention to the presence of flow, even perhaps to amplify it.

But such framing is not necessary for flow production. Flow clearly has strong physiological (including sexual) overtones: flow of milk, flow of semen, flow of blood, flow of urine; there are also metaphorical uses, such as flow of thought, flow of ideas, flow of work, flow of production. Flow clearly crosses the work/leisure divide I spoke of earlier. But the work domain itself is heterogeneous and complex and has its liminal aspects. All these usages imply some kind of psychosomatic basis, and they also imply an endogenous process that has a definite beginning and end. This processual form is not imposed from without by rules: As William Blake said of fire, "Fire finds its own form." So flow finds its own form.

Nevertheless, since we are animals with culture, flow elicitation may well be a function of certain key symbols. Again, it is a matter of particular cultural symbols in concrete situations, not of abstract systems of symbols. Group experience may lead to the selection of certain symbols as the best flow elicitors. My guess is that these would be liminal or liminoid symbols or symbolic actions, precisely those which are associated with social antistructure and which are initially associated with ritual process. They tend to be leveling, frame-breaking, hierarchy-toppling sorts of symbols. They may be in the ludic form of verbal and practical jokes, *jeux de mots*, witty paradoxes, and so forth, or in the serious form of reference in terms of the shared experience of the group to what equalizes us all, the biological facts of "birth, copulation, and death," and "the troubles of our proud and angry dust" which teach us that we *are* dust, to compound T. S. Eliot, A. E. Housman, and the Ash Wednesday liturgy.

If we focus, for example, on the liminoid genres of literature, on scenes and moments famous for the quality of their communitas and flow, such as Achilles's encounter with Priam in the *Iliad*, the episode of Raskolnikov's and Sonya's long, painful discovery of one another in *Crime and Punishment* (so well discussed by Paul Friedrich), the communitas of the liminary outcasts Lear, Tom O'Bedlam, Kent, and the Fool in the scene on the heath in *King Lear*, in the serious vein; and the women's communitas in Aristophanes's *Lysistrata*, and many episodes in *Tom Jones, Don Quixote*, and other "carnivalized novels," in the ludic, my hunch is that there will be key symbols which open up relationships to communitas. And that in life, too, key symbols will emerge to presage experiences of communitas.

Let me conclude by saying that in all societies "flow" symbols are most likely to be found in association with beginnings and transitions, genesis and exodus. In tribal society they are linked with the liminality of rites of passage and seasonal feasts; in complex, large-scale societies, primarily with the liminoid genres of leisure. And flow symbols, often but not always, go with the capacity to play, just as in sexuality and lactation, foreplay elicits physiological flow. The study of such transitional, processual, liminal, and transformative phenomena will surely help us to loosen up structural anthropology, and possibly to disalienate the work process.

4 African Ritual and Western Literature: Is a Comparative Symbology Possible?

I have participated in many performances of African ritual and read many works of European literature. The former's essence is kinesthetic; the latter's, aesthetic. You are moved literally by ritual, figuratively by literature. Action and intersubjectivity dominate ritual, reflection and subjectivity dominate reading. Both abound in symbols, but can ritual and literary symbols be meaningfully compared? The problem is placed in sharper focus by comparing genres drawn not from a single culture but from culture areas divergent to the point of apparent discrepancy. Only very remotely may Central African ritual be genetically connected to European literature, and then perhaps topologically rather than historically, in the sense that in many cultures (those of Japan, China, India, ancient Hellas, and so on) ritual seems to have preceded drama as a major cultural form.

Literature is composed by sedentary writers for sedentary readers. The writers may in their time have been involved in action, including ritual and dramatic action, but their works do not ensue from action; rather, they ensue from reflection upon it. (Melville did not write *Moby Dick* in a whaler's crow's nest.) Readers relate authorial reflections to memories of their own actions. Individual reflection makes accessible to other individual minds a complicated written or printed message. Subjectivity encounters subjectivity through an objective medium of communication, the manuscript or book. The process is one-way; the writer beams out his message in the hope but not the certainty that it will be picked up by readers, but unless a reader is also a critic, the writer will seldom get feedback. As Kierkegaard said, it's like shouting a message to someone rushing past in the night.

In the rituals of preliterate peoples the situation is quite different. Here there is no question of a single author and a single reader or, more generally, of a single transmitter and a single receiver. The form and content of a ritual, on the occasion of its most recent performance, derive on the one hand from recollections of previous performances in the heads of those publicly declared to be its masters of ceremonies, and on the other hand from the flair of those immediately engaged in it, those who appropriately relate traditional components to current social circumstances. Here, inheritance and innovation are both social; in a sense, everyone is both author and authored, maker and made. The liturgical armature is the product of past social action; the way that it is bent and stretched to fit the purposes of the moment is also socially determined. At all points there is reciprocity, interaction, communication, open or tacit.

Again, while sight and imagination dominate literature both for author and for reader, neither direct nor indirect visualization exhausts the sensory codings of ritual. Hearing, touch, taste, smell, and bodily movement are all drawn on to provide a repertoire of formal elements, which is then orchestrated into intricately combined patterns of ritualized action. There is little that is sedentary about African ritual unless it is the role of a novice in an initiation rite or a patient in a therapeutic rite who must maintain a posture of still humility. But this passivity is itself dramatic; it is an attribute of a contrapuntal role which forms part of a system of roles, many of which are extremely active. Moreover, in other episodes the novice or patient may engage in vivid action, notable in the concluding, or "reaggregation," phase of a ritual.

This description of African ritual hardly resembles what we have until recently been accustomed to think of as religious liturgy or church services in the West. Perhaps this is because our rituals are deeply literate. They assume the authoritative transmission of words and gestures based on written rubrics and are often read from a written script to mainly passive receivers (who may, at times, be allowed limited gestural responses but who are not encouraged to perform these in their own idiosyncratic ritual style, as occurs nearly everywhere in the African case).

In any event I am not comparing African with Western liturgy, or African folktales and epics with Western literary genres; I am deliberately making things harder for myself by symbologically comparing a sacred African genre of action, ritual, with Western literary modes. What highest common factors can we find? How may analysis of the former help us better to elucidate the latter, and vice versa?

I

First, a few words on therapeutic (or healing) rituals and communities among the Ndembu of northwestern Zambia, a matrilineal people, about

7,000 in number, in whose company I did two and a half years of field-work. Like many other African peoples, Ndembu use the same term for the malady or affliction and the procedures for curing or removing it. There are several kinds of rituals of affliction, performed for individuals said by Ndembu to have been "caught" (or in some cases "bitten" or "smitten") by the shades of deceased relatives whom they have forgotten to honor with regular small gifts of crops and beer, or whom they have offended by omitting to mention them by name when prayers are made at the village shrine trees planted in their memory. Very frequently people are allegedly "caught" for quarreling with kin or village neighbors, or as representatives of village kin groups torn by quarrels. The ancestral shades act as a kind of collective conscience or superego, punishing the social body by afflicting one or more of its constituent parts, which we would term "individuals." The Leibnitzian notion of a closed "self" would not be recognized by the Ndembu. Selves are open to one another, for good or ill. It is as though each self were festooned with prepositional cords and plugs ("with," "among," "to," "for," even "against"), and thus as though no individual could exist alone, but only when plugged into his group or network.

Being "caught" by an ancestral shade means several things. Both sexes may be smitten by illness: men by bad luck at hunting, women with reproductive disorders of certain specified types. Ndembu distinguish between the shade or spirit which afflicts and its mode of affliction. The shade is a known and named deceased relative of the afflicted person or patient, often one fairly recently dead. The patient is at the same time a candidate for admission into the curative cult community; the doctor is an adept in that cult. The mode of affliction refers to certain characteristics of the shade which are correlated with distinctive features of the patient's misfortune or illness. Mode of affliction and curative ritual have the same name, as I mentioned earlier. The therapeutic ritual is carried out by a number of doctor adepts, both male and female, who have themselves either been patients or else (as in the case of the male adepts in women's rituals) have been closely associated by kinship and affinity with afflicted patient candidates in previous performances of that type of ritual. Such adepts form a flexible ad hoc cult association whose members are mobilized to cure someone afflicted as they had once been. It is a community of suffering and "having suffered" people. Adepts each perform different tasks, but they flow into their roles rather than being assigned them in a hierarchical way.

Chihamba is the most complex and important of all the cults of affliction. Not only an ancestral shade but also a "territorial" or "tribal" spirit or demigod, whose secret cult name is Kavula (an archaic term for "lightning"), are considered to be agencies of affliction. This pair can bestow "all the ills that flesh is heir to," including bad luck at hunting, upon those they have chosen for cult membership. Kavula is male, the afflicting shade is female. The principal candidates are women, but the leading adepts are men. Kavula transcends the localized, particularistic division into villages and chiefdoms; he is the whole land and all its changes of seasons. The ancestresses betoken the villages. Two domains and two logics here interlace. There is not monologic but dialogic form.

When the people of my village, Mukanza, decided to sponsor a big Chihamba performance, they were perhaps driven to it by their internal state of dissension. Three of its factions were constantly contending for the headmanship, for the present headman was old and infirm; there were other sources of conflict, too. But like neurosis, affliction has secondary gains. Chihamba was consciously manipulated to restore friendship not only within the village but also with other villages. One village was indeed a split-off segment of Mukanza (founded by a group that had left the parent body after quarrels and witchcraft accusations). Others were linked to it by kinship, and divided from it by envying and conflicting material interests of various sorts. Here we have a microcosm of international diplomacy, with Chihamba as a sort of United Nations or Olympic Games. Anyway, practically everyone in any way connected with Mukanza village came along to participate as adepts or candidates in the secret or public phases of their ritual (see Turner 1975a:pt. 1).

This symbolic action can best be understood in relation to human social experiences of love and friendship, hatred and rivalry, social constraints and individual identity, determinacy and indeterminacy, continuity and discontinuity, which we, too, have felt and which enable us, with a little guidance as to natural, social, and cultural environmental condition, to penetrate sympathetically the messages embodied in the ritual symbols.

By the time I took part in Chihamba, its symbols were no longer exotic. I knew the landscape from which they were taken, the tree and animal species used, the agricultural cycles and hunting experiences to which they referred. More than that, I knew the people using them as I have never known people before or since that time of first fieldwork— which for anthropologists is akin to the period of heightened sensibility we call "first love" or first anything else of our youth. The basic facts of human sociality, in its health and pathology, are the same everywhere. Ritual and literature, in their different ways (and we'll discuss the "how" of that difference later), provided what it is now fashionable to call metalanguages for discussing sociality, special ways of talking about general ways of talking and acting. To be technical, a metalanguage, as a language used to make assertions about another language, is any language whose symbols refer to the properties of the symbols of another language. Ritual and literature, in a way, are society talking about itself, the reflexivity of society. Yet, paradoxically, ritual language is less discursive and more condensed and cryptic, certainly more potent than ordinary language. Condensation occurs in ritual partly because ritual is society, not one of its components, talking; its speech is thick speech, dense with the past and a distillation of all contemporary social modes.

Ritual is also society evaluating itself; out of its rich, deep experience it asserts that some things—for example, relationships, actions, thought, ideas, images, styles—are "good," others are "bad," others are neutral or not yet fully appraised. Not all ritual is religious ritual, but religious ritual is society not only talking about itself but also talking about what transcends it, about God. As Sally Moore has written of aspects of classification in Chagga ritual symbolism (1976:27): "Part of the message of these [ritual] symbols is that there is an underlying riddle that cannot be rationally solved, a riddle about the source and meaning of life. . . . Comprehensible limited surface orders and underlying unfathomable riddles about meaning and relationship may be the very things that are being represented." In Christian terms, rituals insist upon saving truths that transcend but do not deny rationality: on the paradox of infinity becoming finite, of the Creator becoming part of creation, of God dying, of the body being resurrected. These issues of paradox beset the sequence of field material I shall now present.

Almost at the end of the Chihamba ritual a personal shrine is made a short distance from the doorway of each candidate's hut. The process of constructing this shrine and the articles composing it make up a résumé of many features of Ndembu life and culture. More than this they speak to us, too, once the ritual idiom has been grasped. It must be understood that on the previous day the candidates have symbolically slain an image of Kavula made from a wooden framework covered by a brilliantly white blanket. The head of the demigod is represented by an inverted wooden meal mortar containing a bundle of symbolic objects.

While some adepts prepare this structure, others chase the candidates— naked save for a waist cloth—back and forth along the path between the sacred enclosure containing the image and the senior candidate's house. Songs indicate that the candidates have become slaves of Kavula, and they carry symbolic slave yokes. With each chasing they are brought nearer to Kavula's tabernacle, until at sundown they are brought up individually and serially to make obeisance before the white image of the demideity. They are told to strike it "on the head" with special ceremonial rattles, and then that they have killed him. While "dying," the image shakes violently and keels over. Soon afterward the candidates are told that they are innocent and that he is not dead, and the paraphernalia under the white cloth are revealed to be no more than some everyday implements—although for adepts each item has multiple meanings. Everyone then laughs joyfully.

There is a live sense of communitas, a deep accord among adepts and candidates, eliminating distinctions of age, sex, village affiliation, rank, status, or role. One might say that a "social construction of reality" has been shown to be such that the candidates are relieved to have slain not the god but a symbolic means of portraying and thinking about him. The irony of the situation is that what seems a deception reveals a truth, that the act of being cannot be caught in cognitive nets or adequately presented in symbols.

The following morning the god returns, but in a different way. He is now aligned more closely with nature than with culture. At the same time, it is the turn for the individual candidate. On the day of chasing and apparent deicide, the candidates appeared as a collectivity; now each is singled out as a separate person and assigned a shrine of his or her own. On the first day, the ritual movement was oscillant but ultimately centripetal—all converge to destroy the image of the god and thus assert his reality, his act of being. On the second day, the ritual movement is centrifugal. The god who drew people to him now scatters himself among the single individuals. On the first day, the movement between tabernacle and home culminated at the tabernacle, as a cultural artifact. On the second day, the ritual focus is on the home; the invisible god comes to private shrines and is there embodied in the seeds of edible crops. Before, the many came to the one; now the one comes to the many. Encompassing both is the ritual process which expresses the paradox that the one is the many and the many are one.

The ritual itself, like most Ndembu rituals, is performed with and through simple material things and simple actions and gestures. Their significance is not so simple, however, as we shall see, though it will be accessible to us. My contention has always been that a truly rendered reflexive statement about any isolable natural process of human experience—whether individual or social—consolidates into a sequence and patterning of symbols, each of which is multivocal (susceptible of many meanings) and which together represent a statement of the problems, partial solutions, and abiding paradoxes of the human condition.

Early, then, on the second day, the candidates are taken to a species of tree called *ikamba daChihamba*, literally a "cassava" or "manioc root" of Chihamba (from its swollen shape). A senior female adept bares the white taproot of this tree, which is said to represent—nay, to "be"—Kavula, the god slain previously in effigy. Then a senior male adept cuts off a branch of the root; and this, together with other symbolic vegetable objects, is taken back to the village. Again, this episode is said to be a "wounding" of Kavula, and unguents are applied to the root wherever it has been cut by the adept's hoe. There is something akin to the Western theological notion of transubstantiation here; the substance of the root is the deity Kavula, its accidents are its natural properties. On their way back to the village the adepts stop to draw a white clay image of Kavula (like a cross) on the ground. They conceal this under a medicine basket and make a double arch at its foot with a split sapling. The candidates are made to crawl up to the image and greet it as they greeted the forest image on the previous day. But now it is their turn to be symbolically killed. Kavula, acting through his officiants, ceremonially "beheads" them by passing a knife over their shoulders. Dialecticians might see in this concrete logic a kind of "negation of the negation." Kavula's "death" is canceled by the candidates' "death." Life, health, and fertility can now prevail. Death is dead.

Back in the village, the final important step is the setting up, for each candidate, of a personal shrine, known as *kantong'a*, to the Chihamba spirits, both god and ancestress. These will henceforth be sources of benefit to their former victims. The setting up of shrines begins with that of the senior female candidate, she who was first afflicted and whose house on the previous day represented one symbolic pole of the ritual process. Kavula's tabernacle represented the whole land against her particular home, fertility in general against her specific reproductive power, the bush against the domestic sphere, hunting masculinity against cultivating and procreant feminity, health against illness, and many other oppositions. Now the meaning and power of the whole ritual are being incorporated in the new shrines constructed just outside the house of the candidates.

To make such a shrine, a bundle of twigs cut from trees that are symbolic not only of Chihamba spirits but also of other modes of affliction is thrust into a hole and tamped with cool, black mud from a stream bottom. Sacralized white maize beer is then poured on it as a libation. A clay pot containing medicine made from the bark and leaves of the species from which the twigs were taken is placed near the bundle, and the blood of a decapitated white hen is poured into it, the severed head being placed on the apex of the bundle and the intestines draped around the twigs. A senior male adept then digs a circle in the earth round the shrine with the butt of his sacred, personal rattle. Beans and maize grains are then planted in the trench by all the adepts in unison. A section of the *ikamba daChihamba* root, representing Kavula, is partially buried near the pot on the side nearest to the candidate's hut. Libations are poured at each end of the root. Lines are then drawn in white manioc meal from the medicine pot and root to the doorway of the hut and also to the shrine trees planted to the village ancestors. In this way the auspicious power of the Chihamba ritual is channeled where it can do most good. While these actions are being performed, the senior male adept invokes the spirits of Chihamba, now using the candidate's new cultic name, for she has been transformed into an adept.

Every item, every gesture, has significance at *kantong'a*. Ndembu ritual symbols are what semioticians call "iconic": an icon entails similarity between signifier and signified. This seems to have nothing in common with "icon" in the Christian tradition, but is an idiolect usage of the philosopher Charles S. Peirce. An icon is a type of sign, and since the time of the Stoics a sign has been thought of as made up of two halves, one sensible, one intelligible: the "signifier," a perceptible impact on at least one of the sense organs of the interpreter, and the content that is signified. Charles Morris speaks of the signifier (medieval Latin, *signans*) as the "sign vehicle" and the signified (medieval Latin, *signatum*) as the "designatum." Saussure uses the terms *signifiant* and *signifié*.

Let us look at the bundle of twigs which forms a central part of the personal shrine. Each species of tree is an iconic sign or symbol. In Ndembu ritual, iconicity has three main forms: nominal, substantial, and artifactual. Put simply, an icon's meaning is derived from its name, its nature, and its fashioning by human activity. Thus the name of an object used in ritual may be connected by folk etymology to the name or part of a name denoting some other object, activity, relationship conception, or quality. We shall see how this works in a moment. The natural properties of an object, whether it is a gas, a liquid, or a solid; animal, vegetable, or mineral; plain, striped, or spotted; its color, texture, taste, smell, sound, location, habitus, normal setting, and many more—one or several of these may be selected as foundations for meaning. Finally, a natural object may be worked upon by purposive human activity and shaped into an artifact. This additional cultural elaboration becomes a further basis of meaning.

Let's begin at the "nominal" end of this semantic spectrum. The names of the trees from which twigs are taken are, in order of collection: *mudyi, mukula, musoli, mukombukombu, mututambululu,* and *muhotuhotu.* The prefix *mu-* (pl., *nyi*) commonly applies to the class of trees and shrubs in Ndembu ethnobotany.

None of my informants connected *mudyi* with another Ndembu word or radical, but I have reason to believe that the radical *dyi-* is derived from *dya*, "eat." This would be consistent with its substantial basis, as we shall see.

All Ndembu link *mukula* with *kula*, "to pass a culturally defined point of maturity," such as the transition from childhood to social maturity, or from middle age to elderhood. Roughly, it means "to grow up, mature." Its primary denotation is the onset of the menses in a girl.

Many Ndembu, especially adepts in the various kinds of ritual cults which use it, derive *musoli* from *ku-solola*, "to produce to view, make visible, manifest."

Mukombukombu is derived by informants from *ku-komba*, "to sweep," which is connected by them with *ku-kombela*, "to invoke spirits, to pray."

Mututambululu is associated by informants with *ambululu*, a species of small bee which hovers in clouds around the blossoms of this plant.

Muhotuhotu, according to some informants, is from *ku-hotumuna*, "to fall at once," said of leaves falling together from a shaken tree; according to others, it is from *ku-hotumuka*, "to slip and fall"—one informant added, "like a wind-fallen tree lodged on another one, so a sickness [*musong'u*] lies on a patient's body; they [adepts] want to make it slip off [*hotumuka*]."

At the level of "substantial" iconicity, *mudyi* is a tree which, when cut, secretes a milky latex. I have discussed its semantics in many books and articles. Like all dominant symbols it is susceptible of many meanings. Among these are motherhood, womanhood, matriliny, a particular matrilineage, the mother-child bond, lactation, the learning process, and so on, all derived by association or analogy (that is, in an iconic fashion) from the tree's natural property of exuding white fluid in a way which closely resembles the way beads of milk emerge from a mother's nipple. In Chihamba a further designation of *mudyi* is deemed important: Since this tree is used in primary rites of passage, such as the girls' puberty ritual and the boys' circumcision ritual, as a dominant symbol, it is used metonymically for initiation.

Mukula, like *mudyi*, also secretes fluid. But this fluid is a gum, which is red and thick, not white and fine. Ndembu compare it to blood, calling it "the blood of the *mukula* tree." In their ritual taxonomy there are different categories of blood, as I have shown elsewhere: blood of childbirth, menstrual blood, blood of circumcision, blood of hunting, blood of homicide, and blood of witchcraft (witches are believed to be necrophagous cannibals). The *mukula* tree and *mukula* fluid may be contextually specified to mean any of these. The fluid's propensity to coagulate is stressed in some cases; for example, in cults to cure women's reproductive disorders, *mukula* is used to make the menstrual blood, running away uselessly, cohere to form a fetus and placenta, and in boys' circumcision, to cause the operation wound to scab over. Like *mudyi*, *mukula* in Chihamba is an index of initiation; its very name means "to pass a point of maturation."

The other three species are usually found together in Ndembu ritual, for their branches or twigs are bound together in many rites to form a broom (*chisampu*) used for splashing or sweeping the patient (candidate) with medicine prepared from pounded leaves, bark scrapings, or root parings of ritually significant species. Here we are already dealing with the artifactual basis of meaning, but this is unavoidable. A medicine broom is said by informants to "sweep away diseases" or "sweep away the familiars of witchcraft." But it also contains the positive implication of something swept *on* as well. This is iconically connected with the fact that all three trees have large nectar-filled flowers attractive to bees—as we have seen, the name of one of them is derived from a species of bee. Sweeping with the three-stranded *chisampu* is thought to make the patient "attractive," to draw many people to the rites, and thus to "add power" to them. Women so swept will have many children, a hunter will kill many animals, many will praise the patient. Thus the medicine broom indicates the process it expedites. It purifies from pollution by its sweeping and *eo ipso* creates for the patient an auspicious ritual condition which will draw towards it much success, many benefits, and popularity.

All five tree species are found in many kinds of Ndembu ritual. In some rituals one or another is a dominant or focal symbol about which their entire symbolic repertoire is grouped. Together they constitute the ensemble of the highest, most pervasive values explicitly recognized in Ndembu culture, as well as the lowest common denominators of biological, domestic, and economic experience.

The artifactual basis of meaning may be seen (a) in the tying of the twigs into a bundle (a compendium of Ndembu cults of affliction) and (b) in the position of the bundle vis-à-vis other components of the personal *kantong'a* shrine. My informants told me that the *ikela* or hole in which it was placed made it stand upright, for standing up means strength for the candidate. The *malowa*, black river mud, "is cool, for it comes from water. It is put in the hole so that all the diseases and troubles in the bundle should rest peacefully forever after. For the bundle [*kaseli*] is a collection into one form of every disease that attacked the candidate [*muyeji*]." Water is often used as an initiatory symbol (just as we use it in baptism).

If the bundle is an epitome of "all the ills that flesh is heir to," the horizontally placed root of *ikamba daChihamba*, representing the demigod Kavula, stands for the singularity of the candidate, for her or his specific relationship to the deity. It also indicates the contrapuntal character of Chihamba in relation to all other Ndembu cults. Its half-buried character, said my best informant, Muchona, "means that you only saw the back of Kavula as he came out of the ground." This refers also to the image of Kavula in the tabernacle on the previous day. Kavula is at once a sky god or weather god and an earth god or vegetation god. His name, as I said, is an archaic term for the lightning of the rainy season and is connected with *nvula*, which with its cognates in almost all Bantu languages means "rain." I have shown elsewhere (1975a:pt. 1) that Kavula is also symbolically connected with thunder, with hunting, with the sound of firearms, with high authority, with grandparenthood, and especially with white symbolism, which is at once a sign of the ancestral spirits and of auspiciousness.

Kavula is also a sign of transformation: he dies as rain to become crops and food. Hence the circle of grains and beans and, I should add, the cutting of manioc planted with the bundle of medicine twigs. Those initiated into his cult are transformed, too; they partake of his numinosity, of the immense concentration of sometimes disparate powers and meanings brought together in the symbolic vehicles of his cult and finally deposited in the *kantong'a* shrine. *Kantong'a* means "a memorial," for Ndembu derive it from *ku-tong'ashana*, "to think about," perhaps even to "meditate upon." It is a living reminder of Kavula, whose name must never be mentioned aloud in the mundane world or to those uninitiated in his cult.

When the grains and beans, which are supposed to be a compendium of all Ndembu food crops, have grown to a reasonable height, food taboos laid on the candidates are lifted. The taboos concern mostly striped or spotted animals, fish, or birds, for their marks resemble those made by leprosy—and the sanction against breaking the rules of Chihamba is affliction by this disease, itself the negative power of whiteness, Kavula's color.

There is nothing about these patterns of symbolic objects and actions which we can truthfully say is really alien to our own way of experiencing life. All the big issues are here expressed: life/death; sickness/health; male/female; individual/community; familiar/strange; nature/culture; purification/pollution; the personal crisis that may lead to individuation; the overcoming of conflict to revitalize social cohesion. Local features do abound, of course. There is the contrast not of summer, fall, winter, and spring but of dry and wet seasons—with great Kavula-like storms on the threshold of the rains. There is the overwhelming presence of the savanna, the deciduous woodland, broken intermittently by grassy plains, the frailty of the wattle-and-daub huts in which people live. There is the necessity of surviving on what one grows, hunts, collects, and fishes for, not on what one buys. There is relatively rudimentary technology: hoes, not plows, no cattle nor horses for food or traction. There is a high rate of infant mortality and a short life expectancy for all. Society is disease-logged: malaria, bilharzia, yaws, hookworm, sleeping sickness, relapsing fever, tuberculosis, and many others. Relationships among kinsfolk are close and continuous; some have political value. Men succeed to office and inherit wealth through the mother's, not the father's, side of the family. If you're a headman, your sister's son, not your own son, will succeed to your position and inherit your muzzle-loading gun, if you're lucky enough to have one. Property is simple and mostly movable. Indeed, with shifting cultivation and hunting, the tiny villages pull up stakes and move every five years or so.

There are other major differences from life as we experience it in an industrialized, urban milieu, conscious of millennia of written history and literature, and often abiding among the huge, only slowly perishing artifacts and buildings of our predecessors. But members of a species which has been able to adapt to all kinds of climatic, geographical, and social conditions, whose members learn many new roles in the course of their lives, whose cultural outputs are almost infinitely varied, can easily slip into the skins of Ndembu and see how they use their environment as a source of symbolic forms for experiences all human beings share.

Even the purely religious aspects of Chihamba have an oddly familiar ring for Westerners. There is a deity who is slain by his people, is resurrected, and produces life more abundantly. One recalls the biblical verse "Unless a grain of wheat falls to the ground and dies, it remains only a single grain; but if it dies, it yields a rich harvest" (John 12:24). By entering into the death of their deity, candidates are reborn (the symbolism is clear) as members of his cult and receive new names in religion. The deity comes from the sky, and by his death renews the earth. He is connected with whiteness and water and supreme authority. He heals the afflicted. There is no doubt that Chihamba is a traditional Ndembu ritual that has not been affected by missionary influences from the West.

II

We must now consider whether it is possible to analyze symbols in Western literature in the same way and to compare the results with those obtained in studying tribal ritual symbols. One problem is that literature is a matter of the written word, and writing imposes a linear and hierarchical form, while ritual is act and process and may have several vortices of action going on at the same time—like a three-ring circus. Literary forms relate to earlier literary forms, and no two works are closely similar. Rituals are transmitted orally and often learned in their practice, not from books. But there are deeper differences, and it is to these that I would like to call attention. In 1974 and 1975 I gave tutorials in the Committee on Social Thought at the University of Chicago on Dante, Blake, and Kierkegaard. My method of approach to their texts—and on the Committee we always went directly to texts, probed them as far as we could, and only then sought help from commentators—was to treat them as sequences of multivocal symbols.

In the Dante tutorial, for example, we approached the first canto of the *Purgatorio* (1939:18–30) as if it were the account of a ritual process given us by an exceptionally gifted native informant. We listed all the objects, proper nouns, persons, actions, relationships, attributes, topographical features, and so on, which could be shown to have a symbolic value—that is, in addition to their denotations, they designated a number of other objects, conceptions, religious doctrines, and so on, beyond their literal sense. At first we tried to elucidate Dante by Dante; we looked for exegetical help from other parts of the *Commedia*, or from other works of his, such as the *Vita nuova*, the *Convivio*, and *De monarchia*. Then we invoked the help of commentators such as Charles Singleton, Arnaldo Momigliano, Dorothy Sayers, Umberto Cosmo, and Ernst Curtius.

From these varied sources the following schema emerged for the first book. As we shall see, an initiation scenario emerges which is comparable with the episode of *kantong'a* in the Ndembu ritual. Here Virgil and Cato are the adepts, while Dante the pilgrim—not to be confused here with Dante the poet-narrator—is the candidate. He is to be symbolically purified and humbled before he can ascend the Mountain of Purgatory on his way to Paradise. Dante's book, like the Chihamba ritual, emerged from a situation of social conflict: the poet was exiled by his political opponents, the Guelphs of Florence. I shall not burden you with a heap of particular symbols—it took us a whole term to work our way through the first canto—but will focus on a few relevant to the initiation theme. And, incidentally, I hope to show the virtues of structuralism as a mode of description and ordering of textual materials, if not as a general theory of mind and culture.

The Processual Form of Canto I of the Purgatorio

Canto I begins with nautical symbols—Dante's humble little boat elevates its sails, leaving a cruel sea, Inferno, for better waters, Purgatorio. The notions of elevation, breeze to fill the sails, movement in a favorable element, become prominent. There is also the notion of resurrection, "dead poetry rises again," Muses breathe inspiration into the sails—now, however, as "sacred Muses," pagan goddesses baptized and transformed, a nature good enough for grace to build on. The resurrection theme, associated with female powers, is enhanced by the reference to the Muses' song celebrating Persephone, who rose from the dead after immersion in the night of Hades, against the perverse song of the piebald magpies, the Pierides, who suppose the earth giants to have overthrown the heavenly gods, putting Below where Above should be. In fact, the true course is ever upward, from Hell up to Purgatory, then up the Mountain of Purgatory, where the ascent gets easier the higher one climbs, to Heaven and its successive circles which go up to the beatific vision of the Trinity.

But since the mortal being has fallen in his originally created nature, he has to be re-created or regenerated. Hence the descent of figures such as Beatrice (prefigured by the myth of Persephone) and especially God himself in his Second Person, who harrowed Hell (or, rather, limbo) to raise fallen souls like Dante first to the Earthly Paradise of natural perfection on the top of the Mountain of Purgatory then to the true supernatural Heaven. Even Virgil is raised from limbo to the Earthly Paradise before he must relinquish Dante to the guidance of Beatrice. And Christ raised Cato from limbo to be the guardian of the Mountain of Purgatory, not a jailer like Minos over the Inferno but a liberator urging souls onward and upward toward the earthly and heavenly paradises.

After the water and breath imagery of sea and Muses, we have a set of Ptolemaic astronomical and astrological images, in which the south represents the unfallen world, the north the fallen world, the Southern Cross the four cardinal virtues (shared by pagans and Christians). Venus, mother of the true principle of Roman *monarchia*, represented by Virgil's Augustinian age and his prophecy of the return of a golden age, anticipates the coming of the sun, the true Christian God, just as Beatrice, Matelda, and other female figures are later to lead Dante to the true Christian Heaven. The fishes veiled by the Love Planet may be not only the constellation Pisces but also the fish symbol for Christ, used in the catacombs by the first persecuted Christians. Sea and sky produce a sort of baptism of the Roman principle of *monarchia* in its utopian Virgilian form.

Cato, the mediator, then comes into prominence. He stands between Hell, from which he was taken by Christ, and Purgatory proper. He knows the "laws of the abyss" which separate Hell and Purgatory. On the one side, or rather *below*, is a heap of dark symbols: "dead air, blind stream, eternal prison, deep night, black infernal valley, evil stream, defilement." On the other is the open sky, where the light of the four holy stars representing the four cardinal virtues—Justice, Prudence, Fortitude, and Temperance—makes Cato's face shine "as if the sun [of Christian truth] were before him." His true realm is the limen of the shore of the little island on which the great mountain is perched. But he separates Hell from Purgatory and cannot be won by Virgil's appeal to his love for his wife; a great gulf now separates Cato and Marcia.

Cato has much body symbolism: white-streaked beard, a double tress of hair (to express his duality?), a bright face, eyes that were once pleased by Marcia, a "holy breast" (possibly a reference to Lucan's *Pharsalia* IX. 561–562: "tua pectora sacra / Voce reple," "Fill your breast with the sacred utterance [of the god]").

Virgil, instigated by Cato, then involves Dante in a good deal of body symbolism also. Before that he had "laid hold on me, and with speech and hand and sign made reverent my legs and brow," that is, made Dante bow his head and kneel before the virtuous Roman. Then, on Cato's instructions, Virgil led Dante back a little toward Hell, signifying humility, or *reculer pour mieux sauter*, perhaps to a place where the breeze preserved the dew (perhaps a symbol of God's grace) from evaporation by the sun. Then he performed a kind of ritual which seemed to combine the functions of purificatory ablution (ridding Dante of the sooty stains of Hell which hid his true "color") and baptizing him into a new, more helpful life, by cincturing him with a girdle. The cincture with which Virgil girds Dante, made of a rush, reminds us that a rush or reed was one of St. John the Baptist's attributes in medieval iconography. It was also, of course, a rush that was put in the hand of Jesus as a mock scepter after he had been scourged. The fact that another rush springs up to replace the one taken clearly betokens rebirth and resurrection and their association with humility, the dominant mood of Purgatory.

This whole episode has clear Virgilian echoes, literally so, since they come from the *Aeneid*. For example, when Aeneas, in Book VI, 635–636, leaves black Tartarus and enters the Elysian Fields: "Occupat Aeneas aditum corpusque recenti spargit aqua ramumque in limine figit" (Aeneas gains the entrance, sprinkles his body with fresh water, and plants the bough full on the threshold). In the *Purgatorio*, Dante causes Virgil himself to treat Dante the pilgrim as a Christian Aeneas, sacralizing him to enter a pure realm. Note the literally "liminal" status of both Aeneas and Virgil.

Lévi-Strauss would be delighted by the binary oppositions disclosed in the topography of Purgatory, in its relation to other domains of the cosmos, and in its internal structure. There is the opposition between sea and island, between sky and earth, between left and right, between up and down, between the enclosed domain of Hell and the open domain of Purgatory, between (Cato's) rocks and the ("soft mud" of the) shore, between the northern and southern hemispheres, between the upper world (the Mountain of Purgatory) and the underworld (the Inferno), and (implicitly) between the east with its "oriental sapphire" of sunrise and the west (which we will learn is sundown, when no more activity is possible on the mountain until the next dawn), and between the "solitary plain" around the mountain's base and (as we shall learn) the much-peopled terraces of the purgatorial mountain. Finally, when one looks east, at sunrise, south is to the right, the auspicious side, and north to the left, the inauspicious side.

Further Structuralist Conjectures

Topography is perhaps the most accessible aspect of symbolism to structuralist procedure in the Roman Jakobson–Lévi-Strauss tradition, but while we are on the matter, further binary contrasts might be drawn here. In the temporal order we have—in terms of earlier and later—the Venus-sun dichotomy, the Cato-Virgil relationship (Cato, the best of the Republic; Virgil, the ideal model for *monarchia*); the Virgil-Dante opposition, pagan versus Christian epic poet; then there is the Pierides-Muses competition, which corresponds to the giants-gods conflict, which corresponds to the rebellion of local particularism against the generic, universalistic principle of *monarchia* (for Dante, the modernization process which would overcome the local segmentation of Christendom).

At the level of sex symbolism we have the Virgil-Beatrice complementarity, in which a Christian representative of the weaker sex (in terms of both Roman and medieval patriarchal systems) commands (and in terms of the symbolic actions we considered, there can hardly be any other interpretation—"I was sent to him to rescue him," and so on). In a sense, this is a reversal of the pagan Roman evaluation of the directions. Robert Hertz, for example, in his classical essay "The Preeminence of the Right Hand" (1973:27), writes: "For the Hindus and the Romans the north is the *regio fausta* (the happy, fortunate region) and inhabited by the gods while the south belongs to the dead." Dante keeps the south for the purgatorial dead, but makes it also a *regio fausta*.

Dante's ideal pagan Roman poet, philosopher, and ideologue of benevolent imperialism comes to rescue Dante from the servitude of sins which gave him "little time left to run." Here we have the dichotomy above-below, with the rule that "above is better" operating. There is also the dichotomy "Christian woman–pagan man," with the implication that a structurally inferior female is superior to a structurally superior male in terms of Christian theology. Here, too, we have the notion that the Kingdom of Heaven of the parables is really a sort of *un*-kingdom, in which the weak or structurally inferior are saved—this accords well with the general theme of humility or self-accepted humiliation which is the leitmotiv of the *Purgatorio*. I cite in support of this view such symbolic objects as "little ship," "little island," "little grass," "humble plant," "soft rushes," "tear-stained cheeks," "dew in the breeze" which for a while resists the drying power of the heat, and such symbolic actions as Dante's bowing before Cato and accepting Virgil's act of cincturing him with a reed girdle.

The theme that the historically "later is better" is concretized not only in the Venus-sun, matins-dawn temporal order but also in the Marcia-Beatrice comparison. Cato is "moved no more" by Marcia because she dwells "beyond the evil stream," that is, in a downward direction, in the Inferno, even though in that dread realm she is in the limbo of the good pagans. But Virgil, himself from limbo, and therefore, in a way, inferior in state to Cato, *is* induced by the prayers of Beatrice, "a lady descended from heaven," to come to the rescue of the almost damned Dante—damned perhaps through lust and pride.

Christian "paradoxes" abound here: in the secular-cultural antilogic of this frame, woman is better than man, another man's wife (Beatrice) is better than one's own wife (in the case of Cato), *above* is humility (Heaven approached by the purgatorial mountain) and *below* is pride (Hell), Virgil (though from the Inferno) ascends higher than Cato (who has been released by Christ's "harrowing of Hell" from the "laws of the abyss"), yet Cato will eventually attain Heaven while Virgil will not. Before one may mount, one must be abased—shown in the rush cincture and the descent to the shore of the "little island" on which there stands such a huge mountain. In Dante's Christian scheme, humility rises and pride sinks. Or perhaps we might say, with St. Francis de Sales, that "love is humility rising, while humility is love descending."

Some Dantean Paradoxes: Beatrice-Marcia

But, as we have had occasion to note, there remain some paradoxes of Dante's own. These often concern the nature of the relationship between pagan Roman and various Christian figures and ideas. What, for example, are we to make of the Dante-Beatrice and Cato-Marcia relationships? In the former case, Dante, for whatever reason, failed to marry an idealized woman, who married another and died young without children; in his imagination, she posthumously descended from heaven to save her lover (whom, living, she is not known to have loved equally) from damnation. In the latter case, Cato married Marcia when she was young—she was his second wife—and she bore him three children. After that, Cato gave her to his friend Hortensius, to whom she also bore children, fruit of her obedience to the stern Cato. When Hortensius died, she returned to Cato, in Lucan's words, "wearied and worn out with child-bearing" and implored him: "Grant me to renew the faithful compact of my first marriage; grant me only the name of wife; suffer men to write on my tomb, 'Marcia, wife of Cato'" (*Pharsalia* II.338–344).

We have here a classic case of Lévi-Straussian "structural inversion." The idealized and fantasized Beatrice tries after death to save the man she did not marry, Dante; the real and rejected Marcia tries before death to save her own marriage to a husband who had given her away. Beatrice, who, if we are to believe the *Vita nuova*, once jested with her friends at Dante's expense, had no children; Marcia, who always took Cato very much in earnest, bore him and his friend children. There is another thread to the story, of course. Dante was for a time, by his own confession, highly unfaithful to Beatrice's memory; Cato, although he "put Marcia away," was virtuous in all ways. But Dante puts Cato now in the vestibule of Purgatory, awaiting Heaven, and hence with hope, above Marcia, who exists without hope but also without pain, in limbo. Beatrice is above Cato, stationed at a high level of Heaven, and above Dante, although he hopes to reach Heaven eventually through Beatrice's aid. Yet Cato will also reach Heaven after the Last Judgment, according to the text we have just read. It may or may not be significant that Dante mentions in his poem neither Beatrice's husband, Simone de' Bardi, a member of one of the great banking houses of Florence, nor Marcia's second husband, Hortensius, Cato's friend.

What is Dante trying to say, then? Is it, in the language of inversion, a message that first love is best love, and that just as Cato received Marcia back in marriage at the pagan level of virtuous earthly life, so will Beatrice receive Dante back in nonmarriage at the level of heavenly life, which is a life of grace, not natural virtue? But in the afterlife, Cato "may no more be moved" by Marcia, "now that she dwells beyond the evil stream," in limbo, beyond Acheron, "the river of pain or woe." Beatrice "moves and directs" not only Virgil but also Dante, as we shall see, and moves him toward the beatific vision. Perhaps here the Christian doctrine that "in heaven, there is neither marriage nor giving in marriage" but instead the infinite and generous reciprocity of *all* souls, is a factor in Dante's argument.

I have already discussed the paradoxical position of Cato, pagan, suicide, and putter-away of a virtuous wife, who caused her to bear children in adultery, according to Christian standards. The roles of the female pagan deities, Venus and the Muses, in a Christian didactic-cum-epic poem have also been mentioned.

Now let us go back to themes detectable in the symbol vehicles. One can, for example, array symbols under the pagan-Christian contrast.

Pagan symbols would include Muses, Calliope, Pierides, Venus, fishes, wain, Cato, Marcia, the evil stream, Virgil, and Minos. Christian symbols would include Hell, Purgatory, Heaven, lady of heaven, Beatrice, Dante, rush, humility, angel, breeze (of grace), sun, little island, grass, boat, matins, purificatory washing, resurrection of the body (I.75), four stars, and first people. There are also ambiguous symbols: "sacred" Muses, Cato (pagan freedom from tyranny and Christian freedom from sin), the sun (as both Apollo, god of medicine, music, and prophecy, and the Christian God), Dante's act of obeisance to Cato as both a pagan act of filial piety and a Christian genuflection to a *figura* of God the Father (as Dante himself states in *Convivio* IV.xxvii.15–19, when he says that Marcia's return to Cato after Hortensius's death symbolizes the noble soul returning to God in old age).

III

The Christian-pagan contrast, ambiguity, and tension stress the difference between African ritual and European literature. For the literatus is working in a culture of papyrus and vellum, later of paper and printing, in which descriptions, observations, commentaries, and interpretations of the world have been accumulated over the centuries, and to which he has access. The composers of tribal rituals—and there are innovative geniuses of liturgy, too—work in oral traditions in which precise historical time depth is relatively shallow and becomes blended with mythical thought and imagery. Dante had time, in his long exile, to ruminate over Christian and pagan written works and documents. They could be embodied in his subjectivity, his inwardness. If they raised problems for him, these problems could be ventilated in poetic forms which themselves were products of literary traditions. For the tribal ritual "artists," their creations came out of the heat—the "effervescence," Durkheim might have said—of intersubjective, corporate action, forming themselves like the motifs and phrases of jazz musicians in the crucible of the living event. Live communion generated metaphors and symbols of its own sensuous incarnation.

Tribal rituals are conceived of as "work" and have a central place in cultural dynamics. The whole society participates in life-crisis rituals, in calendrical feasts, and everyone undergoes therapeutic ritual at some time in life. It is obligatory to pass through major initiations. But in an advanced phase of the division of labor, the domain of religion has contracted and is occupied by a plurality of churches and sects. Moreover, ritual has become an issue; some religious groups eschew it on principle, others water it down. With the contraction of the religious domain and its relegation for the masses of the surviving faithful to the sphere of leisure time, many of its former attributes have been secularized and have then fallen under the influence of the division of labor.

In Ndembu ritual, for example, what we could call art, music, sculpture, poetry, and drama are all strands of ritual action. In western European culture, with nodal points of change at the Renaissance, Reformation, and industrial revolution, these aesthetic processes have become increasingly specialized, secularized, diverse, individualized, voluntarized, and controversial. These, too, belong mainly to leisure, particularly as regards their consumption. Individuals generate artworks—which often become commodities on the market—out of freedom and subjectivity. Thus Dante's vision was by no means the *summa poetica* of medieval culture (equivalent to St. Thomas's *Summa theologiae*) it has often been held to be. It was often a somewhat subversive metasocial commentary on politics, religion, contemporary morality, and current poetic practice in a changing liminal age—as might have been expected from a political exile who was strongly critical of the forms of government of the Italian city-state produced by the new merchant-aristocrats and of the role of the church in its dealings with the empire, the French monarchy, and the Italian city-states.

Ndembu ritual often contains what we would call "ludic" (playful) or joking episodes. Sometimes its symbols portray reversal of the normal social and political structure. But this merely relates to experiences of the cyclical, repetitive character of the universe, of life and death, of village growth and decay. The reversive is not the potentially subversive. Again the focal ethical unit is the corporate group of kin, not the single individual. Though Chihamba does in fact give greater weight to individual destiny than most Ndembu rituals, it is still mostly performed as a remedy against social conflict in the interest of the wider community.

With all these differences go many similarities. Both rituals and literary works are highly complex semiotic phenomena. Both are systems of multivocal or polysemous signs (symbols). In both cases the symbols concentrate and bring within a single limited context many designations that in ordinary life are scattered widely through the events of each day and year in the lives of individuals and societies. As Barbara Babcock (1975:912) has written of the relation between ritual and the novel: "Just as ritual may combine and recapitulate the cultural repertoire of performance types and communicative relationships, so the novel is sufficiently flexible and 'open' that it may introduce the different voices of any and all other literary genres, not to mention extra-literary ones." Both ritual and literary opus are metalanguages, in the former case a nonverbal as well as a verbal one, confronting in their symbolisms and within their frames, forms and values that would otherwise be regarded as separate, discrepant, or even opposed.

Dante confronts ancient Roman with contemporary Christian principles and practices. In Chihamba, systems based on kinship are juxtaposed with systems based on territory and friendship. Both the poem and the ritual take stock of the cultures in which they are embedded and of which they constitute, so to speak, the reflecting mind and feeling heart. Since the symbol is the semantic molecule, the ultimate unit of specific structure, in both ritual and literary contexts, it is not surprising to find it a microcosm of the whole process or opus. That is why both Ndembu ritual symbol and Dantean poetic symbol share the following attributes:

1. Multiple meanings (*signifiés*)
2. Unification of disparate *signifiés*—essentially different signifieds are interconnected by analogy or by some link of association in fact or thought
3. Condensation—many ideas, relations between things, actions, interactions, and transactions are represented simultaneously by the symbol or icon vehicle (the ritual or poetic use of such a vehicle abridges what would otherwise be a lengthy verbal statement or argument)
4. Polarization of signifieds—referents especially of dominant symbols tend often to be grouped at opposed semantic poles: one refers to components of the moral and social orders (the ideological or normative pole of meaning); the other (the sensory or orectic pole) refers to phenomena and processes that may be expected to arouse feelings and desires, including sexual, metabolic, aggressive, and work activities. Thus in Chihamba, the *ikamba daChihamba* root stands both for the wounded body of a deity and for all the virtues and values he represents.

In Canto I of the *Purgatorio* the lines

> *Lo bel pianeto che d'amar conforta*
> The fair planet that prompts to love

> *feceva tutto rider l'oriente*
> was making the whole east smile

exemplify all the attributes I have been assigning to dominant symbols. It is at once a description of satisfying visual experience; a reference to Venus and to the sunrise which its own rising as Morning Star portended;

a reference to classical mythology, especially to Virgil's poetry; and a condensed account of Dante's political ideology. For Venus was the mother of Aeneas, whose Trojans were held to be ancestors of the Roman people. *Venus genetrix* was venerated as mother of the Roman people, especially of the Julian house, descended from Iulius, grandson of Venus, whom the Iulii, following Cato's lead, identified with Ascanius, son of Aeneas. Julius Caesar belonged to this house, as did Augustus Caesar, first emperor who presided over the Augustan age, which both Dante, and before him Virgil, his psychopomp, admired.

Virgil's famous Fourth Eclogue, written in 40 B.C., predicts the return of a golden age, and a newborn child is to rule a pacified world with the virtues of his father. Dante, like most educated Christians, supposed that Virgil, under divine inspiration, was referring to the dawn of the Christian era. Venus heralding the dawn was imperial, pacifying Rome, heralding the birth of Christ. For Dante, the sun nearly always signifies God; as it is Easter morning when the poets emerge from the Inferno onto the shoreline of the island of Mount Purgatory, Venus now appears not only as precursor of Christ's nativity but also of his resurrection. At yet another level, Venus may be said to prefigure the coming of Dante's guide through heaven, Beatrice, who will take over Virgil's role of guide and teacher in the Earthly Paradise on the summit of the mountain. Venus means "charm" or "blooming nature"; her name may even be derived from *venia*, "the grace of the gods" (Grant 1971:65).

The difference between Ndembu and European dominant symbols is not in their semantic structure but in the oral versus written traditions in which they are embedded. Venus, in Dante, has orectic and normative poles. Later (xxvii.94–96) he will write in passionate terms of the goddess who is a "planet" (and who in the *Paradiso* presides over the Third Heaven): "In the hour, I think, that from the east first shone from the mountain Cytherea, who with the fire of love [is] for ever burning." Dante knew well that the epithet "Cytherea" came from the island of Cythera, off the Peloponnesus, near which Venus rose from the sea. Here the erotic as well as maternal overtones of Venus are striking, linked to the opposite feminine qualities possessed by the blessed Beatrice and perhaps hinting at the presence of the Magdalene and other holy women at the empty tomb on Resurrection morning.

I have abundantly shown how Ndembu symbols, such as *mudyi*, the milk tree, and *mukula*, the blood tree, have physiological and ideological poles of meaning. It is my argument that it is through their dominant symbols or iconic signs, which constitute the molecules of both African ritual and European literature, that the action genres of the former and the written texts of the latter may best be compared. Dominant symbols provide the fixed points in the total systems, ritual or literary. They designate the major themes of the culture for which they are supreme modes of expression. Sometimes they also embody critiques of those principles and values, or enunciate new, unprecedented themes. Analysis of dominant symbols and the clusters of ancillary symbols which they organize is perhaps the best way to reveal differences in the implicit postulates of dynamical cultural systems. It raises questions which determine the shape and style of further, broader-gauged comparative research.

5 Sacrifice as Quintessential Process: Prophylaxis or Abandonment?

"Sacrifice" is a word with many dictionary definitions used in many different ways by anthropologists and biblical and classical scholars. Here I relate what I have learned about sacrifice to some previously published views about the nature and form of social and ritual processes.

In the first place, I have come to see sacrifice neither as a single act or event nor as an intellectual structure perhaps further reducible, as Lévi-Strauss has done for totems, to deep-lying rules, but as a process with several stages (one common sequence runs invocation-consecration-immolation-communion). The whole process, furthermore, may itself be a stage in a longer ritual process. That process, too, may be a phase in a protracted social drama or crisis, with secular as well as ritual moments. Or it may be fitted into the calendrical process of the agricultural year.

I am, of course, discussing sacrifice here as public religious worship or veneration, not internal sacrifice as the inward offering of oneself or something one deeply cherishes to God, the gods, or other transcendental beings or powers. I am beginning by asking what Allan Hanson (1975) calls "institutional questions" of the data on sacrifice, not "individual questions." I am trying to make sense of customs, values, norms, concepts, forms of social organization, and other institutions in forming the behavior from which arises the sacrificial process. I am not at the outset primarily concerned with the intentions, needs, drives, motivations, emotions, or habits of those engaged in that process—though I will adopt that perspective later.

But first some definitions. Many scholars from a wide range of disciplines have entered the definitional field—which is strewn with their broken lances. The splinters of mine will probably join them, but I will make the attempt. "Sacrifice" derives from the Latin *sacrificium*, and means "the action of making sacred (*sacer*)." There is much speculation about the etymology of *sacer*. Some would derive it from the Indo-European base *sak-, "to sanctify, make a compact." The old Norse *sattr*, "reconciled," and the Hittite *saklis*, "law, ritual," are derived from this base and appear to be cognates of *sacer*.

Most religious sacrifices involve an offering of some kind from a visible human agent, or a specialist acting on his or her behalf, to an invisible entity usually thought of as more powerful than the offerer, and capable of helping or hindering him/her by preternatural means. A compact is thus anticipated in the offering. Aquinas held, in the *Summa theologiae*, that while offering or "oblation" is the genus, sacrifice proper is a species. Some addition must be made to the oblation which determines, specifies, and reserves the sensible thing offered to the deity or power to whom it is offered. The "something done" to the offered thing Aquinas calls "immolation." Immolation is derived from the Latin *immolare*, which means to sprinkle with flour (from Latin *in-* and *mola*, coarse meal or flour, what in Virginia we call "grits," usually of spelt, a primitive species of wheat which, mixed with salt, was sprinkled on victims before sacrifice). In ritual "to immolate" meant, then, to sprinkle a victim with sacred meal preparatory to sacrificing it.

Even in Latin, but especially in English, immolation acquired the sense of "devoting to death," even of "slaying," of "blood" sacrifice. In fact, however, immolation need not be bloody but is according to the nature of the victim or offering. While animals may be killed (bloodily or unbloodily—by strangulation, for example), liquids may be poured out (making libation a species of immolation), and solids, including grain and flour, burned. I mention this because some thinkers, such as René Girard (1977, 1982), have placed blood sacrifice—regarding it as sacrifice *pur sang*, so to speak—at the center of theories of religion and culture.

Moreover, offering something and immolating it are only two acts in the chain of acts which make up a sacrificial process. As an anthropologist I have been present at many rituals of sacrifice and have often witnessed the events which led up to them. My fieldwork in Central Africa among the Ndembu and Kosa Lunda of Zambia involved long stays in two villages where my family and I came to know the residents quite well and were privy to much of the news and gossip about their problems. We knew only too well as facts of daily experience the high morbidity and mortality rates of Zambian rural society. And the quarrels and disputes which intermittently erupted between individuals and groups occurred quite literally a few yards from our threshold. For a time we were part of the village's social experience, woven into its developing and declining pattern of social relationships.

We found, as I have often written, that sickness and death were seldom thought to be consequences of what we would call "natural causes"—viruses, bacteria, fatal accidents—but were almost always held to be the result of invisible preternatural agencies: ancestral spirits, sorcery, witchcraft, breach of taboo, and the like. It was thought, furthermore, that such entities were roused into action by the state of men's and women's emotions or by the pressure of their wills. Hatred, envy, sexual jealousy, and covetousness could activate the *ndumba* or *tuyebela* (female witches' familiars) to kill the targets of these feelings. The theory existed also that strength and long life could result from killing one's fellows—indeed, one's close kin or affines—by the medicine-manufactured familiars of masculine sorcery. Death then was usually from the malignant occult power of the living, as was sudden, severe illness, its frequent precursor.

But most illness stopping short of death was thought to be sent as a warning by the patient's deceased relatives, the ancestral shades. It was a warning because, the Ndembu thought, the ancestors, the *akishi*, are offended by prolonged quarreling among their living village descendants and afflict one or more of them "prophylactically," to guard against the witchcraft or sorcery that must inevitably result from indulgence in passionate ill-wishing. Sickness is an indicator that all is not well in the state of the social body. The afflicted person is not necessarily the worst offender but may often be a child, in the role of scapegoat for the quarrel-ridden community.

When there is severe or protracted illness and death, Ndembu resort to divination, to an expert skilled in detecting the unseen causes of visible maladies and misfortunes. My book *Revelation and Divination in Ndembu Ritual* (1975a) discusses various types of Ndembu divination and diviners and what is held to be their relative efficacy. The main point I want to make now is that the diviner is a diagnostician who not only discovers the kind of preternatural being or power directly responsible for the patient's condition but also unravels, in the course of his séance, the complex tangle of open quarrels and secret rancors which provoked the affliction. The diviner has the further task of prescribing what type of ritual should be performed in order either to exorcise or to propitiate (both methods may be employed in a single performance) the inimical agency. Thereafter, the therapist or *chimbuki* (from *ku-uka*, "to cure") takes over, and a ritual selected by the diviner from a large repertoire of types is performed for the patient. The ritual is sponsored by a senior kinsman of the afflicted one, acting representatively for a corporate group of matrilineal kin.

In brief, we have a community's social process, its failure at times to run smoothly, the occurrence of illness, misfortune, or death during this disharmonious phase, the decision to go to a diviner, his diagnosis, and the performance of a specific type of ritual aimed directly at removing the affliction from the patient but also quite consciously concerned with restoring harmony to the disturbed group. In the case of death the process may involve the punishment and banishment of someone divined as the witch responsible, followed by the purification of the village—which may take the drastic form of abandoning the site where death occurred and building anew elsewhere.

But where only illness or bad luck—especially at hunting—is at issue, a ritual is performed for the patient. It is often elaborate, rich in symbolism, and may contain more than one phase of sacrifice. Ndembu do not have autonomous sacrificial rituals; sacrifice is always encompassed by a sequence of activities which includes many other ritual types—the collection of herbal symbols or "medicines," the erection of a shrine, lustrations, petitions, sacred songs and dances, medication of the candidate–patient, and so forth. In this respect they are in sharp contrast with the Nilotic peoples, such as the Nuer and Dinka, described by Evans-Pritchard and Leinhardt, for whom purely sacrificial rites are central in their religious practice.

Nevertheless, Ndembu offer a wide range of birds and animals, as well as vegetable substances of many kinds, as sacrificial victims to the ancestral spirits or as a means of driving away the creatures of sorcery or witchcraft. In *Revelation and Divination* (1975a) I have described the Chihamba ritual in some detail. In it, on separate occasions, a red cock and a white hen are beheaded, the former with reference to a woodland demigod, Kavula, the latter to an ancestress who had afflicted the patient in collusion with Kavula but who would now become her (or his) tutelary spirit. I say "with reference to" Kavula because the cock's blood is represented by adepts to be the blood of the deity whom the candidates (also "patients") believe or are supposed to believe they have slain in the crucial episode of the ritual.

Whether this symbolic slaughtering of Kavula and the subsequent symbolic beheading of the candidates are to be defined as "sacrificial" acts is problematic. As Ndembu see the situation, the deity is "beheaded" (*ketula hamutu*) by the candidates, and the following day, through his adepts, he "beheads" them. Similarly, but on different occasions, his red fowl is beheaded and their white fowls are beheaded. His animal equivalents are feminine and plural. And just as in the circumcision ceremony and in the hunting–cult rituals red is often a masculine color while in the girls' puberty ceremony and in many gynecological rituals white is a feminine color (the principal candidates in Chihamba also being women), the color of the sacrificial victims is clearly appropriate in the sacrificial context. I say "victims" advisedly, for it is not a matter, as some of my colleagues have thought, of merely magical action—the blood of the victims constituting a sort of vital force adding to the efficacy of the procedure. No, the red cock is clearly identified with Kavula and the white hen with the candidates.

I cannot go into the elaborate symbolism here, but my book shows how Kavula, originally a singular and dangerous numen,[1] after his slaying is transformed into a beneficent power expressing itself in the fertility of a variety of cultivated crops and of human beings. The One—symbolized as lightning—becomes the Many. In contrast, what is originally a large group of candidates, both male and female, after each has been symbolically decapitated one by one, is divided into its individual components; a special shrine is set up for each new adept near his or her own doorway. Each receives a special cultic name, and each is given personal insignia. I should mention that Chihamba is usually performed a year or two after some major crisis in a large village or local community, and that both adepts and candidates are drawn from factions formerly at sharp odds with one another—it is thus not only a healing rite but also a ritual of reconciliation, since former foes must collaborate to fulfill the ends of the ritual.

Clearly the symbolic beheadings are central episodes in the ritual sequence. It is important to note that the fowls are not eaten in a communion meal. There is a communion meal, but the sacred food eaten is not meat but beans and cassava (manioc). Moreover, the communion takes place at the time that Kavula, impersonated by a leading adept, gives each of the candidates his or her cultic name. I cannot refrain from quoting in full what my best informant, Muchona, had to say about why cassava and beans are used, for it is highly pertinent to the theme I am about to develop:

Cassava is important both at birth and death. When a child is born it is given thin porridge, *kapudyi*, made from cassava meal. When a sick person is nearly dead, before he expires, he asks for thin cassava porridge. He laps it and dies. These things, then, act together both at birth and death. Again, when women pass a grave, they throw down cassava roots for the dead. These are food for the dead. Cassava is the most important food of the Lunda people. Truly meat is just an addition to it.

But the big food of Chihamba is *ikundi* [the singular form, meaning "bean"]. It is to cause love, *ku-kundisha* [this is the causative form of *ku-kunda*, "to love": by folk etymologizing, Ndembu derive *ikundi*, "bean," pl. *makundi*, from *ku-kunda*, "to love"], between Chihamba [that is, Kavula] and the people. (Turner 1975a:70)

Here we have a veritable agape, a bean feast as a love feast. This communion takes place during the evening following the symbolic slaying of Kavula in effigy and before the symbolic slaying of the candidates the following morning. It is a liminal episode between complementary acts of sacrifice.

My readers will be fully aware of the almost universal presence of symbols of birth and death in rites of passage. Symbols of love, even physical love, are also prominent. Muchona's explicit association (corroborated by other informants) of cassava meal with both birth and death, and of beans with love (ku-kunda primarily means marital sexual love, not merely liking or affection), exemplifies these oft-repeated themes. With the god Kavula and with the afflicting ancestress the candidates and adepts partake of the death, birth (or rebirth), and love of this entire sacred community "under the species" of white cassava meal and white beans (the makundi beans are carefully divested of their colored outer cases before cooking)—white representing not only purity, as it does for us, but also health, strength, beauty, social amity, and right relationship among men and the ancestral spirits. Many texts and observations support this. The love feast is a significant step on the way toward the full ritual individuation of the candidates, which will be consummated on the morrow by their symbolic beheading, the sacrifice of the white hen, and the setting up for each of his or her personal shrine.

Now let us take stock of what we have learned before making broader comparisons and considering theories of sacrifice. The deity and the candidates undergo opposite but complementary transformations as the ritual process continues. The god and his avian equivalent, the red cock, are slain, a love feast and cultic naming rite follow, then the candidates and their avian equivalents, the white hens, are slain. The love feast is where each category, the invisible singular deity and the visible plural human candidates, passes through the other in mutual death, love, and birth—the deity on his way to materialization in the form of manifold crops, losing his secret name Kavula as he does so; the people on their way to ritual individuation, representing the partition of a social body into separate identities, each betokened by a unique cultic name. It is rather like William Blake's great formulation of the Christian doctrine of the Incarnation: "Therefore God becomes as we are, that we may be as He is" (1965:2).

Hubert and Mauss might have said in their celebrated Essay on Sacrifice (1964) that through sacrifice Kavula is "desacralized," and the sacrificers (both adepts and candidates) "sacralized." But this would be inadequate, for it is not here a matter of mana, or impersonal supernatural force, being concentrated in the victims (the red and white fowls) and then discharged for the benefit of gods and men, as Hubert and Mauss supposed. It is true that the adepts eat the red cock after sprinkling its blood on the meal mortar (which, covered by a whitened blanket, is believed by the candidates to be Kavula's head, to be struck by them with sacred rattles, *yileng'a*). Hubert and Mauss had postulated that in sacrifices of sacralization, supernatural forces are transmitted through the victim to the sacrificer, who gains, often by partaking of its flesh, a sacred character he lacked before the symbolic killing. But in Chihamba the adepts have already been sacralized. Here it is rather that by eating the cock, they become one with the god and in this capacity will symbolically behead the candidates on the following day.

But notions of impersonal force, such as mana, are inapposite here. Rather, we are witnessing a series of transformations and countertransformations of persons, visible and invisible. The love feast, the bean feast, is the archliminal moment when the One on its way to becoming the Many coincides with the Many on their way to being One, as a communitas of singular persons rather than as a system of social-structural status roles. There is a nondual mutual "flow," not the exhibition of a structural model.

We must see the "beheadings" and "deaths" as ritual processes encompassed by ritual processes, and the total sum of ritual processes as being encompassed by the processes of everyday, mundane social life in the village community. Thus envisioned, Chihamba emerges as a series of transformative symbolic actions designed to convert a preliminary situation of major social disunion into a situation of profound union among community members—including its invisible but morally active members, the ancestral spirits—and between society and the personalized powers of nature as represented by Kavula, who as lightning and storm brings destruction and as fertility multiplies crops, animals, and human beings.

Lévi-Strauss has written of "the manner in which, through their myths, their rituals, and their religious representations, men try to hide or to justify the discrepancies between their society and the ideal image of it which they harbor (1960: esp. 53). Whatever may be the case for myths, I think his formulation does not apply to rituals such as Chihamba. It is not a question here of hiding or justifying discrepancies between real and ideal societies. Rather, it is a matter of transforming the group as a whole, and its main individual members, from a social state of mutual antagonism to a social state of communitas. It does this by drawing on the power of symbols of death, love, and birth which influence the interiority as well as the manifest character of the social situation. Discrepancies are not "hidden," but aired and repented. Death symbols indicate the end of a bad era; birth and growth symbols, the hopeful beginning of a good one.

Almost any way of structuring a society—tribal, feudal, oriental despotic, bureaucratic, and so on—into hierarchical or segmentary arrangements of corporate groups, levels of authority, statuses, and roles produces conflicts, either through defects in social engineering or through the disparity between men's aspirations and their achievements, leading to frustration, jealousy, envy, and covetousness, and other "deadly sins" of social structure. Ritual concepts such as pollution, purification, sacrifice, and the like emerge from the recognition that social groups, in the course of time, get increasingly clogged by these negative sentiments, so that if there is any sense of generic human communality at the foundation of the group, it becomes harder to find as people identify themselves more and more with their statuses and their ambitions to rise in status and power.

But human society as a whole has been around long enough for it to have developed all kinds of cultural means for periodically striving to cleanse the polluted generic bond, which we may call, with Hume, the sentiment of "humankindness" or even agape, spontaneous, altruistic love. Perhaps the most successful as well as the least successful of these means have included religious ones. Whether such means are solitary and contemplative, or social and ritualistic, their symbology often includes sacrificial imagery and acts. In apotropaic sacrifice the negative, polluting, or evil outcomes of social action in social structure are "given a body," as William Blake said of error, "in order that it may be cast off (1965:153). This body very often is quite literally represented as a sacrificial animal, which may be either totally immolated as a holocaust or burned offering, or loaded symbolically with the sins of the social body and driven out, as a scapegoat, into the wilderness. Quite often, as in ancient Hellas, this type of sacrifice is offered to deities and powers of the underworld, the chthonic powers, connected with decay and excrement.

In sacrifices aimed at restoring true fellowship or communitas (human relationship without formal structure), the ideas of gift, expiation, and communion all find expression. Here the notion is not to thrust evil away so much as it is to abandon oneself to good—good with a knife in its hand. This is painful, for the self to be abandoned is polluted, and polluted by one's own wants. One gives up what one has impregnated with one's desires. Here the sacrificer expiates by becoming himself the victim. As in Chihamba, sacrificer is transformed into victim, and victim into sacrificer, that all may be one outside structure and inside communitas.

I have always thought it worthwhile to ask members of the group whose religious life I have been studying how they interpret their own rituals. Naturally, some are readier to answer than others—there are degrees of esoteric knowledge—but, to complicate matters, some who know most are least willing to communicate their knowledge to outsiders, while others, though verbally fluent, know less. It has been argued by structuralists, most recently by Dan Sperber (1975), that a religious system is like the grammar of a language—we all "know" its deep structure unconsciously, in the sense that we can generate not only intelligible but also novel sentences by using its rules, but even the greatest linguists find themselves hard pressed to articulate deep structural rules. Hence, one must infer meaning from institutional structures, not elicit meaning from adept informants. Despite these difficulties I dislike self-denying ordinances (the reverse of sacrifices, which usually have a certain generosity), and am glad of valid information wherever I can get it.

Beheading by knife is a common mode of sacrificial slaying in Ndembu ritual, though other means are also used, such as cutting the throat of an animal or biting through a fowl's neck. I was curious about the Ndembu theory of ritual beheadings and asked ritual specialists about it. The deity Kavula, as I mentioned, is only symbolically beheaded. What happens is that each candidate in turn advances toward the white effigy of the deity, creeping along on his belly in the humble posture with which one should approach a great chief, then strikes it on its head—a concealed meal mortar—with a ceremonial wooden rattle the butt of which is carved into curious geometrical designs, a different pattern for each individual, again representing his or her ritual uniqueness. A concealed adept makes the hidden framework, covered by a whitened blanket representing the god, shake violently after its "head" has been struck. These agitations are said to be its "death throes."

Afterward, as I said, the candidate is shown blood on the mortar and told that it is Kavula's; then he is reassured that the blood is only the sacrificial cock's while the adepts sing "He [the candidate] is innocent, he has been acquitted, he went with cries into the grave [but] is now innocent." The candidate is "innocent" because, appearances notwithstanding, he did *not* slay Kavula (or, as some thought, a hidden adept impersonating him). Of course, there is a deeper meaning in all this, a meaning which, frankly, I have inferred from data not obtained directly from informants. The candidate, who has been afflicted with illness or other misfortune in a situation of social crisis, is, in a sense, "killing"—that is, eliminating—the source of his and the community's troubles, the negative valence of the spiritual power. To regain innocence (*ku-ying'a*), he has to cut off guilt.

Ndembu adepts do not put it in precisely this way. They talk a good deal about the meaning of "head" and of "beheading" in a ritual context. Thus Muchona, my best informant, in speaking of the beheading of the white hen at the personal shrine (*kantong'a*) set up for each candidate, told me that "they sacrificed [literally *aketwili*, "cut"] the white hen so that the candidate's body should be white [*mujimba atooka*]." Metaphoric whiteness is intended here—whiteness ranges from purity to health, fertility, and strength, as I have often pointed out. That this is not merely a magical act is shown by Muchona's next words: "The sprinkling of blood [*kusansa*] on the *kantong'a* shrine is for the Chihamba spirit [that is, for the ancestress, not directly for the deity Kavula], who is given blood. The head of the hen is food for the spirit. In the same way a hunter keeps an animal's head for himself—it is the most important part."

Clearly, the idea of immolation is present here. Part of the sacrificed object, the head, is reserved for the ancestress, while the rest is eaten by the candidate. The meal might even be said to have aspects of a communion, with multiple identifications. The white hen stands for the candidate herself or himself; it is also partly a symbol by color for Kavula, the "white spirit," and by gender for the ancestress. Yet ideas of offering and immolation are also present. Distance between and union among deity, ancestress, and candidate are represented by different acts and objects in this sacrificial process. So, too, is the idea of propitiation—the spirit is being placated by the gift of a white hen. White is also the typical color of ancestral veneration rituals, in the form of such symbols as white clay, a shrine tree with white wood, a libation of white maize beer, white clothing, and the blowing of white tobacco smoke over the shrine by the ritual officiant.

The notion of apotropaic sacrifice is not absent either. The beheading is partly the removal of life as "animus"—the lively hostility of the invisible being, deity or ancestral shade, is "cut off" by beheading. Muchona and many other Ndembu have told me, "The head [*mutu*] is the place of life [*wumi*]." In this case, punitive life.

Hubert and Mauss's neat pattern breaks down in this sacrifice. For the candidate not only is being "desacralized" in the sense that he or she is being separated from the ancestress as source of affliction, but also is by the same act being "sacralized" in the sense of being consecrated or dedicated to Kavula through entering his cultus. The shrine is a sign of this.

I mention these aspects—honorific, apotropaic, communicative, piacular, dynamic, tributary, and the like—because we can see here that they clearly belong to a single process, viewed by Ndembu from various perspectives. Each of these aspects has been made the basis of a separate theory of sacrifice by scholars, and in the heyday of evolution theory much ink was spilled in arguing which "form of sacrifice"—gift, communion, expiation, and so on—came first and what was the chronological or developmental order of successive dominant forms. For example, Robertson Smith and Wellhausen argued that early Israelite worship was centered in a joyous sacrificial meal, unshadowed by any sense of sin, and that sin offering, guilt offering, and the Day of Atonement had no existence before the Exile—a point of view which R. J. Thompson has sought lustily to rebut (1963: ch. 1, *passim*).

In fact, we have a many-faceted process of symbolic action, expressed in the medium of multivocal symbols, which is saying something about the way human relationships develop over time, how they wax and wane, blossom and decay, are built up and become dilapidated. Most of all, sacrifice points to a dual causality. Some manifest social effects have "visible" social causes; men and women pursue their aims and use open or readily inferable means to obtain them. Nevertheless, it is a constant fact of human group experience that "the best laid schemes of mice and men gang aft agley," that what even the powerful and knowledgeable patiently strive to bring about encounters mysterious obstacles and often fails miserably. Invisible causes seem to be involved. Untoward events are thought to have transcendent sources. These may result from the capriciousness of powers, or they may represent a principle of justice, transcending human formulations, which operates through invisible agencies, punishing the secretly wicked and defending the innocent.

I have argued in *Schism and Continuity* (1957) that where there is a social crisis in Ndembu village life in which generally recognized laws and norms have been transgressed, it is usually resolved by recourse to legal and judicial action, by recourse to the courts, formal and informal. But when people come to be motivated on opposite sides by equally valid moral and ethical principles, when there is no shared frame of values in which to assess the righteousness or unrighteousness of public behavior—and where, additionally, misfortune is running rife in the community—the group, acting through its senior representatives, betakes itself to ritual action, offers itself to the arbitrament of the invisible powers, so to speak, in ritual action which invariably contains inbuilt sacrificial processes, major or minor.

For example, in one protracted performance of the Chihamba ritual, sponsored by a village I had known intimately for two and a half years and had lived in for fifteen months, every source of tension not only in the village but also in a cluster of related villages was at one time or another ventilated in ritual contexts, mentioned in prayers and invocations, reflected in the choice and relative seniority of adepts and candidates, shown particularly in the sacrifices (who sacrificed for whom and the words of their petitions to Kavula and the shades), and made quite explicit in the "wings" of ritual action—in the comments and behavior of actors during the dances and commensal activities that interrupted the phases of the ritual proper as it extended over three days and nights.

The point I am trying to make is that the "purposive action-pattern" (to use Nadel's phrase), which we may call "sacrifice," had for these people no merely abstract theological significance—it was an act of great moment for their lives as members of a community, as part of a developing and changing web of social relationships.

My contention is that this view of sacrifice as a process within a process within a process enables us to focus attention on its existential rather than on its taxonomic, structural, or other cognitive capacities. The "lamb to the slaughter" is an emblem and instrument of the dealings of "man alive" with "man alive," and of visible people with the invisible influences that inhere in human actions—the continuing presence of the immediate dead, kinsfolk and affines of the living, whose will can still endorse or ban acts contemplated by their descendants. Beyond this presence are mightier powers making for righteousness or vitalizing unrighteousness, in any case exceeding ordinary, nonritual human attempts to curb or channel them and apparently able to intervene when things go wrong for a community or its component members. Here only the greatest human experiences—"birth, copulation and death," as T. S. Eliot sparingly cataloged them—can serve as the ritual codes of communication. Visible domain can communicate with invisible domain only through a liminary object whose destruction or immolation opens a channel between them.

In animal or human sacrifice, killing totally terminates the victim's life, perhaps as a surrogate for the sacrificer's. But it also gives life—and so many scholars have commented on the identification of blood and the internal organs (the Roman *exta*, the Ndembu *yijila*) which secrete or contain blood in large quantity, that I refrain from giving many examples. It may be even thought to reanimate that which is dead while deanimating that which is alive. The fact that blood is present at birth as well as at slaughter gives bloody sacrifice a rebirth as well as a life-terminating quality. This fact is explicitly noted by Ndembu. For example, there is Muchona's comment that "to sacrifice [*kuketula*] means life [*wumi*] for everyone" (Turner 1975a:84–85).

Transformation as the mode of sacrifice is not, therefore, a gradual remolding of a human essence. In Ndembu ritual, such a metaphor could be and is used in connection with initiation rites when a boy or girl is "grown" into an adult member of the tribal community. But sacrifice transforms, like revolution in some modern doctrines, more violently and rapidly by an act of slaughter that both ends and begins. The hasty and extreme character of blood sacrifice may well be linked in the simpler societies with social pressure for speedy and drastic action to resolve a crisis.

Nevertheless, sacrifice, whether bloody or unbloody, like most ritual actions may, and often does, in the course of time and in societies of greater technological and political complexity than the Ndembu and similar peoples, become a regular feature of public ceremonials. Such ceremonials in well-established communities founded on advanced agriculture with many specialized handicrafts may be built into the annual cycle as regularly recurrent performances marking the limits or changes of season—in which spatial boundaries may also be confirmed or redemarcated. Sacrifice in such cultures may become a boundary-regulating or -sustaining process. No longer a major means for restoring communitas in social-structural crises, it may become the means for maintaining order and structure at the level of the state or polis. However, the sacrifice of crisis may be retained in the private or peripherally public domain.

The notion of sacrifice as marking a terminus, both to and from, and providing a limit between periods of time and portions of space, is well developed both in ancient Roman and in post-Exile Jewish societies. Here the components of sacrifice, sacrificer, officiant, victim, sacralized space, sacred time, instruments of sacrifice, accompanying prayers, and so on receive a formidable elaboration. What Lévi-Strauss has called sensory codes—hearing, sight, touch, smell, and taste—are put to full use. Animal, avian, and vegetable codes are also used—relations among sacrificial animals, for example, are seen as homologous with relations among different classes of persons, types of social events, kinds of redressive action to end untoward happenings, and so forth. Every event involving sharp transition or necessitating clear demarcation among phenomena and relationships is conceded its own variant on the sacrificial model. Let me, for example, quote briefly from Fowler (1911:179) to bring out something of the diversity and orderliness of an advanced system of sacrifice. He discusses the role of the victim in public sacrifices:

It must be of the right kind, sex, age, color [for the particular sacrifice]. It must go willingly to the slaughter, adorned with fillets and ribbons (*infulae, vittae*), in order to mark it off from other animals as holy; in the case of oxen, we hear also of the gilding of the horns. . . . All these details were doubtless laid down in the *ius divinum* [the "law governing the relations between the divine and human inhabitants of the city, as the *ius civile* governed the relations between citizen and citizen," p. 169], and in later times, when the deities dwelt in roofed temples, they were embodied in the *lex* or charter of each temple . . . all victims, so far as we know, were domestic animals, and in almost all cases were valuable (*pecunia*), such as belonged to the stock of the Latin farmer, ox, sheep, pig, varying according to age and sex. Goats were used at the Lupercalia, and a horse was sacrificed to Mars . . . on October 15, and at the Robigalia in April a red dog was offered to the spirit of the mildew.

One might comment here that most well-established ritual systems utilize the diversity of animal and vegetable species of victims to signalize differences in the nature, ends, occasions, and social contexts of sacrifices. The Ndembu do this, but I will, for variety, draw examples from other African religious systems.

Francis A. Arinze (1970) mentions a wide diversity of sacrificial offerings in the ritual of the Ibo of Nigeria:

> Food crops offered include kola nuts, nuts, yams, coco yams, fruits, tender palm leaves, *ogilisi* leaves (*Newboldia laevis*), *ogbu* leaves, oil, sliced cassava, fou-fou (pounded yam or cassava), *ighu* (an edible root, sliced), banana stems and plantain. Kola nuts are necessary as an introduction to the more joyful sacrifices, especially those to the ancestors. "Kola-nuts symbolize friendship," says Geoffrey Parrinder, "and if split and partaken of by others, constitute a pact of loyalty and communion." An Ibo proverb says "if kola is not first brought, a cow will not be killed." (Arinze 1970:80)

You will recall the role of shelled beans in Ndembu sacrificial communion at Chihamba. Kola seems to have a similar significance among Ibo. But whereas Ibo and many other West African peoples stress the red color of kola and point out its similarity to blood, Ndembu stress the whiteness of the beans. Christians who partake of Communion in both kinds combine these colors—the whiteness of the bread or host,[2] and the redness of the wine.

Arinze includes among animals offered in sacrifice

> . . . small chickens, hens, cocks, dogs, lizards, goats, sheep, and cows. The fowl figures so much in Ibo sacrifices that one would not be wrong to say that the majority of fowls in Iboland in the past lost their precarious lives in honour of the higher powers [he adds somewhat wryly]. The fowl is the classical Ibo sacrificial victim [as it is, indeed, among the Ndembu]. . . . In the joyful sacrifices [a category Arinze distinguished from the "joyless" sacrifices of exorcism of malevolent beings, what we might call apotropaic sacrifices, whose aim is to drive away an invisible power rather than commune with one] the victim is often what the people can eat; hence the proverb: what a person feeds on, that he gives

to the spirits. Sometimes a special spirit prefers a special victim; thus rams are normally the proper offering for Amadioha, the spirit of thunder. Lizards are offered in sacrifices which have a rather sinister character [involving sorcery]. . . . The supreme victims when the gravest causes were at stake were human beings. (1970:81)

In the works of Evans-Pritchard and Lienhardt on the Nilotic Nuer and Dinka peoples, it is stated that even though these groups mainly use cattle for sacrifice to deity or to spirits and ancestors, these animals are divided into numerous types by their colors and markings, and each named spirit has as his sacrificial beast an animal of a particular color or configuration of markings—spotted, striped, brindled, and so forth. Thus the oxen appropriate for sacrifice to the Dinka "free-divinity"[3]— Macardit, "the Great Black One," who presides over the ending of good things—are black, the inauspicious color (Lienhardt 1961:30), while "the colour of the sacrificial beast ideally appropriate for the [rain and fertility] divinity *Deng* is pied, with bold markings, or boldly spotted in black and white—explicitly related to the Dinka representation of thundery skies" (1961:93). The divinity Garang is "associated with red-brown, and red and white combinations whenever they occur in cattle" (1961:85), and such cattle are therefore his appropriate sacrificial beasts. As with the Romans and the Ibo, the simple sacrificial process here becomes discriminated into numerous parts; the One, passed through experience and reflection upon it, becomes the Many. Each part—sacrificer, victim, mode of sacrifice, officiant, place, time of sacrifice, and so on—has many "allelomorphs."

I will not discuss here the Jewish, Vedic, and Hellenic sacrificial systems in the full richness of their lexica—types of actors, objects, relationships, aims, and occasions—each system having its own rules for generating sacrificial processes appropriate to culturally recognized types of situations, periodic or dramatic. I would prefer to speculate, on this occasion, drawing both on data I have presented and on recent reading, upon what appear to be certain universal features of the sacrificial process and upon certain major historical changes in the form and meaning of sacrifice as societies have increased in scale and complexity and have become literate.

Dinka, like Ndembu, as Lienhardt makes clear by giving texts of invocations to divinities and ancestors made by those about to sacrifice cattle, keep sacrifice close to the give-and-take, the triumphs and struggles of social life.[4] The invocations always relate to the quarrels of known, named persons. It is the corruption or pollution of ego's relations with the other or others that has to be removed by sacrifice. The invisible entities that control the health, strength, and fertility of bodily visible life, and bring good or bad fortune to the living, are activated either by sustained neglect of one's ordinary moral duties toward kin, neighbors, and friends or by one's suddenly stirred, vehement passions. In either case, the mysterious equilibrium—what Jakob Boehme called (in William Law's translation) the "temperature," what A. E. Housman called "the pact of things," and what Aristotle called "the golden mean," which should exist between person and person, group and group, the moral and the natural orders—has been disturbed, sending echoes of that disturbance through the whole social world.

The Invisibles are prompted to action. Some Invisibles, such as African creatures of witchcraft or the Greek powers of the underworld, the chthonic deities, are held to increase the disturbance, to spread the rotlike Robigas, the Roman spirit of the red mildew.[5] These have to be placated, bribed to go away. One does not eat with them in communion. They are given the wholly burned offering, the totally immolated sacrificial object. They are the powers of the "joyless sacrifice," as the Ibo understand it, and of what Jane Harrison called the "rites of aversion . . . gloomy and tending to superstition," of Greek religion. The Invisibles of the Ibo joyful sacrifice, of Harrison's Greek "rites of service," are the powers of joyful order, who seek from men repentance and atonement and the restoration of the basic social bond at every level of the community's existence. If they have punished some, they have done it to bring people to their senses. They demand sacrifice not principally for their own benefit but because it is only just that those who have sinned or erred should give up the fruits of their selfish action.

At the level of social relationships among men, there seems to be a distinction made between what in each person belongs to himself and what belongs to the community. If he withholds from the social circulation not only certain material things—property, dependents, and the like—but also his willing assent to what is for the general good, he is thought to be transgressing, to be sundering himself from a social compact which lives only in a constant circulation of giving, receiving, then giving again.[6] God, the gods, the spirits, the ancestors, in various ways and in different kinds of situations, preside over the flow. When all goes well, they do not need to interfere. It is held that when the whole group flows, when it is truly a communitas, a shared flow, men remember the Invisibles, make them offerings of food and drink, speak their names with reverence on the appropriate occasions.

But when selfish or sectional interests are put above the great circulation of thoughts, feelings, and goods, then the Invisibles, however they may be conceived or imaged, act to put pressure on the transgressing party, individual or collective, to give up blocking the equilibrating movement. Sacrifice is one very important means of restoring the flow. Metaphorically, it often literally involves a flow of blood or a flow of sacrificial smoke. It is a destruction of that part of the self which impedes the flow and an abandonment of the self to that which is greater than it, the total process of self and significant others in their living together. To give up is often painful. Here to give up in sacrifice is a necessary piece of social surgery. For the Invisibles the sacrifice would be a gift; for men, an atonement.

But all flow requires a channel. In tribal societies such as the Ndembu, Nuer, and Dinka, that channel is often ad hoc, improvised in accordance with rules certainly but adapted to the specific occasion. The kind of object sacrificed, the officiant to make the sacrifice, the type of shrine used, the particular words of invocation and petition, the ancillary nonverbal symbols used—all these are situationally patterned to be in tune with the social context of crisis or discord, or of sudden prosperity to be celebrated, which preceded and, as it were, secreted the sacrificial rite.

In more complex societies with settled agriculture (Nilotic peoples are mainly pastoralists, Ndembu combine hunting with slash-and-burn horticulture), the frame becomes more rigid. In literate cultures rubrics are written down and transmitted through the generations of officiants who have become specialized priests. Regular, calendrically determined rituals prevail over the ad hoc ritual responses to crisis. I have recently been fascinated by that remarkable series of inscriptions in the Umbrian dialect, the Iguvine Tablets, seven bronze tablets discovered at Gubbio in 1444 on the western slope of the Apennines.[7] The tablets contain the records of the priestly order of the Fratres Atiedii, a brotherhood which resembles the Fratres Arvales of Rome, the ancient agricultural priesthood discussed at some length by Fowler and which seems to have held at Iguvium a position as powerful as that of the Pontifical College at Rome.[8] The tablets include

> directions for the purification or lustration of the sacred mount or citadel of Iguvium; for the lustration of the Iguvine people themselves; for the decurial festival of the allied *curiae* of Iguvium;[9] for several private sacrifices; for the annual ceremonies of the Atiedian brotherhood. In addition there are several decrees of the college which stipulate the duties of the officers of the Fratres in relation to the sacrifices and the reciprocal functions of the Fratres and the federated families or *curiae* participating in the decurial festival. (Fowler 1911:11)

One can hardly imagine a system more different from the Ndembu than the Iguvian. Structuration prevails over flow in many ways. The major religious ceremonies take place on fixed dates in the annual cycle; Ndembu rituals are not calendrically connected. The procedures of each Iguvian ritual are fixed in written rubrics and must be performed in a set order, though there is a fallback mechanism of ritual redress in case of error or failure in the performance. Rituals involve a hierarchy of deities, each of whom has his or her sacrificial beasts and prescribed forms of worship. But the main difference perhaps is in the Iguvian stress on limits and boundaries and in the association of sacrifices with such *fines*. Sacrifice for Ndembu and many other African peoples is dominantly associated with the termination of flow—with the sharp cutting off of a social process, the ending of a relationship in a form that had become unviable.

Iguvian and other Umbrian and Latin sacrifice is linked with the demarcation of frameworks in space and time. It is a cultural mapping device for establishing contours, limits, and bounded spaces. Perhaps this "plotting and piecing" is appropriate for a culture of skilled and committed farmers. In the Roman case, certainly, the methodical farming style was transferred to the political realm just as Mars, originally an agricultural numen, became primarily associated with war in the religion of the state.

Death enters both the African and the Iguvian forms, but in the former, symbolic death as expressed in sacrificial acts punctuates the behavioral "speech" of changing social relations, while in the latter it imposes sacred legitimacy on the ritually discriminated, one might almost say "constructed," social and cultural orders seen as expressions of the invisible divine order. Sacrifices express discontinuities and thus create structure in this ritual system dedicated to demarcating, separating, and framing.

An example of this structuring or restructuring sacrificial ritual may be found in the *lustratio* of the sacred mount or citadel of Iguvium, known as the Arx Fisia. In Latin and Umbrian ritual a *lustratio* was a ritual process aimed at effecting purification and protection from evil or inauspicious influences—it began with taking the auspices, an observation of the position of birds entering a *templum* or rectangular space in which the augur sits looking southward for favorable avian indications (flight or song) on the east or unfavorable on the west. The *lustratio* consists essentially of a solemn procession around the thing to be purified—city, fields, army, or flocks—and the offering of prayer and sacrifice at certain points.

Virgil describes such a lustration after the funeral rites for Misenus in the *Aeneid* (VI.229). The Iguvian tablets mention that in the lustration of the citadel, three gates and two shrines form successive places of sacrifice.

Sacrifices are made first before each gate, then behind it. Any structuralist worth his salt would be delighted by this highly formalized process. I will not give all the details but cannot refrain from mentioning that each of the eight sacrifices is offered to a different deity and that each consists of the slaughter of three animals. Each performance is associated with the worship of a separate deity and has five stages thrice repeated: libation; invocation; a long prayer; slaughter of an animal; and an offering of the *exta* or vital organs of the animal, a cake of spelt (a primitive species of wheat) and a flour cake, with wine or *posca* (inferior soured wine). The *exta* are offered in a litter. The whole sacrificial process is terminated by a prayer recited in low tones generally summarizing the sacrifice.

Before the Trebulan Gate three oxen are sacrificed to Iuppiter Grabovius; behind it, three pregnant sows to Trebus Iovia. Before the Tesenacan Gate three oxen are offered to Mars Grabovius (then mainly an agricultural diety); behind it, three suckling pigs to Fisus Sancius. Before the Porta Veia three oxen with white foreheads are offered to Vofionus (or Vofio) Grabovius; behind it, three lambs to Tefer Iovius. The seventh sacrifice is made at the Jovian shrine: three bull calves to Mars Hodius. The eighth and last stop of the circuit is made at the shrine of Coredius for the sacrifice of three bull calves to Hontus Cerifius. Details of minor offerings vary slightly from site to site. "The inscription states that if any fault is committed by any omission in the prescribed ritual, then the sacrifices are vitiated. It will be necessary to observe the birds again, to return to the Porta Trebulana, and to begin the entire sacrifice and procession anew" (Rosenzweig 1937:31).

Followers of Dumezil will have already noted the triads in sacrifice: the number of beasts slain on each occasion, the triad of gods with the title Grabovius: Jupiter, Mars, and Vofionus—"to make whom a triad in the technical sense, only a common shrine is lacking" (Rosenzweig 1937:67). Kretschmer has derived the term Grabovius applied as adjective to three deities, Iuppiter, Mars, and Vofionus, from the Slavic *grabz*, an oak tree, considering it to have been borrowed by the Umbrians from the Illyrian, with the meaning of "belonging to oaks, oak god" (Rosenzweig 1937:68). The association of Jupiter and the Greek Zeus with sacred oak groves used for oracular purposes (for example, Dodona) is well known. But I will not here go into the fascinating detail of these rites. Enough data have been presented to show that they are concerned with general processes of inclusion and exclusion, of delimiting, of protecting the known against the unknown, and presenting models of symmetry and hierarchy. They impose cosmos on the city at regular, calendrical intervals. They also have a strong prophylactic intention; they prevent or guard against pollution or inauspicious intervention.

Whereas the Ndembu and other African rituals respond to crises, these Umbrian rites ward them off. The words of the invocation and prayer made in front of the Trebulan Gate (one of the ingresses into the citadel, thus constituting a potentially dangerous threshold of *limen*) make this clear:

> Iuppiter Grabovius, I invoke thee with this ox, a rich expiatory offering, for the Fisian Hill, for the Iguvian State, for the name of this hill, for the name of this state. Iuppiter Grabovius, honored with this, if on the Fisian Hill a fire had broken out, if in the Iguvian State the due rites are omitted, overlook it. Iuppiter Grabovius, if there is any fault in thy sacrifice, any offense, any diminution, any neglect, any defect, any fault seen or unseen, Iuppiter Grabovius, if it is permitted, let it be expiated with this ox, the rich expiatory offering. Iuppiter Grabovius, purify the Fisian Hill, purify the Iguvian State, the nobles, the rites, the men, the cattle, the fields, and the fruits of the Fisian Hill. Be propitious, be favorable with thy peace to the Fisian Hill, to the Iguvian State, to the name of the hill, to the name of the state. Iuppiter Grabovius, preserve safe the Fisian Hill, preserve safe the Iguvian State. . . . (Rosenzweig 1937:28)

The *lustratio* rites, like all other Iguvian rites recorded in the tablets, are frame-maintenance rites. The city or the state has taken over the sacrificial system, and acting through its twelve Fratres Atiedii, the priestly college, has elaborated and systematized the material of sacrifice as perhaps it was known in earlier times among the Umbrian tribes. In so doing, sacrifice has been put directly at the service of the overarching cosmological and political structures, losing to a great extent its interior quality and its sensitive responsiveness to important changes in specific personal and social relationships. The formed has been made to prevail over the forming, law over the living, in these sacrifices.

Now let us return to the Ndembu sacrifices at Chihamba in which the deity Kavula first allows himself to be sacrificed, then, in a new mode of being, sacrifices the former sacrificers, the candidates for admission to his cult, who are also patients aspiring to be cured of illness or ill luck brought about by neglect or transgression of the kinds of rules binding on a localized moral community of living and dead kin. Here there is some sense of abandonment, not merely prophylaxis. You will recall how Hubert and Mauss in the final pages of their seminal essay, while characterizing sacrifice as a mingling of disinterestedness and self-interest (1964:100) since "no sacrifice [does not have] some contractual element," made one exception.

This is the case of the sacrifice of the god, for the god who sacrifices himself gives himself irrevocably. This time all intermediaries have disappeared. The god who is at the same time the "sacrifier" [by which the translator, W. D. Halls, means the sponsor of the sacrifice] is one with the victim and sometimes even with the "sacrificer" [that is, the officiant or priest]. All the differing elements which enter into ordinary sacrifice here enter into each other and become mixed together. But such mixing is possible only for mythical, that is, ideal beings. This is how the concept of a god sacrificing himself for the world could be realized, and has become, even for the most civilized peoples, the highest expression and, as it were, the ideal limit or abnegation, in which no apportionment occurs. (1964:101)

The French scholars seem to have only the high historical religions in mind, but we have seen the same principle of total mutual identification in death and rebirth of god, victim, sacrifice, and sacrificer operating in the religion of a remote West-Central Bantu-speaking tribe of Zambian forest dwellers. There is no question of "totemism" here,[10] except in the Lévi-Straussian sense that an "animal code" (the sacrifice of fowls) is used as part of the sacrificial process, and that the real death of fowls is homologous with the symbolic death of adepts and candidates. But the whole process suggests that it is only by "losing one's life" that one will find life more abundantly, only by entrusting oneself to the invisible powers that one will renew one's own visible social existence. But I do not want to fall into Hubert and Mauss's trap: that of blithely identifying what they call "the sacred things in relation to which sacrifice functions" as "social things," a statement which they say "is enough to explain sacrifice" (1964:101). "This character of intimate penetration and separating," they say, "of immanence and transcendence, is distinctive of social matters to the highest degree. They also exist at the same time within and outside the individual, according to one's viewpoint. Sacrifice . . . is a social function because sacrifice is concerned with social matters" (1964:120).

Here one would have to say that if sacrifice is "ambiguous," the school of Durkheim has not resolved its ambiguity by invoking the deus ex machina, "society," which they have placed on the throne of the God who is dead—murdered, one supposes, not sacrificed, since sacrifice presupposes a resurrection or at least a regeneration. Society may perhaps better be thought of in this idiom as Augustine's "Terrene City" or "social structure," in which the person is masked in the persona, subjugated to the rules and customs hedging his status role and group membership, and driven by self-interest, enlightened or otherwise, to maximize his gratifications at the expense of his fellows. Here the dynamic principle is *amor sui*, "love of self." Or it may be Augustine's "Heavenly City" of disinterested communitas that is being presented as the model for postsacrificial behavior, where persons unmask themselves and freely become friends and lovers, where William Blake's formulation prevails: "Mutual Forgiveness of each Vice, Such are the Gates of Paradise" (1965:256). Sacrifice, too, relates to these opposed models for "society": The lamb may be slaughtered to maintain the structured order, as in the system maintained at Iguvium by the priestly college. Or it may be an indicator of the dissolution of all structural *fines* or boundaries, an annihilator of artificial distances, restorative of communitas, however transiently.

In the sacrifice of abandonment, the classical theological notions of sin, redemption, and atonement find their places as phases in a process which seeks personal and social renewal through the surgical removal—interiorly in the will, exteriorly by the immolation of a victim—of the pollution, corruption, and division brought about by participation in the domain of social structure. Sacrifice is here regarded as a limen, or entry into the domain of communitas where all that is and ever has been human, and the forces that have caused humanity to be, are joined in a circulation of mutual love and trust. In the sacrifice of prophylaxis, structure is cleansed but left intact; here enlightened self-interest prevails. Hubert and Mauss put the matter very well:

> The two parties present [gods and men] exchange their services and each gets his due. For the gods too have need of the profane. If nothing were set aside from the harvest, the god of the corn would die; in order that Dionysus may be reborn, Dionysus' goat must be sacrificed at the grape harvest; it is the *soma* that men give the gods that fortifies them against evil spirits. In order that the sacred may subsist, its share must be given to it, and it is from the share of the profane that this apportionment is made . . . we know that with no intermediary there is no sacrifice. Because the victim is distinct from the sacrificer and the god, it separates them while uniting them: they draw close to each other, without giving themselves to each other entirely. (Hubert and Mauss 1964:100)

Major religions, such as Christianity, move between these poles of the sacrificial process, between Chihamba and *lustratio arcis*, so to speak, which themselves correspond to the dual nature of "the social," communitas and structure. On the one hand Jesus, at Gethsemane, "abandons" himself: "Not my will but Thine be done." On the other hand, theologians, beginning with Saint Paul, draw out all the implications of the ransom or redemption metaphor, with its structural implications of slavery and the market. At one pole, self is immolated for the other; at the opposite pole, the other is immolated for self. Between the poles there are many gradations of offering: part of self may be offered for some others; part of the other may be offered for the whole self. These nuances may be coded in many ways: in the type and quantity of victims, in the manner of immolation, in the kind of officiant, in the time and place of the sacrificial occasion.

In summary, anthropology knows many theories of sacrifice, including those of the evolutionists, diffusionists, functionalists, and structuralists. Each has tended to focus on a component act, object, relationship, or concept of what is, in reality, a complex ritual process, verbal and nonverbal, which has to be grasped from the outset as a totality. Gift exchange, tribute, propitiation, penitence, atonement, submission, purification, communion, symbolic parricide or filiocide, impetration, and many more ideas of practices have been advanced as clues, even keys, to its understanding. Sacrifice, as we have seen, may be performed by or for individuals, groups, or types of persons. It may involve the offering of a gift or the immolation of a victim—which may be partially or totally destroyed, consumed totally or as a special portion by officiants, or eaten by all present, often after special preparation. Prayers as well as objects are offered. Most sacrifices, whether embedded in seasonal, curative, life-crisis, divinatory, lustrational, or other kinds of rituals, or performed as isolable ritual sequences, are intended to transform the moral state of those who offer them, through the intermediacy of a victim, as Hubert and Mauss have eloquently shown.

The sacrificial process, especially when it involves the immolation of something highly valued (directly or figuratively), posits the antinomy of an unblemished self (directly and spontaneously related to other such selves) and a blemished self (or, in most non-Western contexts, multiple selves) closed or distanced from each other by conflicts and jealousies attendant upon the occupancy of positions in the social structure. Two notions of power are contrasted: power based on force, wealth, authority, status, tradition, or competitive achievement; and power released by the dissolution of systemic and structural bonds. The sacrifice of abandonment collapses hierarchical and segmentary differentiations. The first kind of power is offered and abandoned; the second, sometimes thought of as deriving from God, the gods, numina, spirits, ancestors, or other types of generous "Invisibles," is tapped to purify and simplify relations among group members and the "mental sets" of individuals. The structural self is immolated to liberate the antistructural identity.

Of course, different types of sacrifices deal with this process in different ways, some stressing total renunciation of the structural order both subjectively and objectively, others its cleansing and renovation. In the majority of public sacrifices, the order of social structure is ultimately reinstated or reconstituted on the understanding that it must pass periodically, wholly or segment by segment, under the knife or through the fires of sacrifice, dying to be reborn in symbol, surrogate, or ordeal. Renunciatory sacrifices stress the interiority of the act; prophylactic sacrifices, the performative, institutionalized details. And while the former uses the imagery of sharp, almost surgical death to bring about the rebirth of the identity and the existential communitas, the agapic feast of identities, the latter employs the metaphor of death to establish or reestablish the limits, boundaries, and frames of legitimately constituted structures of society and culture, within which orderly life may be lived. One destructures, the other restructures, soul and city. Both renew, both respond to the human condition, oscillant and liminal between the Visible and the Invisible, the Many and the One.

6 The Kannokura Festival at Shingu: The Symbolism of Sun, Fire, and Light

In January and February 1978 I visited Japan under the auspices of the Japan Society for the Promotion of Science. One of the most interesting "incidents of travel" occurred when a graduate student, Paul J. Swanson, son of an American Methodist missionary in Shingu, on the east coast of the Kii Peninsula in southern Honshu, invited a group of us, participants in a lively seminar on pilgrimage at Sophia University, to sally forth on February 6 to witness the dramatic Kannokura Torch Festival. This took place in the awesome easterly region of Kumano on the Kii Peninsula, which I now know to be a veritable *omphalos* (world navel) of Shinto religion and a wellhead of imperial mystique. There were seven of us: Professor Miyake Hitoshi, an authority on Shugendō, from Keio University; Paul Swanson, who studied mountain pilgrimage under his supervision; Araki Michio of Tokyo Science University, whom I knew well at the University of Chicago as a student of Dr. Kitagawa's; a new friend, Dr. Nakamaki Hirochika, a fellow of the National Museum of Ethnology at Osaka and a former student of Professor Yanagawa's; and two graduate students of the Department of Religion at Tokyo University, both countercultural communards. A motley bunch, we called ourselves "The Seven Samurai."

I had visited temples and shrines and observed ritual in Tokyo, Nara, Kyoto, Osaka, and Tenri City, but only briefly and without expert exegetical guidance. Now I sensed that I was on the track of complex ritual processes comparable with initiation rites I had studied in East and Central Africa. But I had the major disadvantage of not knowing the social, cultural, and historical contexts of the *matsuri* we were about to see. And, of course, I did not know Japanese. I could be considered a cultural innocent. However, I was in the company of folklore specialists and scholars, and had been promised an interview with the *guji* or *kannushi*, the priest-guardian of Shingu's principal Shinto shrine, Hayatama Jinja. My ignorance of Japanese was partly counterbalanced by the presence of Araki Michio, who was well acquainted with my writings and theoretical notions, having attended my seminar on ritual and myth at the University of Chicago. He acted as my main interpreter.

Fieldwork in Central and East Africa, Mexico, and Europe had sensitized me to the importance of collecting and analyzing vernacular terms for key concepts in religious and ritual systems, and I plied Araki-san with etymological questions. This possibly enabled me to make more sense of the scholarly literature in English on Kumano than I would otherwise have done, since it is often provokingly peppered with untranslated Japanese terms. Other assets mitigating my ignorance were papers on Shugendō by Miyake and Swanson which they discussed with me, and the photographic skill of Mr. Nakamaki of the National Museum of Ethnology.

The data I have gleaned about Kumano consist of observations of Kannokura ritual, some interpretations by the priest (which he called *kaishaku* or *kaisetu*, "explanation" or "exegesis"), unpublished papers by Miyake and Swanson, my reading in the *Kojiki* (1969), *Studies in Shinto and Shrines* by R. A. B. Ponsonby-Fane (1962), *Gods of Kumano* by Shinichi Nagai (1970), *Folk Religion in Japan* by Ichiro Hōri (1969), "Kingship, Theatricality, and Marginal Reality in Japan" by Masao Yamaguchi (1973), and sundry scattered references in journals and books. This paper intends no more than to provide a preliminary analysis of the torch festival (*ōto matsuri*) and to give the reader an idea of how a student of ritual performance like myself goes to work in an initially unfamiliar culture— later he will have to unwind his preliminary skein of interpretation and begin again, often with new strands of thread and even new braiding techniques. However, I am determined to persevere until I have at least a preliminary grasp on this most fascinating, beautiful, and satisfactorily laminated strip of cultural behavior.

In Tokyo I was told that the Kannokura Festival takes place on the night of February 6, when boys dressed in white and with white hoods and/or headbands[1] climb to the foot of a huge boulder known as Gotobiki Iwa (literally Toad Rock), up a steep path carved into five hundred steps from the living stone of a thousand-foot-high hill. They carry pinewood torches containing white pinewood shavings and bedecked with a beard of long, trailing wood shavings. Each wears a rice straw rope coiled around him seven times. Miyake associates this with Shugendō, in which the Shugenja ascetics use ropes to climb rocks and cliffs as part of their ascetic practices (see Swanson 1978:14–33). Such a sacred rope is called a *shimenawa*. A huge *shimenawa* is tied around Gotobiki Iwa itself. When the gate of the fence that encloses the rock is opened, the boys run down the steep flight of steps, holding blazing torches high over their heads, amid shouts of the massed spectators. Paul Swanson has often witnessed the final stage, well summarized by Shinichi Nagai in his *Gods of Kumano* (1970:33): "There is a running stream of fire from the top of Kannokura to its foot, and the skies themselves seem to have been ablaze."

No one in our party, not even Paul or Hitoshi, knew much of what this meant. Some said that it was, perhaps, "the equivalent of a boys' puberty rite," since the majority of the participants were young men about fifteen to eighteen years old. I was not quite convinced of this because further questioning brought out the fact that old men and little boys, all dressed in white, ascended the hill. What was clear was that females were prohibited from climbing the Kannokura Mountain. Whatever else it might be, the Kannokura Festival was a celebration of masculinity. As a comparative symbologist I was intrigued by the dominance of white symbolism, and by the association of the whiteness with fire. I am, of course, aware—and it was often communicated to me by Japanese friends—that Shinto is not interested in *credenda*, but in *agenda* (works rather than beliefs). Thus, in *matsuri*, I was told, verbal expressions (let alone interpretations), with the exception of incantations, have little or no place, and all is expression of feelings. However, I found quite a number of people who were willing to express opinions as to the meaning of ritual objects, actions, and sacred spatial contexts. We shall take up these points later.

At Tokyo, no one had mentioned that the Kannokura Festival might be connected with Shinto mythology, especially with the birth of the imperial polity, through the conquests of Jimmu Tenno. And yet much of this argument was implicit in a paper Paul Swanson gave me, "Shugendō and the Yoshino-Kumano *Nyubu*[2]: An Example of Mountain Pilgrimage." Let me quote from it:

Shingu: Located at the mouth of the Kumano River, this area is the home of the Kumano-Shingu Hayatama Shrine and the Kannokura Rock or Mountain. Hayatama Shrine enshrines the *kami* (god) Hayatama-no-Ō. This *kami* was created from the spittle of Izanagi as he was cleansing himself from the defilements accumulated from his visit to the Nether World.[3] In the *Kojiki* and *Nihon Shoki*, he was believed to be the *kami* who presides over the ceremony for purification from the defilement of contact with death. [We will observe many aspects of cleansing or purification in the symbolism of the rites.] Kannokura is a mountain overlooking Shingu City from the north and also refers to a large rock

formation on its side. This is believed to be the site mentioned in the
Kojiki nearby which Jimmu Tenno landed with his invading army, was
visited by the Sun Goddess, Amaterasu, in a vision, and granted a large
eight-legged sun-crow (*yata-garasu*) as a guide to the interior where he
defeated his foes and set up the Imperial line which continues today. [It
should be mentioned here that *yata* means "eight," but the iconography
of the shrine portrays the bird with three legs. The only other place,
according to Ponsonby-Fane, where a three-legged bird is represented is
on pottery found in an excavation in Phrygia. The "eight" may refer to
some ancient unit of measurement. The sun-crow was evidently of great
size.] The original Shingu shrine is believed to have been at this location,
but was later transferred to the riverside where ascetic and purification
ceremonies took place. Thus the name *Shingu* = "New Shrine." Kannokura still attracts many pilgrims and ascetics, who in the Tokugawa
period were known as Kannokura *hijiri* ("sages, saints"). A fire festival
(Ōto-matsuri) is still held on this site every year in February. (Swanson
197:7) [Kumano itself is often regarded as a domain of the dead—indeed, its southern location supports this view, since in Indian religious
thought the realm of Yama, god of death, is symbolized by the south. In
the *Nihon Shoki*, Izanami after her death was buried in the village of
Arima in Kumano. Kannon had her abode in the south, too, on Mount
Fudaraku.]

Commentary

Paul Swanson gave me this text during our train journey to Kumano. I
could make little of it at the time, beyond speculating that the "fire festival" was somehow linked both to Shinto cosmogony (the creation of
Hayatama-no-Ō from the spittle of Izanagi) and the establishment of the
imperial line by Jimmu Tenno. These speculations had little to do, it
seemed, with the concept of Kannokura as a boys' initiation, though
fieldwork experience had shown me that rituals often retain form but
change function.

When I came back to Virginia, I began to look for scholarly interpretations of the proper names in Paul's text. Here I was greatly assisted by
Philippi's glossary and notes to the *Kojiki* (1969).

Kumano is mentioned in the *Kojiki*, Chapter 49, where it is visited by
Emperor Jimmu. He encounters a mysterious bear—indeed *kumano*
means "bear plain" (*kuma* = bear, *no* = plain)—thought to be a form
taken by "the unruly deities of the Kumano mountains." The bear casts a
spell over Jimmu and his men. What follows seems to be pertinent to this

exegesis. The priest (*guji*) of Shingu's main Shinto shrine told me that the shrine *kami* (god) was Taka-kuraji and that the procession of white-clad, torch-bearing males started off for Kannokura Mountain from that place, after offerings and *norito* (prayer) had been made to the *kami*.

In the *Kojiki* in Philippi's translation,

> A person called Taka-Kuraji of Kumano came bringing a sword to the place where the child of the heavenly deities (that is, Jimmu Tenno) was lying. . . . At the very time that he received that sword, all of the unruly deities in the Kumano mountains were of themselves cut down; and the troops, who had been lying in a faint, all woke up and rose. (1969: ch. 49, 3–5)

In other words, the magic power of the sword—which, Taka-Kuraji tells Jimmu, had been given him by two deities in a dream (one of them was, in Old Japanese, Ama-Terasu-Ō-Mikami, "the Heaven-Illuminating Great Deity," ancestress of the imperial family and goddess of the sun)— was in itself, writes Philippi, "sufficient to vanquish immediately all the unruly deities." Dare one speculate that this incident may refer to the conquest of a proto-Ainu population (whose Bear Cult is still a prominent ritual feature) by Bronze Age or Iron Age invaders? The Shinto priest at Hayatama Jinja speculated that Jimmu's people were from "Oceania" (possibly Malayo-Polynesians). Philippi hints that there may have been references to practices among the *kami* (ancestral to Jimmu) reminiscent of Siberian shamanism in *Kojiki*, Chapter 34, where mourners dress as birds of various species (1969:126). Birds are, of course, widely distributed symbols of the shamanic flight. Other scholars suggest a Korean origin for the invaders (for instance, Ponsonby-Fane 1962:36, 44; Bradley-Smith 1964:23).

The Shingu priest told me that the Kannokura ritual was a reenactment of the origin story in *Kojiki* and the *Nihon Shoki*. I took him to mean that the boys in white, known as the *agariko* (*agarisuru* = to rise), "the children that go up," represented Jimmu Tenno's army, who received magical power from the *kami* Taka-Kuraji, and then went on procession to the Taka-Kuraji shrine at the base of the mountain, before climbing to the Toad Rock. This procession followed the path reputedly taken by Jimmu Tenno. He agreed that was part of the meaning of reenactment, but that a deeper meaning connected the ritual with the descent of the three original "invisible" deities—Ame-no-Minaka-Nusino-Kami (Heavenly Center Lord Divinity), Taka-Mi-Musubi-no-Kami (High Generative Force Deity), and Kami-Musubi-no-Kami (Divine Generative Force Deity)—in the Japanese cosmogony who rose out of primordial chaos, and were neither begotten nor did they beget. More recently, it was related to the descent of the three gods of Kumano: Hayatama, Ketsumiko, and Fusumi.

Professor Miyake told me later, as we made our way back from the mountain, following the *agariko* through the now-silent streets of Shingu to Hayatama shrine, that he had been informed by participants that the seven coils of white rope round their bodies represented the "seven generations" (*Yu*=age, era) "of the age of the gods come into existence," mentioned in the second chapter of the *Kojiki*. I was delighted, of course, by the "looseness of fit" between ritual and myth (rather than tight logical series of transformation), a constant feature I found in Africa and elsewhere.

If we are to use the geological metaphor of stratification, it is that of mobile plates rather than of static layers. The past is never quiet or frozen in the form of major rituals. And there is often not a single *illud tempus*, that creative, generative time so often mentioned by Eliade, to which the ritual refers, but several *illa tempora*, both mythological and putatively historical. Thus, connections have been made between the ritual at Shingu and both cosmogonic and political beginnings, the descent of the three *kami*, and the arrival of Jimmu Tenno.

Kannokura, the second term used in Swanson's account, is discussed as follows by Shinichi Nagai:

> The name "Kannokura" has a strange sound to Japanese ears, and it does not mean, as its characters would indicate, "warehouse [storehouse] of the gods" but rather "where the gods live." One etymological theory is that it is the same "*kura*" (= warehouse) as in *takamikura* (connected with *takameru*, to raise, exalt, ennoble), the imperial throne, while another contends that it is the "*kura*" of "darkness," suggesting a place full of dark and towering trees.
>
> Broken bits of ancient bronze bells have been found recently under the rock, indicating that they were originally used in ritual worship at *Gotobiki Iwa* ("Toad Rock") [*hikigaeru* = toad, rock = *iwa*] and also that it has been an object of reverence for a long, long time. (Nagai 1979:33)

The Shingu priest told me that he had found a bell-shaped bronze object when excavating near the base of the rock which he assigned to the Yayoi culture (300 B.C.–A.D. 300; wet rice cultivation) and which he described as a "ritual vessel."

Hayatama is a major shrine, known as Hayatama-no-Ō (king, ruler, great) of Kumano-ni-imasu Jinja (*jinja* = shrine), dedicated to the *kami* Hayatama-no-Ō. When we visited it later, the priest, Mr. Ueno, told us that according to tradition Emperor Keiko Teno visited the shrine. His reign was officially reckoned to be from A.D. 71 to A.D. 130, when he died at the age of 106 (according to the *Nihongi* 1972, 1:214). The shrine, he said, was already well established. It is situated a mile or so from the base of the Kannokura mountain.

I mentioned earlier that the shrine *kami*, created from the cleansing spittle of Izanagi, presides over the ceremony for purification from the defilement of death. I should now place Shingu and its shrines in the wider Kumano context. There are in Kumano three great shrines— Hongu, Shingu, and Nachi—known collectively as Kumano Sanzan, "The Three Mountains of Kumano." Hongu, or Kumano-ni-masa Jinja, is the abode of the *kami* Ketsumiko, one of the numerous names of Su- sano-O-no-Mikoto, and is said to have been founded in the reign of the tenth emperor, Sujin. Ketsumiko, according to Swanson, is the *kami* of food. Nachi Shinto shrine is dedicated to Fusumi, who is identified with Izanami. Swanson points out that all three *kami* are connected with the world of the dead (*yomi*), and reflect the belief that the Kumano area is the gate to the other world of the dead. Susano-O of Hongu was expelled from the upper to the nether world (Ne No Kuni). Hayatama-no-Ō of Shingu, as we have seen, was made from Izanagi's spittle as he purified himself from the pollution of contact with the world of the dead. Izanami of Nachi, Izanagi's consort and goal of his visit there, became a *kami* of the land of the dead after she died giving birth to the *kami* of fire.

Hirata Atsutane, in commenting on Chapters 7 and 8 of the *Kojiki*, which describe the fiery death of Izanami and the transformation of the blood of the fire deity, slain by Izanagi, into various deities, connects fire (*hi*) with blood (*chi*). He says that Izanami's giving birth to fire (the fire deity) reflected either the afterbirth or the menstrual blood. In Hirata At- sutane's time (late nineteenth and early twentieth centuries) the menstrual period was referred to as "fire," and he surmises that the practice of re- maining in seclusion during the menstrual period may be connected with Izanami's "sickness" (H. A. Zenshu, *Complete Works*, I, 233, cited in Philippi 1969:399). I mention the connection of fire with birth because I was interested in the color symbolism of the Kannokura Festival, notably the white dress and accoutrements of the *agariko* and the red symbolism of fire. It should be remembered, too, that white is associated in these rites with masculinity, and that women are forbidden to climb the moun- tain. The red symbolism of menstruation here might be connected with the exclusion of women, as polluting; and the fire, as we shall see, of the burning torches is "white," not red.

Among the Ndembu of Zambia, I found during fieldwork that in cer- tain contexts whiteness was ritually associated with seminal fluid, which was described as "blood whitened [or purified] by water." In the same contexts, including the Twin Ritual (*Wubwang'u*), red was linked with "the blood of motherhood" (*mashi amama*) "revealed" or "made visible" (*kusolola*) during parturition. Menstrual blood, also represented by red symbolism of various kinds (red clay, red gum, red feathers, and the like), was adjudged to be "impure" or "lacking in whiteness." Among Ndembu, however, fire (*kesi*) was considered to be "white," as were sunlight and moonlight.

In the *ōto-matsuri* on Mount Kannokura, masculinity is clearly associated with whiteness. Quite explicitly, whiteness is also associated with the purification rite known as *misogi*, a kind of lustration made facing running water, which the *agariko* performed before going to the rallying point at the Shingu shrine. On our return from the mountain Professor Miyake, Mr. Araki, and I asked one of the older men, who had an organizing and policing role in the ritual, what the prevalence of white things (white clothing, *shirokiji*; white rice rope, called *nawa* by Mr. Ueno; and *nawa chi*, white pine torches and shavings) represented. He replied, "Purity" (*kiyome*). He connected with this the fact that the *agariko* had to eat only "white" (*shiroi*) foods during the week preceding the *matsuri*: these included white shelled beans of a certain species (*shiroazuki*), rice, some white fish, and other foods I was unable to record.

Mr. Ueno, who was *guji* on my second visit, said that the white clothes were "to purify the body"—they included a white jacket (*happi*), white socks (*koshita*), and the white rope, always in seven turns around the body. The rope was to make the person sacred. A rope, about thirty meters long, is tied around Gotobiki Rock, and adorned with *gohei*, the white paper cutout rectangles so typical of Shinto ritual. This big rope is renewed each year before the *matsuri*, when the first buds begin to appear.

Purity seems to be connected as much with aesthetics as with ethics in Shinto, as has often been noted in the literature. There is a need to maintain aesthetic order in the world, and anything that blemishes that order may be seen as impure. However, the "purity and beauty always go hand in hand" theme does not take adequately into account the veiled Shinto admiration of wildness and of wandering (that is, chaotic) behavior seen in myths about Susano-O-no-Mikoto and Yamato Takeru in the *Kojiki*— as Professor Yamaguchi has noted. During the procession and climb up the hill only sake was to be drunk—as indeed it was, copiously!—since it was white. My elderly informant said suddenly, in English, "Sake is white fire!" The deities and expressions of chaos, as well as those of cosmos, of the disorderly and unruly, have their representation in the nature of things.

Let me now return to our conversation with the priest of Hayatama shrine. I asked Mr. Araki Michio and Mr. Nakamaki to obtain from him his interpretation of the term *hi*, since there is a major *hi matsuri* at Nachi

Falls on July 14, with some symbolism in common with the Kannokura *matsuri*. Its principal objects are giant white pine torches and large portable shrines decorated with twelve gold fans, eight mirrors, and objects known as *hikari* (shining light, brilliant radiance). Legend associates this festival, too, with Emperor Jimmu, in particular his landing at Kumano. According to one story the portable shrine, called the *ōgi mikoshi* (portable fan shrine or tabernacle), a long, narrow plank covered with satin damask, represents the imperial army, and torches symbolize the army of the Nishikitobe, Kumano's ruling family at the time. Following the ritual drama of the "battle," the divine *ōgi mikoshi* remains after the torches have all burned out.

Since both the Nachi and Shingu festivals emphasized fire, I was interested in the priest's explanation. *Hi*, he explained, "may be light, the sun which produces life," but it is also fire, the destroyer. Therefore, we see in *hi* both fear and thanksgiving. However, "sun" and "fire" are represented by different characters. He went on to note that there are many Buddhist fire rituals, such as the *goma*, which I saw performed in Osaka during 1978 for the local fire brigade. *Goma* is derived from the Sanskrit *hōma*, and plays a major role in Shugendō asceticism. The priest then told us that the stone steps up Kannokura-Yama were made during the Kamakura period under Shugendō influence.

I have not yet mentioned the importance of Shugendō in the Shingu Kannokura Festival, but Professor Miyake assured me that it was deep though not obtrusive. Paul Swanson described himself as a *shugenja*, "one who accumulates power and experience" in the mountains. He recounts the Saito Goma ritual in which he participated in July 1975, at the Ōmine Bridge (*mine* = peak, ridge) at the foot of Mount Ōmine in the far north of Kumano. Part of the ritual involves the catechizing of wandering *shugenja* who have come to participate, to see if they are true *shugenja* of the Hozan-ha, a group, according to Professor Miyake, which considers En-no-Gyoja as the founder of the sect in 659, the fourth year of Empress Saimei.[4] Swanson records the Honzan-ha catechism (*mondō*) as it concerns Shugendō notions of fire and sacrifice:

Q. What is the meaning of the burnt offering of the Great Saito Goma?
A. The burnt offering of the Great Saito Goma is the secret offering of
   Shugendō. It is comparable to the Buddha's wisdom which like fire
   completely burns and consumes all the passions and attachments to
   this world. The ceremony expresses clearly the rational aspect of the
   Law, burns away the polluted accumulations (*karma*) of life and
   death; leads one to rely on the foundation represented by the letter
   [the first letter of the Sanskrit alphabet]; encourages us to make our

residence in the land of the five Buddhas; [teaches us] to enter the Six
Great Concepts; and signifies the nonduality of ourselves and the
Buddha. The ritual, activity, and appearance of the *goma* all have
varying significance.

(Swanson 1978:22)

In considering this answer one is once again struck by the way in
which the fundamental Shinto beliefs and symbols and those of Buddhism constitute a coincidence of opposites, a dynamic unity based on
cognitive contrasts; the former stresses fire as the source of life and fertility, the latter, as a destroyer of karmic pollution. Yet the unending stream
of paradoxes produced by this opposition glitters with aesthetic trea-
sures: the vanity of sensory loveliness and the loveliness of transience
form a series of conjunct opposites. The novel and the Noh play provide
many examples—the notion of *yūgen*, the "mysterious depth" which
Seami Motokiyo (1363–1444) considered to be the goal of the Noh actor,
involving a passionate attachment to nonattachment in which beauty is
also "the dark profound tranquil color of truth," speaks of an acceptance
of paradox in the heart of things. Japanese poetry, too, is full of this sense
of the pathos of life in time which is simultaneously the annihilation of
time. No great culture can live without fruitful tension between its deepest principles. As William Blake wrote, "Without contraries there is no
progression."

But back to Shingu. The priest made a further interesting comment on
the fire aspects of Kannokura. I asked why it was that small children, as I
had been told, dressed in white like their older brothers and fathers, were
carried or made to climb the steep steps. It was to unite them more
closely with their male kinsfolk, was his reply. He then said that when a
boy is born, the infant is taken at the next *ōto-matsuri* up to the Gotobiki
Iwa, since, when he is exposed to the fire and smoke of blazing torches,
his tears will come down. The tears are white, and whiteness is purity.

The Festival, February 6, 1978

According to some (such as Shinichi Nagai 1970:34) the *ōto-matsuri* her-
alds the advent of spring in the mountains of Kumano. We have already
considered some of the evidence that connects the festival with Emperor
Jimmu Tenno, who set out, sacred sword in hand, to conquer Yamato;
the torch festival is said to honor the *kami*, Taka-Kuraji-no-Mikoto, who
gave the emperor his magic sword. From what we have seen of the symbolism, it also seems to mark the descent of the *kami* on Japan from the

High Heavenly Plain in the beginning, and also the movement of the *kami* from the Gotobiki Rock to the lowland at the base of the mountain. I was told at Kumano that the deities retire to the mountains during the winter and return to make the land fertile in the early spring—which indeed comes early to the coastal plain of Kumano, as I know from my experience. White plum blossom was already out in February of the year of my visit.

The ritual also represented a purification of the masculine principle through austerities and by fire. Professor Miyake suggested to me that just as the *goma* fire rite burns off sin in Shugendō, so does the *oto-matsuri* purify those who take part in it. He further suggested that evil deities might be exorcised and malign planetary influences reversed by the rites. The use of fire might have an exorcising function, he hinted. It would seem that the ritual was a kind of Shugendō for the ordinary man, just as the austere Irish pilgrimage to Saint Patrick's Purgatory in Lough Dearg (Turner and Turner 1978) represents a sort of brief monasticism for the ordinary Catholic layperson.

Mr. Ueno, the present priest, told us that in the medieval period, Shugendō priests (*yamabushi*) came to Shingu for training, and then spread all over Japan as missionaries of that form of mountain asceticism. He mentioned that the day before, a number of *shugenja* from Ōmine, a mountain sacred to the cult in the north of Kumano, had visited the Hayatama shrine. In the past, he said, the Kumano pilgrimage was called "the pilgrimage of ants," due to the myriad pilgrims. There had been, he said, 144 pilgrimages by emperors who had left many gifts at the shrine (they are now in its museum). Each emperor would be attended by some eight hundred retainers.

Before the procession began, roughly at sunset, many *agariko* and *kaishakunin*, senior men who organized and policed the procession, gathered in the courtyard of Taka-Kuraji shrine (that is, the Hayatama). They included the mayor of Shingu and several other local government officials, all dressed in ritual garments and each with a white pinewood torch. If I had been doing sustained fieldwork in Shingu, as I have done in other societies, I would have collected data on the relationships among the festival, local government, neighborhood associations, and the temple organizations at Taka-Kuraji and Hayatama shrines, and tried to ascertain residents' attitudes to the festival. I would have tried to elicit the structure of festival roles, statuses, and rankings—and, importantly, the maneuvering and politicking that almost inevitably attend competition for office in all societies.

I was soon told that the young men who formed the bulk of the participants were organized in terms of *chō* and *machi* (city blocks and wards).

Shingu's other big festival, the boat *matsuri*, involves a race of nine boats manned by young men from the city's nine wards and dedicated to the deity Hayatama, who has a special shrine constructed for him annually about two kilometers up the Kumano River. Today it costs about $1,000 to prepare each crew for the festival. Perhaps *chō* and *machi* are similar to the wards (*contradas*) which become rivals in the Siena Palio in Italy described by Don Handelman—units of local administration whose members are probably interlinked in many networks of kinship, affinity, and occupational interdependence. Fighting between youths of different wards or sections could be quite violent, I was told, and this was later confirmed by observation. The youths used their three-foot pine torches (*tai-matsu*) as bludgeons; when the torches were later ignited near the Gotobiki Rock, they could be formidable weapons; indeed, a number of casualties were brought to the first-aid post set up on an overlooking knoll where we "Seven Samurai" watched the milling, swarming young warriors. Most were "flown with strong spirit" (sake), as the poet has said.

Because Shugendō has many shamanistic features, including possession, I inquired if the youths were thought to be possessed. "Only by sake," my friends replied. But I would guess (and in my present state of inquiry, can only guess) that the *agariko* were, at least in the past, regarded as vehicles of the *kami* of the mountain, bringing them down to the cultivated land and the fishing villages below. It may be significant that in the Nikko Fire Festival, fire is said to be obtained "by magnifying the rays of the sun." This may well indicate the turn of the year toward the cultivating season. Fire is being brought down "from heaven." Sake on this occasion was clearly regarded as a sacred drink, and it was obligatory to drink it.

At the Hayatama shrine, the *guji* intoned a prayer. The *agariko* and the "Samurai" were offered sprigs of the sacred *sakaki* tree (*Cleyera japonica*). The procession began and continued all the way through Shingu City. The older men, known as *kaishakunin* (sodality members), carried, in addition to their torches, large cudgels. I was told that these were to keep order on the climb and to discourage tarrying on the way. From time to time *agariko* would join us, singly or in groups. Occasionally we would meet white-clad groups going the opposite way to meet associates at some other rallying point. When the two groups met, they exchanged a stereotyped formula of greeting, which I was unable to record. Our group broke into songs with choruses which I was told were obscene. Whenever our younger men saw women, they pretended to threaten them, even chasing them down the street, shouting rude remarks in rough, throaty voices. Altogether it was the very type of universal adolescent machismo. The *guji* and other officials turned a blind eye, even when the young *agariko* grabbed bottles of sake, apparently without paying for them.

Obviously there were aspects of ritual reversal, or at least permissiveness. Certainly the behavior of the young men was in sharp contrast with the politeness and deference to age and femininity prescribed by customary norms. When groups of *agariko* met, they had brief battles, wielding their torches as weapons. I learned from one young man in our party that the *agariko* of different quarters were traditional rivals, each quarter having its own songs and greeting formulas. One of the aims of the ritual was to establish not only the individual champion for the year—that is, the winner of the downhill torch race from the summit of Kannokura Mountain to the torii (gate) of Shingu Taisha—but also which group could place the greatest number of its members among the leaders. Traditionally, the winner received nine kilos of rice, but this has been discontinued.

But it was not only city wards which sent youths to the summit. I met, near the top, a young American member of the celebrated Aikikai Kumano Juku Dojo private school, an aikido school, who told me that the *sensei* had sent his male disciples there, both to venerate the *kami* and to test their prowess in the dangerous torch-carrying gallop down the 538 steps at a terrific speed.

Women, prohibited from setting foot on those steps during the ritual, congregated in great numbers outside the torii of the shrine at the base of the mountain. I saw what I had often seen in Africa. In certain rituals, social categories (men/women, circumcised/uncircumcised, married/unmarried, and so forth), as against corporate groups, are isolated from the complex matrix of social interaction and exposed, so to speak, to concentrated ritual attention. The corporate group is unraveled, the social category appears in its purity. Here males and females are segregated; males are purified, even stand situationally for purity, and are linked with the pristine *kami* on the mountain's summit. Women remain outside the sacred precinct, and situationally represent the profane world of everyday. Men are active, climbing and descending; women wait passively at the mountain's base. The interdiction on women, we were told on our 1981 visit by Mr. Ueno, was connected with the ban on women's participation in the Shugendō mountain pilgrimage. I was told, with much chuckling, however, that when men descend, bearing fire, the women had better beware—every year the birth rate goes up nine months after the *ōto-matsuri*.

The *guji* joined other Shinto priests in performing rites, which we did not observe, in the Shingu shrine at the base of Kannokura Mountain. In the shrine precinct more sake was consumed by the *agariko*, preparatory to the ascent. Then the procession resumed, this time up the steep flight of steps to Kannokura shrine. According to Shinichi Nagai (1970:32), "the steps are a masterpiece of man's ability to make his handiwork fit in with the surroundings that nature has provided." Utilizing a hillside, the architect placed natural stones one above the other; their shapes were unchanged, and they were obviously chosen with a view to harmony among themselves as well as with the overall site. They were said to have been an offering of Yoritomo Minamoto, the first Kamakura shogun.

The "Seven Samurai" had been supplied with small flashlights and warned not to lag, lest we be cudgeled by the *kaishakunin*. It was hard going for me, the "Scotland-jin," with my osteoarthritis, but I was able to see the rambunctious throng of white-clad youngsters surging up before me, singing, cursing, and fighting. About halfway up the hill the cliff retreated, leaving a fairly wide, rocky platform, on which was placed a portable shrine. Several senior participants remained at this location, which played an important role in the ritual, a "liminal" role.

At the top of the flight of steps was a small Shinto shrine hugging the base of the Gotobiki Iwa. The *guji* entered it to perform private rites and invoke the *kami*. Before entering, he told me the Gotobiki Iwa "is" the *kami*. Araki explained that just as in the theological doctrine of transubstantiation in Christianity the substance of Christ is present under the appearances or accidents of bread and wine in the sacrament of the Eucharist, so were the *kami*—he used the English plural—"really present" under the appearance of the *iwa*. I had encountered a similar notion among the Ndembu of Zambia. I witnessed the sacralization of a tree of a certain species (*mukula*) which then became the dominant symbol of the last phase of the Nkula ritual. My informants told me, "Now the *mukula* tree *is* the spirit [*mukishi*]." Here symbol becomes sacrament; there is an interlocking of visible and invisible orders of being.

Some thirty or so steps below the shrine was another area of flat ground overlooked by a small knoll. Around the platform had been erected a fence. A ritual door or gate (torii) was set in the fence, through which the *agariko* passed; most of the *kaishakunin* remained outside the gate. More and more young men passed into the compound behind the fence, forming groups based on blocks and neighborhoods. Fighting continued. We "Seven Samurai" were assigned places on the knoll, which we shared with the Shingu Firefighters' Auxiliary, the local police, and a hospital unit. While we waited, I counted twelve casualties, who received first aid for head injuries obtained in scuffles, contusions from falls—the sake had done its work—and, later, burns. The police maintained a discreetly unobtrusive presence. It seemed that modern agencies of law and order provided a frame within which traditionalism could flourish. No arrests were made for disturbances of the peace. Aggressive behavior was recognized to be a symbol of the pure masculinity which was being ritually manifested. Eventually the corral or paddock-like space was entirely filled with young men and boys.

Meanwhile, the *guji*, having concluded his offerings and invocations, "made pure fire," we were told. There were two ways of doing this. One was by rubbing a stone (generally a flint, *hiuchi-ishi*) or a piece of metal against a piece of hardwood, or flint against metal. In one variant I have since learned, in the Fukuoka Sumiyoshi-jinja, a very special fire, called *bekka*, was obtained by rubbing a stone against a piece of wood which had previously been smeared with sulfur (*sukei*). Traditionally, I was told, persons were purified by "fire-striking" (*kiribi*) or sparks made by steel and flint. This was done over offerings made to the *kami-dana-* (domestic Shinto shrine) at the door when someone began a long journey or pilgrimage, or by a wife every morning when her husband left for work. In the *ōto-matsuri*, fire obviously has a similar purifying function.

The priest's assistant then lit a small torch from the "pure fire" and ran down the steps with it to the platform halfway up the Kannokura-yama. There a gigantic torch was lit from it. A priest had to chop this open with an ax, so that the shavings it contained could be ignited. The ax, Mr. Ueno told us, was a reminder of the pioneer who first entered the forested Kumano mountain thickly clad with pines. The great torch was made of the extremely hard wood of the Japanese cypress (*hinōki*). This was carried back up the steps to the enclosure, where the boys had been laying down heaps of pinewood shavings around which they grouped themselves in traditional units of kin, friends, and neighbors. These shavings were kindled from the big torch, and then each lad lit his own torch from it. Each torch was inscribed with *kanji*, Chinese characters or ideographs. The owner's name was sometimes part of the inscription, and possibly a prayer for health or wealth. The torches were made in a special shop in Shingu. The shavings were hung up for a long period to dry and became readily combustible. The torches were hollow, their sides tied by bark string. As the young men were lighting their torches, the older men closed the torii aperture with a new door, and bolted it with a stout wooden bar.

Now began the most dramatic episode of the whole ritual. The young men inside hurled themselves against the door, fiery torches in hand, while the older men pressed against the door from the outside to contain them and poked their cudgels through the fence to further frustrate the would-be escapers. Finally the bar snapped, the door collapsed, the marshals beat a hasty retreat, and a torrent of youth and fire came tumbling through the holy portal at agonistic speed. Each lad sought to be first to reach the profane feminine crowd awaiting the *agariko* in Shingu City beyond the torii of Kumano Hayatama Taisha.

The theophoric torchmen were bearing spring, sunlight, purity, virility, and general fertility back to the winter-silenced land in the *shōkan* (the minor cold) season. More than this was surely meant. For not only was a cosmic drama being played out but there were also overtones of the first emperor, Kamu-Yamato-Ipare-Biko-no-Mikoto (Divine-Yamato-Ipare-Lad-Lord; Ipare is a region in Yamato famous for its pond), better known as Jimmu Tenno, as he began the eastward march of the Yamato ruling family. It may be significant that the movement of the *agariko* had been from Hayatama shrine in the west of Shingu to Kannokura-yama, across the Kumano River, to the east (really northeast, but I found that the dominant directional axis in Kumano was regarded as west-east, *nishi-higashi*).

History, albeit mythical and speculative, represented a semantic layer deposited on the seasonal metaphors. Mr. Ueno told us that during the Edo period, before the Meiji period began (c. 1863), there had been a huge building in the space now enclosed by the fence. The *agariko* and others, after their torches were lit, had to remain there, praying, "hot with fire," to the *kami*, until they could not stand the heat any longer and pressed out of the narrow entrance. He did not know whether there was then a restraining door. One of the "Samurai," who shall remain nameless, suggested that the sudden bursting forth of the white and fiery tide of young men could be likened to a male orgasm. It could perhaps be more convincingly argued that it represented an ordeal imposed by male elders on male juniors, followed by a test of the latter's strength and capacity to represent the masculine principle well in the future. Perhaps we can see in these male/female, elder/junior oppositions an echo of the *onmyō-dō* system, the way of Yin-Yang, borrowed from Taoism. There is certainly sense in the view that regards the *ōto-matsuri* as at least in part a male initiation ritual, a life-crisis ritual.

One interesting though unsubstantiated suggestion made by one of our number, was that the breaking out of the young men represented the birth of the fire deity, Kagu-Tuti-no-Kami (Radiant Earth) or Pi-no-Kagu (First Shining Spirit Deity). When his mother, Izanami-no-Mikoto, bore him, she died, since her genitals, so says the *Kojiki* (bk. 1, ch. 7, v. 18), were "burned"; and "because she had borne the fire deity [she] divinely passed away" (v. 22). The violent "birth" of the young men through the torii, destroying the restraining doorway, would lend some support to such a view. Mr. Ueno said that it was more likely that what he called "the very dynamic and violent character of the festival, its darker spirit," was connected with the storm god, Susano-O-no-Mikoto,[5] than with the fire god, Kagu-Tuti-no-Kami.

When we returned, in my case limpingly, to the shrine at the base of the mountain, most of the younger men had dispersed. However, we managed to mobilize a small procession of dignitaries and elders. We retraced our steps to the Hayatama shrine, where we received hot, sweet sake. When the *matsuri* is over, three cut-paper prayers are dedicated to the three great deities of Kumano at the shrine on the mountain. This recalls the original descent of the gods on the rock before they dispersed to the shrines, Shingu, Nachi, and Hongu. Ueno said that the torches used by the *agariko* represented the torch used by the deity Taka-Kuraji to guide the first emperor, Jimmu Tenno.

Let me conclude this impressionistic and speculative account by saying that the Shingu shrines seemed to stress Shinto rather than Buddhist myths, symbols, and rituals, although, as Paul Swanson and Professor Miyake insisted, Buddhist influences have been incorporated through Shugendō (itself described, however, by Ichiro Hōri [1969:52] as "Buddhist asceticism mixed with Shinto, Buddhism, Taoism, and popular shamanism"). The three great Kumano shrines, Hongu, Shingu, and Nachi, known collectively as Kumano Sanzan, "the Three Mountains of Kumano," according to Ponsonby-Fane (1962:145), were dedicated to Shinto deities: Hongu to Ketsumiko, one of the numerous names of Susano-O-no-Mikoto; Shingu to Hayatama-Ō; and Nachi to three deities, Ketsumiko, Hayatama-Ō, and Fusumi. According to legend, Hongu was founded in the reign of the tenth emperor, Sujin; Shingu, in that of the twelfth, Keikō; and Nachi, in that of the sixteenth, Nintoku, in the early centuries of the common era. However, as we have seen, Mr. Ueno would place the founding of Hayatama shrine at Shingu at an even earlier date.

Ketsumiko, according to several Kumano informants, seemed to be an indigenous *kami* associated with agriculture rather than a storm god of the Great Tradition of Shinto. Mr. Ueno, the Shinto priest at Shingu, told us that he believed, from recent archaeological evidence, that Shingu had been a sacred site in the Jōmon period (at least c. 5000 B.C.) and confirmed that his predecessor had excavated an object from the wet-rice-cultivating Yayoi Culture, which existed from approximately 300 B.C. to A.D. 300. It would seem, therefore, that Shingu was a ritual center long before the establishment of Yamato government. It may well be that the Shinto aspects of Kumano religion prospered in the Meiji period, with the consolidation of the cults of the emperor, and that Shingu prospered most from the nationalist mood which gave Shrine Shinto its status and strength (see Fridell 1973:3–10) in the late nineteenth and early twentieth centuries.

On the other hand, Nachi and Hongu became associated with Buddhist pilgrimage with special devotion to the Boddhisatva Kannon, venerated in thirty-three temples. The main Shugendō pilgrimage (known as *nyubu*, "entering the peak") is through seventy-five stations (*nabiki*) located mainly between Hoshino and Hongu, although the pilgrimage is concluded by visiting the Kumano Sanzan. Japanese pilgrimages tend to be made around circles of several shrines, rather than as a linear progress to a dominant shrine, as in Christian pilgrimage. The pilgrimage circles intersect at key points, as at Nachi, where the Buddhist pilgrimage circle intersects with the Shugendō circle.

Elsewhere I have discussed dominant ritual symbols as having opposed yet complementary semantic poles. The entire ritual process of the Kannokura *matsuri* seems to have this bipolarity. At one pole there is imagery of a physical and material nature, with sexual and aggressive features—this I would call the sensory or orectic pole of meaning. At the opposite pole of meaning stress is laid on purity, light, and illumination, and there are frequent references to the foundation of Japan as a political order under the first emperor—this I would call the normative or ideological pole. The former energizes, the latter articulates the ritual process.

At the level of social relations it is clear that ordinary, day-to-day social relationships are suspended, and a new ritual set of ranks comes into being. The *agariko* enjoy a kind of normative communitas despite their contestation. And they unite to break down the gate held shut by their elders—there is an element of ritual rebellion here. What Paul Swanson (1978:14) wrote about Shugendō seems to hold good for Kannokura participants: "There is a saying in Shugendō that in the mountains all people, laymen and priests, are on equal footing, as it were. Anyone, be he businessman, farmer, priest, or whatever, may join and rise in the ranks." Shugendō ranking depends on the number of pilgrimages one has undertaken and the degree to which one has mastered the esoterica of several ceremonies (such as the secret meanings of certain *goma* rites; proficiency in the Saito Goma; walking across fire; the fire ceremony for personal protection; prayers for sickness; and so on—Swanson 1978:15). But these criteria represent stages of spiritual experience and achievement, and *not* differences in political-jural-economic status.

As in the Kannokura ritual, women were forbidden to climb the sacred mountains between Yoshino and Kumano, and boys entering adult life were encouraged to undertake mountain pilgrimages (*nyubu*) as "novices" (*nyui*). The rank *nyui* is the first of seven or nine ranks (according to the Shugendō sect), culminating in the rank of "true *sendatsu*" or "guide," or, in the Honzan-ha sect, "eminent senior *sendatsu* of the mountains" (*buchū shusse daisendatsu*, "success, promotion, eminence"),

THE KANNOKURA FESTIVAL · 131

one of whose qualifications is that he has made fifty Ōmine pilgrimages. Professor Kitagawa, in his pioneering article "Three Types of Pilgrimage in Japan" (1967:158), suggests that "The stiff mountain climbing, conducted by experienced guides, essential for spiritual and physical disciplines . . . was often considered an initiatory ceremony for boys." I have argued that the same holds true for the Shingu rites. And like all genuine initiatory rites, symbols of birth, procreation, death, and rebirth are prominent, and the individual life cycle is linked to the seasonal cycle at the same time that the historical past, the beginning of the empire, is symbolically restored.

7 Morality and Liminality

Much of my recent work in social and symbolic anthropology has been on the nature of those passages from one state of society or mind to another, when the past has lost its grip and the future has not yet taken definite shape. Following the noted folklorist Van Gennep, I have called such passages "liminal," literally "threshold," movements betwixt and between the formerly familiar and stable and the not-yet familiar and stable. The African societies I studied in the field in the 1950s and 1960s were very good at providing rituals which took care of these perilous personal journeys in everyone's life from one brightly lighted familiar area (and set of habits) to another, through a medial darkness of liminality, illuminated only by the candles of guesswork and mythological speculation. Such societies try to aid the traveler, the neophyte or initiand, by declaring to him or her, usually in symbolic form, the central beliefs of their cultures, the crystallized wisdom of their collective experience. The cards are laid on the table, even if, like all cards, up to and including the Tarot pack, they are sufficiently enigmatic and gnomic to provide a lifetime of thought for the thoughtful.

Rites of passage, as Van Gennep called these symbolic journeys, have been found cross-culturally to cluster particularly around birth, marriage, and death. Rites of initiation into full membership of a male or female moral community may take place at puberty, particularly in the case of women, where first menstruation or breast development may provide a visible, biological marker of maturity. The age range for such initiations may sometimes be quite wide. In the case of males, for example, operations on the body, such as circumcision, tatooing, tooth removal, body painting, and so forth, represent cultural equivalents of the natural changes conspicuous among females, but can be performed at any age between birth and young manhood.

Cultural fiat rather than biological necessity here plays the dominant part, though it is interesting to note that many of the symbols of male initiation are borrowed from the repertoire of female physiological change. For example, it is common among West-Central Bantu-speaking peoples to find recently circumcised boys being identified with menstruating girls. I mention these differences not to discuss how sex roles are established in culture but to show how human experience, both male and female, is ransacked for telling symbols, metaphors, and images which can provide the building blocks—or better, the alphabet blocks— for a liminal language, as much nonverbal as verbal, in which potent messages are delivered to those undergoing changes of state.

While all ritual processes are "liminal," in the sense of being temporally located between and outside ordinary times, or at thresholds between regulated spheres of pragmatic action, they are often divided, as Van Gennep discovered, into three major stages or phases, the second of which, the liminal stage proper, represents a state of being and of culture almost completely at odds with the ordinary and mundane. Van Gennep's stages of ritual action begin with what he called "rites of separation." The second phase consists of "rites of margin or limen." His third phase consists of "rites of reaggregation," through which the neophytes are returned from liminality to the world of legal and customary practices and usages, the world of "social structure."

I have used the term "antistructure" for many liminal events and relationships not because I consider liminality to be essentially chaotic or amorphous, although some of its central symbols and behavior do hint at a primary void of precosmic freedom, but because its general manner of organization or construction seems to rest on principles different from those governing quotidian social life. This is not to say that everyday social structure is essentially static, for it is constantly being influenced and modified by antistructure, just as antistructure is continually being curbed and penetrated by structure which sets limits on its capacity for experimentation and critical reflection.

Cultural Processes in the Subjunctive Mood

The world of what the Marxists would call "productive forces" and "productive relations," including the increasingly bureaucratized relations of technical and social control of large-scale productive institutions from industries to factories, and banks to unions, falls within the purview of structure. Political action to alter or maintain the systems and personnel of control in this world is therefore structural action. One might add that action and reaction in this world are in culture's "indicative mood." This linguistic analogy suggests that such sociocultural processes have to do with what most cultures would label by terms translatable in Western languages as "actual," existing or happening as or "in fact," not merely seeming to be so—pretended, imagined, fictitious, or ostensible.

But just as verbs in many languages possess directly (in terms of suffixes, infixes, or prefixes) or indirectly (as in the English "may," "would," and "might") subjunctive and optative moods, so do cultural processes, and so does experienced life or lived-through experience in all cultures. Let me give Webster's definition of "subjunctive": "designating or of that mood of a verb used to express supposition, desire, hypothesis, possibility, etc., rather than to state an actual fact" (as in the mood of "were," in "if I were you." A good deal of what I have called antistructure would be in the subjunctive mood, so defined.

The optative mood, as in Greek, expresses wish or desire, as the term's derivation from the Latin *optare,* "to wish or desire," itself traceable to the Indo-European base *op-, "to choose, prefer," clearly shows. Rupert Brooke's cry in his poem "Grantchester": "εἰθεγενοίμηγ, would I were in Grantchester, in Grantchester," is, of course, in the optative. There are ritual overtones to this term, for Priscian, the great Latin grammarian, who introduced it in the early sixth century, used it to translate the Greek *euktike egklisis* (εὐκτικη εγκλιóις). *Euktike* means "votive" or "expressing a wish," and derives from *euchomai* (εὐχσμαι), "to pray, offer a prayer, pay one's vows, make a vow" (similar to the Latin *precari*, "to make a vow," or *vota facere*, "pay one's vows"), originally to make a tangible offering or sacrifice in a ritual situation. Sacrifice often occurs in the liminal phase of a ritual, so that we may perhaps trace the grammatical mood to a cultural mood, a mode of thought to a mode of action. Ritual liminality, containing sacrifice and stressing wishes and vows, here seems to underlie a grammatical mode of framing language.

The liminal or central phase of elaborate ritual is clearly dominated by the subjunctive mood of culture. So, too, are the productions of artists of all types, whether religious or not. For they are masters of the *"paraliminal"* or "limin*oid*," if not of the liminal. Their works may not be overtly concerned with invisible or ultrahuman beings and powers, as are the works of religion, the *opera dei*, but they are surely concerned, just as religions are, with the assignment of meaning to the moral complexities and paradoxes of human social and individual life, with the glosses, commentaries, and evaluations of the stream of intersubjective events that compose the lives of communities—systems of connective persons and individuals. Furthermore, they are concerned with possibilities, not merely with what seems to be the case at the given moment in terms of the authoritative assumptions of the given culture. They are concerned with variants, with alternatives, with that which is nobler or baser, more beautiful or uglier, purer or more corrupt, than the current dominant social construction of reality accepted as fact, as culture's indicative mood. They are inherently skeptical of the received wisdom, the wordly wisdom.

Religious liminality perhaps evaluates human behavior in terms of its lapses from simple ideals—for example, from the Ten Commandments, the principles of the Sermon on the Mount, Koranic law, Krishna's injunctions to Arjuna in the *Baghavadgita*. Skepticism can, in fact, proceed from the religious perspective as readily as from the secular standpoint, if by "skepticism" we mean the doctrine that the truth of authoritative knowledge must always be in question. The prophets of Israel were, in this sense, skeptical of the policies of the kings of Israel.

Artistic liminality, in addition to its concern with formal excellence, is tuned to the problematic and many-leveled character of human relationships, and the difficulty of making honest judgments on them if one eschews simple moral rules as absolutely binding and universally applicable. I personally suspect, with Tolstoy and his idealized peasants, that cross-culturally the simple may be the true; but human history has, alas, always evaded this issue. Great artists delineate the superimposed arabesques of this evasiveness. Every memorable play or novel is about apparently irresolvable moral contradictions. Every act and interaction is shown to be "laminated," many-leveled, while, as Auden writes, "the desires of the heart are as crooked as corkscrews." Artists are thus often skeptical of simple solutions and forgiving of individuals who choose to reject not only the prevailing mores, but also the religious and ethical axioms currently prestigious, in response to what they feel in "instinct" or "love."

Analysis of rites of passage in Central and East African sociocultural systems, followed years later by study of theater and narrative in the literate cultures of large-scale societies, has given me cause to think that human life, both singular and plural, requires its moments of antistructure as well as its days of structure if it is to remain healthy and achieve self-mastery. I say "*moments* of antistructure" because quantitatively these passages between structured times, whether in initiation rites, or watching a play, or listening to music, are brief though rich in implications for the future. Clock time and experienced time are quite different, as we all know. When we are deeply implicated in an activity, we cease to count the minutes. The moments of antistructure are felt to belong to one's "authentic self," beyond playacting: action and awareness then merge and one ceases to keep one's eye on the clock.

I have written at length on the strange cultural phenomena that appear during the liminal stages of initiation rituals in preindustrial societies—symbols of birth and death, male and female, nature and culture, these opposites often being represented by the same ambiguous symbol: androgynes, theriomorphic figures, caves that represent, at once, womb and tomb, the presentation of monstrous beings in the forms of masks, paintings, sculptures—which are nevertheless composed of elements drawn from everyday experience, though now combined in bizarre and original ways; the telling and enacting of creation myths or the deeds of culture heroes; the use of archaic or secret language; the playing of special liminal music, sometimes on instruments never used outside ritual occasions; the chanting of songs certainly never rendered in mundane situations—and many other fascinating liminal features and qualities whose subjunctive (and sometimes speculative) framings manifest release from conventional lineaments of order.

Liminality has its own structures—as Lévi-Strauss's analyses of myths have abundantly demonstrated—but these have emerged as reflections *upon* the matter-of-fact world rather than as a reflection *of* it. Some would say that they add up to a set of metalanguages, nonverbal as well as verbal, transcending the languages in which members of societies transact their daily business. In liminal and liminoid situation we develop grammars and lexicons, some mathematical, for talking about our indicative ways of communicating with one another. We take ourselves for our subject matter, distance ourselves from ourselves to know ourselves better—and hence, oddly enough, to become close to ourselves—a process never finally resolved, since we are endlessly in motion, endlessly, through our minds, evolving. Social groups, by means of metalanguages, may be thought of as periodically coming to a realization of how their present state relates to their mythical and quasi-historical past, and how far actual experience has strayed from idealized social categories. We find here at least the germ of a reflexive moral self-critique. Such a critique may sever its moorings from the past or reinterpret the past to give more flexibility to the present.

Antistructure and the Durkheimian View of Religion

I now want to focus attention upon certain social and individual aspects of antistructure, since they speak more directly to the problem of moral action than do most consolidated cultural forms. When initiands—those undergoing a change of state, status, or being—move into liminality, they experience a change in the quality of social relationships. On the one hand, they find themselves shorn of all their preritual attributes—symbolized in various cultures by the loss of their names, removal of clothing, separation from kin, withdrawal of insignia or other signs of rank, wearing of uniform clothing, blackening or whitening of the body—while, on the other hand, they are compelled to obey implicitly the apparently arbitrary commands of the elders and instructors. They are reduced, so to speak, to a generic *prima materia* which is to be reconstituted and repersonalized by the potent gnosis or traditional ritual knowledge imparted to them by the elders. Their new selves will thus be adequated to the new lives they must lead as incumbents of new status roles.

In other words, social structure does not disappear; rather, it is drastically simplified into a command-obedience, almost a boot-camp, relationship between initiators and initiated. Nevertheless, among the initiands themselves something unstructured emerges: They confront one another as integral entities and not as segmentalized occupants of statuses and players of roles. Stripped of ascribed structural being, they are wholly in becoming. For a time there is no inequality between them; as David Schneider might say, they "share substance," even if this "substance" is not that conferred by kinship, as in his analysis. Rather, shared essence is conferred through gnosis, that kind of knowledge which is believed to reshape the novice's being, not merely to be stored in her/his memory as a cognitive possession.

After observing African initiation rites of boys and girls, seeing them stripped during their period of seclusion of all the attributes of their former social-structural status, even their personal names, and not yet given new signs of status (clothing, tattoos, circumcised genitalia, insignia, hair style, new names, new privileges and duties), nevertheless communicating as good friends with one another, I finally arrived at the notion that the "social" is not to be regarded as being identical only with the "social-structural."

Durkheim and his followers of the *Année sociologique* school seem mainly to have upheld the structural view, though Durkheim's concept of collective "effervescence" when new social structures are generated, as in the French Revolution, admittedly points to a different view of the social. Beyond the structural lies not just the Hobbesian "war of all against all," as such contrasting figures as Konrad Lorenz and René Girard have argued, but something else—which I have called communitas. I have sometimes spoken of it as a "generic human bond," almost in the language of sociobiology, but I am closer to what I intend when I formulate communitas as "a relational quality of full unmediated communication, even communion, between definite and determinate human identities [William Blake's phrase], which arises spontaneously in all kinds of groups, situations, and circumstances" (1977:46).

A Dutch anthropologist, Matthew Schoffeleers, has used my notion of communitas to highlight what he calls "a curious ambivalence in all of Durkheim's writings on religion" (Schoffeleers and Meijers 1978:14). This ambivalence appears in Durkheim's *The Elementary Forms of the Religious Life* (1915:283–294), where he discusses the transition from the "religion of the clan" to the "religion of the tribe." In that context he argues that the two may be contrasted in terms of "totem worship" (at the clan level) and the "worship of supernatural beings" such as gods (at the tribal level). Totem worship, Schoffeleers writes, summarizing Durkheim, "may be described as a kind of religion which emphasizes the values and interests of a particular community, whereas the worship of supernatural beings implies their subordination to a set of wider ideas and values. The contrast is thus one between particularism and universalism" (1978:14). Later Schoffeleers remarks that Durkheim failed to comment on the tensions which must of necessity be provoked by the coexistence of these modes of religious sociality. Situations must arise where loyalties to clan or tribe are in opposition.

Gluckman has seen such "cross-cutting ties" as acting as a brake on the spread of the feud in tribal societies. Durkheim does, however, pay attention to the tensions between national and wider values in modern, large-scale, complex societies. Here his ambivalence is patent. On the one hand, he condemns each and every kind of narrow nationalism, which he rejects as "immoral" (now we are beginning to touch upon one of the main themes of this paper) and a "regression to paganism." On the other hand, he puts forward a conception of the nation and the state which, in Schoffeleer's words, "comes dangerously close to the very thing he condemned" (1978:14). Briefly, the nation is elevated to the status of "the sacred" and, as Robert Bellah insists in *Emile Durkheim on Morality and Society* (1973:xxxv), the ideal nation in this conception is the equivalent of a congregation of believers, and one of the tasks of the state is to watch over its orthodoxy. Here the obvious danger is totalitarianism. Durkheim tried to avoid this by stressing that the nation must always be aware that it is part of an *inter*national field, and its values must therefore be in accord with the universal values of mankind. There is a contradiction in this position which Durkheim never resolved, for if the nation is to be seen as a kind of sacralized macroclan, providing existential meaning, particularism is thereby merely reinstated at a higher level of social organization, at odds with the humanistic ideals Durkheim simultaneously upheld.

At this point Schoffeleers notes the contrast I made in my book *The Ritual Process* (1969:132) between communitas and Durkheimian "solidarity," the force of the latter depending upon an in-group/out-group contrast. Schoffeleers writes (1978:15):

> [Turner] argues on the basis of a wealth of empirical evidence that religion may sacralize *both* "structure"—by which he means broadly the existing organizational arrangements of a collectivity—*and* "antistructure" or "communitas." Structure and communitas are two major models of human relations, one of which articulates and legitimates differentiation and inequality, while the other emphasizes "humankindness" [or, in David Hume's terms, "the sentiment for humanity"], the view that all human beings, despite their cultural diversity, are ultimately equal. If social life is to be viable, it must combine these two elements, for structure without the tempering influence of communitas would soon become arid and oppressive.

Individual and Communitas/Person and Structure

Durkheim, in another aspect of his work, was concerned with what he called the "cult of the individual," a formulation which first appeared in 1893, in his early work on the social division of labor. Not only are such groups as the totemic clan and the nation-state sacralized but also, in modern industrial societies, the individual. Steven Lukes quotes Durkheim as writing, at the time of the Dreyfus affair (1975:340–341):

> The human person [by which he means, in the terminology I will shortly employ, the human individual—V.T.] whose definition serves as the touchstone according to which good must be distinguished from evil, is considered as sacred, in what one might call the ritual sense of the word. It has something of the transcendental majesty which churches of all times have given to their God. It is conceived as being invested with that mysterious property which creates an empty space around holy objects, which keeps them away from profane contacts and which draws them away from ordinary life. And it is exactly this feature which induces the respect of which it is the object. Whoever makes an attempt on a man's life, on a man's liberty, on a man's honor, inspires us with a feeling of horror in every way analogous to that which the believer expe-

riences when he sees his idol profaned. Such a morality is therefore not simply a hygienic discipline or a wise principle of economy. It is a religion of which man is, at the same time, both believer and God.

The cult of the individual, in other words, addresses itself to all humanity, but in doing this it must transcend the sacralized nation, the nationalist ideal.

Durkheim considered God to be a symbol of society. But if one distinguishes social structure from communitas, this symbol may be seen as having two senses which are at opposite semantic poles. God may be regarded a "symbol of structure," by which is meant everything that has to do with social differentiation and with the authoritative ordering of that differentiation. Per contra, God may be symbol of antistructure or the negation, hereditarily ascribed, of hierarchical and segmentary differentiation: I believe that is the sense in which the Declaration of Independence defined America as "one nation under God." In my own work I have argued that the individual, who is the human unit of communitas, is at the root of all religion, including primitive religion, insofar as such religion is the manifestation of antistructure. Durkheim tended to see the concept of the individual or, as he also called it, "individualism" as a later development and, as Schoffeleers and Meijers write, "something which manifested itself, as it were, on the fringe of primitive society in such concepts as personal totems and guardian spirits" (1978:47).

The unit of structure is the persona. *Persona* in Latin first meant a mask used by a player, then later a player himself or herself, one who played a part, or for a character acted (as in dramatis personae). It came in time to mean the capacity or character in which one acts—and here the modern sociological sense of "person" as the sum of an individual's roles and statuses, or of his incumbencies of positions in a social-structural system, comes close to the Latin sense. The Latin verb *personare* means literally "to sound through," as a voice sounds through a mask. It can also mean "to perform upon a musical instrument," as in the sentence "Cithară Iopas personat" ("Iopas plays the cithara [a kind of lyre or lute]").

Whether as mask or instrument, *persona* suggests a medium, something through which a communication is made or an action effected. It also induces the idea of an artifact, a creation of culture, not of nature. It is indirect, fabricated, an interposition between simpler, more fundamental entities. It is part of the social construction of reality. Since it is this latter "reality" which I have previously called "the indicative mood," and which now reveals itself in the ambiguous guise of theater, it would seem that language itself abets the melancholy Jacques's view in Shakespeare's *As You Like It*: "All the world's a stage, And all the men and

MORALITY AND LIMINALITY · 141

women on it merely players" (read *personae*). But Jacques's "players" were "persons," not "individuals," some of them, like the furious soldier and the "lean and slippered pantaloon," drawn directly from the masked-role repertoire of the Italian *commedia dell'arte.*

The adjective "individual" was found only rarely before the seventeenth century, in the sense of "existing as a separate entity." It was this fact that caught the attention of Durkheim. He did not deny that individuals were recognized in premodern cultures, but argued that the concept of "the individual in general" developed rather late in the social history of humankind, parallel, he thought, with the steady contraction of the domain of traditional religion. Durkheim saw the cult of the individual as replacing other religions, including what Robert Bellah was to call "civil religions." Bellah, indeed, quotes a passage from Durkheim in which he relates the individual to a sort of secularized religion of humanity (1973:48–49):

> After all, individualism . . . is the glorification not of the self but of the individual in general. It springs not from egoism but from sympathy for all that is human, a broader pity for all sufferings, for all human miseries, a more ardent need to combat them and mitigate them, a greater thirst for justice. Is there not herein what is needed to place all men of good will in communion?

Durkheim's problem was to establish, on a firm basis of scientific sociology, social and political frameworks which would be based upon and would extract the maximum benefit from "the individual in general." He wanted to eliminate symbols, rites, temples, and priests from his "religion of humanity," considering religion as "essentially nothing but a group of collective beliefs and practices that have a special authority" (Bellah 1973:11). In this religion, as in all others, "the individual is a product of society more than he is its cause" (Bellah 1973:12). But let us look a little more closely at this tricky concept, "the individual," before we consider the social and moral experiences in which human beings engender meaning and express it in cultural modes, whether rites, books, or conduct.

An excellent contemporary anthropological treatment of the individual/communitas, person/structure question, one which also confronts its moral and ethical dimensions, can be found in Kenelm Burridge's *Someone, No One: An Essay on Individuality* (1979). Burridge defines "individual" and "person" much as I have done; for him the person is also an "identity"—a "someone"—who conforms to social roles and norms, and is structurally defined as an occupant of roles and statuses in an ordered role-status system, while the individual is a "nonidentity"—a "no one"—who may hold particular nonconformist perceptions of truth that result in conscious and independent moral discrimination and innovation. Burridge also uses the term "individuality" as "a movement from the person to the individual, a movement from apprehension to comprehension" (1979:74), a formulation which has something in common with my notion of human life as moving back and forth between experiences of social structure and experiences of antistructure, the latter often in liminal situations, thresholds between structured domains, as when one undergoes a rite of passage or takes part in a carnival.

For Burridge, the "integrative/disintegrative energy which gathers particular relations either into the person or into the individual" (1979:6) may be called the self. Alternatively, the self is "an energy which either inhibits or makes possible the movement between person and individual." Burridge's usage, of course, reverses the senses which such religious philosophers as Maritain and Berdyaev apply to the terms "person" and "individual." For them the person and personhood are associated with moral choice and creativeness, while the individual is merely a single instance of humanity in the mass, of Ibsen's Dr. Stockman's "damned compact majority." But on reflection, I favor Burridge's usage because it has its roots in the British anthropological tradition which Burridge and I share.

Since Burridge's treatment of the semantic family "self-person-individual-individuality" is so important for the development of communitas-liminality theory in relation to morality and ethics, I will quote his most explicit statement of the relationships among these terms, interpolating comments to stitch his argument into mine.

> Within the European or Western tradition we tend to think of ourselves as unique beings in whom others, a computer, and God perhaps, take a particular interest. Yet in practice each one of us *is*, not necessarily because we *think* or because thoughts come or even because there are papers which say who or what we are. (1979:4)
> [One thinks here of the young student at the beginning of the Japanese movie *Woman in the Dunes* who gazes in disgust at all the identity cards and other papers in his wallet which appear to sum up his social existence—bureaucracy is the iron cage of the individual-in-general. Later, of course, he realizes the liberated individuality in himself as he applies his mind to solving the problem of the dune water table and of providing a water supply for the very villagers who have closely imprisoned him, relishing his inner freedom so much that he opts to remain in the permanent liminality of the dunes as a "no one" rather than return to the iron cage, as a "someone" defined once more by cards.]

Back to Burridge:

> We *are* because in immediate objectivity in relation to others each one of
> us is life: genes in movement, a nervous system, a mouth to be fed. In
> interaction with a sociocultural environment and through a mind or
> brain capable of a variety of operations we *become*. Not so far from
> George Herbert Mead [Burridge is referring here to Mead's seminal
> work *Mind, Self, and Society* (1934)], but reformulating, taking the en-
> ergy of the peculiar integration of these features as provisionally con-
> stituting the *self* [italics added throughout quote]. Whether god-given, in
> which case this energy becomes the soul journeying back to its creator
> [rather like John Keats's notion of life as a "Vale of Soul Making," for
> Burridge speaks of the self as the energy in a process of *becoming*], or
> gene-given, or simply intuited, the fact of integration—some sort of co-
> herence or coordination of the parts or constituents of being—does not
> detach the integrative energy or *self* from its constituents, but still makes
> it more than the sum of parts and, in that sense, conceptually and em-
> pirically distinct.
>
> In its integration of animal and sociocultural parts, a self may show
> forth in the *person*: "a single instance of the species," the conformist
> who, in reproducing in word or deed the norms of the given traditional
> social order, manifests the relations of that tradition. Put another way,
> the constitutive relations of one who *conforms* to the given social tradi-
> tions reveal the *person*. Going further, the self may also integrate the
> parts into the *individual*: not merely the non-conformist or one who has
> the qualities or attributes of the single instance in greater degree—one
> who runs faster, talks better, or works harder or the like—but, giving
> the "special attributes" and the inherent ambiguity of the word their full
> force, one who manifests relations *opposed* to those indicated by the per-
> son. That is, the *moral critic* who envisages another kind of social or
> moral order, the creative spark poised and ready to change tradition [the
> prophet, the nabi, the religious founder, the ethical innovator, the politi-
> cal innovator, the cutting-edge philosopher, the poetic genius—not the
> eccentric whose unconventionality is often an unrequited love for con-
> vention]. Yet if some people are wholly *individuals* and others are *persons*,
> it is a matter of common observation that most people are in some re-
> spects and most frequently persons, while in other respects and at other
> times they can appear as individuals. And this apparent oscillation or
> movement between person and individual—whether in a particular in-
> stance the movement is oneway or a return is made—may be identified
> as *individuality*. Or, individuality refers to the opportunity and capacity
> to move from person to individual and/or *vice versa*. . . . (1979:4–6)

["Individuality," for Burridge, would seem to be an ever-shifting ratio between individual and person, either the sum of their mutual compromises or a regular or irregular polar movement from one extreme to the other.]

The [person] is content with things as they are, the [individual] posits an alternative set of moral discriminations. . . . Because the self is capable of moving towards an integration of now one and then the other, the interplay between person and individual can yield either a dilemma—indicative of a self in disintegrative mode—or an apperception of own being *in relation* to traditional or alternative categories. Without this interplay and apperception, sociology and social and cultural anthropology would not be possible. Which makes of the self a necessary if mute assumption. (1979:6)

Burridge explicitly relates his individual/person model to my characterization of liminality:

The liminal period becomes an introduction to, and test of, *moral being.* Generally re-enacting the transformation from nature to culture, pubertal rites bring the components of being together and confront the cultural faculties with the oppositions and correspondences between animal, moral, and spiritual being. To use another idiom, the initiand is asked to measure communitas and antistructure—wherein human beings, stripped of their roles, statuses, memberships, and moralities, are in communion as human selves—against the demands of organization and structure.

In this situation most initiands, responding to the past pressures of kinsfolk and conformists, yield to the more obvious and overt side of the ritual. Some, intuitively grasping that symbols and symbolic activities contain a mysterium—a latency, a promissory note, an invitation to realize that which lies behind the obvious and overt—may perceive and order a truth which, because they cannot withstand conformist pressures, they will hold in their hearts all the years of their lives. Others lose themselves in the chaos, unable to bring it into order. A few persevere and are led into areas which the overtness of the cultural symbols hide from most. But while the affirmation of a truth discovered calls a halt, one negation breeds another and discovery becomes a continuing journey. Truth's center seems to grow more distant with each successive launch from closing peripheries. Each arrival entails a further moral choice if it is to make a new point of departure, and each departure requires a further transformation of the self in relation to otherness. In Turner's phrase [Burridge goes on], man grows through antistructure and conserves through structure (*The Ritual Process*: 203). (Burridge 1979:146–147)

There are, of course, many paradoxes in Burridge's position. For example, one may play a structural role with verve and creativeness as if one were an "individual" in Burridge's terms. Obviously there are creative civil servants and administrators in the very center of the structural domain of the "person." Without them the structure undoubtedly would not work, for "working to rule" is not working resiliently. Again, in culturally, and especially religiously, "plural" societies, if one belongs to a minority culture of which one is an exemplary person, one is by that very fact considered to be a nonperson or an inferior person from the standpoint of the dominant culture. However, in this case, the differences among cultures in a single nation-state may provoke many persons into individuality as they strive to integrate the self in an arena of conflicting values and rules. It is perhaps not surprising that the concept of the individual-in-general in the West arose most explicitly in the Judeo-Christian tradition among peoples belonging to minority and often diasporogenic cultures whose strongly held worldviews were under constant assault from a vast range of powerful environing polities and belief systems.

But the emancipation of the individual from the person, as tribal and feudal societies crumble, as the division of labor destroys hallowed, corporate ties, may lead, as Burridge well recognizes, to societies driven by individualistic greed, selfishness, self-interest, and the exploitation of others. The backlash to this social Darwinist outlook, involving a struggle among individuals for environmentally limited resources and the elimination or subordination of the "less fit," may be an attempt to regress to a monstrous tribalism supported by heavy industry, where "dogmas and procedures are substituted for living morality." Here the pseudo individual is replaced (in totalitarianism—monopolistic, coercive retribalization controlled by a self-perpetuating elite) by the pseudo person, amoral antistructure by ideological structure which has no place for the creative individual.

The modern individual-in-general, therefore, exists in a state of alienation, not only from the means of production, as in the Marxist interpretation, but also, and perhaps more devastating psychologically, because he/she is sometimes embodied in what David Apter (1963) has called a "theocratic state," in a monstrous pseudo communitas from which the critical and creative individual is excluded as a hero or renegade. In theocracies, Apter claims, political and religious associations are one and the same. Some specialization and independence of political roles are possible, but these have their significance in a religious or quasi-religious system. The king is a spiritual counselor as well as a warrior, he is a defender of the faith in addition to being a lawgiver. Many forms of leadership are possible, but leaders in such states have two main qualities.

First, they are roles that are personalized and institutionalized. Second, they are representatives of the deity.

Theocracies are communities that are part of a natural and wider order both of nature and of transcendence. Thus there is no sharp contrast between the natural universe and the state, nor is there a sharp dividing line between the living and the dead, or between the real state and the transcendent state, that is, between the kingdom of God and the kingdom of man. Of course, in practice, as I tried to show in my case study of the conflict between Henry II of England and Thomas Becket, archbishop of Canterbury in the late twelfth century in England, in medieval Europe church and state were often locked in competition over temporal (and at times spiritual) power. From Australian aboriginal communities to the Greek polis, and some modern Middle Eastern states, the human entity derives his/her personal identity as well as his/her moral objectives and general philosophy of life from the political community, which is itself regarded as sacred (Apter 1963:70–72).

In such societies, which in all their variety preceded the industrial leviathans of the modern age, the individual emerged more rarely than the person. Burridge does draw attention, however, in his chapter "Prescribed Positions" to the "ways in which something like the individual or individuality with which we are familiar occurs in other cultures" (1979:116). Even in relatively simple societies, he argues, it is possible to recognize individuality as a thematic fact of culture with varying expressions. He considers some examples in which "individuals or their likenesses are forced to occupy prescribed roles and positions within the community, and may *not* be individuals or *like* individuals *outside* those positions" (Burridge 1979:116). In other words, we do not have the generalized individual, as in Western societies, but the creation of specific cultural niches in which the creative and critical attributes of the individual can legitimately manifest themselves—rather like the state of "permanent liminality" which I described in *The Ritual Process*, where, paradoxically, what is essentially a phase or process of becoming or transformation is fixed into a status role (like monks and mendicants in the major historical religions).

Also relevant is Burridge's fascinating examination of such prototypical or foreshadowing individuals in societies of varying scale and complexity: the shaman, the Nuer leopard-skin chief of the Sudanese Republic, the Melanesian manager and/or sorcerer, the Australian man of high degree, and, at a much more sophisticated level, the Hindu *sanyasi*. These particularized individuals stand opposed to the persons of the normative social structure, who "confirm the given system of roles and statuses. In the relations between such persons and individuals or their likeness or refraction the structure becomes evident to all, and, more than this, possibilities of innovation and moral variation are indicated" (Burridge 1979:116). In the mythologies often associated with shamans, diviners, and prophets, such symbolic types as the Hero, the Clown, and the Trickster point to further attributes of the individual held in abeyance by conformity with structural norms.

Now, in my view, in all societies liminality belongs both to the person and to the individual; to the social structure, as it transforms and is transformed by the transition of human entities from one social position or status to another, representing a movement and alteration of personhood; and to the antistructure, as it brings into transient visibility both the positive and the negative aspects of the individual, the creator and destroyer of the vested mores. The antistructure is also ambiguous, for it may represent nihilistic solitude for the temporarily exposed individual, or it may be the epiphanic uncovering of a new depth of human communion, brotherhood and sisterhood, transcending the kinship terms through which it is often metaphorized.

In various writings I have stressed that the liminal phases of initiatory rituals contain episodes where the dominant symbols of cultural order, and a fortiori of social-structural order, are displayed to the initiands, as well as episodes where order is mocked, reversed, criticized, or ignored. I have been implicitly rebuked, in Evan M. Zuesse's penetrating study of sub-Saharan African religions, *Ritual Cosmos*, for failing to distinguish "two *types* of liminality" (1979:35). These are, he writes, "applicable throughout African religions" and consist (1) of "*positive liminality*, which integrates structure and builds up a divine order, and (2) *negative liminality*, which destroys order and isolates its victims (Zuesse 1979:35). Zuesse obviously writes from the characteristic perspective of person and structure—which often presents liminality as a sort of Manichaean confrontation of "good" with "evil," "evil" being indeterminacy or structurelessness.

Zuesse has it in for liminality per se when he writes: "The liminal purely in itself acts on the human order as an uncontrollable destructive force; it is chaos" (1979:54). He expands on this view in his reanalysis of Mary Douglas's discussion of the Lele pangolin hunters' cult in her article "Animals in Lele Religious Symbolism" (1957). The pangolin or scaly anteater is destined to be a liminal beast if ever there was one. The Lele, a Zairean people, say of it: "In our forest there is an animal with the body and tail of a fish, covered with scales. It has four little legs and climbs in trees" (Douglas 1957:237). Like humans, it bears its young one at a time (not in a litter), and it neither fights nor runs away from the hunter but curls up into a ball and awaits the spear's thrust. Zuesse says: "It offers itself to sustain the Lele" (1979:69). He claims:

All the categories of the Lele universe are brought together in this liminal being, and in its self-offering to the chosen hunter, humanity is allowed to participate in the transcendence of all normative structure, the
return to primordial generative formlessness. Yet the cult members are
given great powers to *reaffirm* the normative order by their communal
feast on the pangolin sacrifice. Although transcending the taboos that
constrain others, they *regenerate* the structures that are defined by the
taboos. The pangolin embodies *positive* liminality, which contributes to
the upbuilding of the divine order. It is in effect the monstrous inter-
mediary between formlessness and form. (1979:69; italics added)

For me, the two types of liminality are not Zuesse's "order" and
"chaos"; rather, they consist of a confrontation between that domain
which pertains to the person, that is, social structure and cultural order,
and that which belongs to the individual, that is, the critical and potentially creative destructuration of that order. The intent of individuals in
antistructural liminality is not to produce chaos but to realize a new and
more effective integration of the components of experience for which
there is no traditional precedent. This may look like chaos to the representatives of traditional order, but may in fact be a creative response to
conditions that require societal reordering.

Here I recall to the reader my earlier distinction between indicative and
subjunctive moods of culture. Indeed, Zuesse seems to recognize the
subjunctive potentiality of what he otherwise castigates as "negative"
when he mentions that the Lele hunters, through the pangolin's sacrifice
of abandonment to the spear, "return to primordial generative formlessness." However, he does not mention the cognitive activities of individuals, particularly the play of ideas, which often occur during the liminal phase of passage ritual. He seems to suggest that there is only a
profound immersion in a kind of collective unconscious—and, indeed,
symbols of womb and tomb *do* abound cross-culturally in liminal settings—but he fails to note the frequent presence of play, including the
play of ideas and plays on words, which also characterizes many of these
contexts.

In her authoritative work on children's play—which extends to many
kinds of adult play— *Transformations: The Anthropology of Children's Play*,
Helen B. Schwartzman shows how in various societies, institutionalized
play in ritual (usually in ritual liminality) "sanctions insults and derision
of authority figures, social status inversions, parody, satire, lampooning,
and clowning" (1978:124).

Brian Sutton-Smith, who has made extensive studies of children's
play, and who has also generalized from them to adult play, has argued

that "play is the learning of variability"—in other words, a function of individuality as Burridge conceives it; Sutton-Smith, in a seminal article, "Games of Order and Disorder" (1976), suggests that play and games are not always socializing or social-ordering activities (such as would lead to the fabrication of social personae), for they may seek to challenge and reverse the social order. Games may model the social system "only to destroy it," as in ring-around-a-rosy or, as we call it in Britain, "ring-a-ring-a-roses," where everyone acts in concert and then collapses— "Ashes, ashes, we all fall down"—with a lot of happy giggling—obviously in praise of antistructure. Games of order and disorder also often mock conventional power roles (such as the adult as parent, teacher, law official, or political figure):

> Roosevelt in the White House
> Waiting to be elected;
> Dewey in the garbage can
> Waiting to be collected.
> (Withers 1947:218)

Sutton-Smith expanded on my notions of structure and antistructure to hypothecate that children's games of order and disorder (which he calls "antistructural phenomena") make the system (the sociocultural system of which the players are members)

> tolerable as it exists, and, therefore, with respect to possible change. Each system has different structural *and* anti-structural functions. The normative structure represents the working equilibrium, the antistructure represents the latent system of potential alternatives from which novelty will arise when contingencies in the normative system require it. We might more correctly call this second system the *protostructural* system because it is the precursor of innovative normative forms. It is the source of "new culture." (1976:20)

The protostructural system is also the matrix of individuality, where the social persona is no longer the focus of attention in the game.

I would be inclined to extend this formulation from children's games to many adult liminal situations, both ritual and nonritual, particularly those of the performative arts; these are, so to speak, legitimated space-time "pods," "pockets," "capsules," or "enclosures," set apart, "framed," or hollowed out from the ongoing processes of mundane social life, pods of becoming in which the subjunctive mood prevails, the mood of "maybe," "might be," "could be," and "as if." Here play, in the full ambiguity of the term, may reign.

Gregory Bateson moved from the observation of mammalian play (monkeys, otters, canids, dolphins) to the notion that in human play particularly we not merely learn how to behave as players of roles but also that there are frames and contexts of behavior. And that there are "*sorts* and *categories* of behavior." He gives the example of a child playing at being an archbishop. The point, he insists, is not that the child is learning to be an archbishop from playing the role, but that he learns that there is such a thing as a role. He is not just learning how to put on the persona defined as archbishop.

> He learns or acquires a new view, partly flexible and partly rigid, which is introduced into life when he realizes that behavior can, in a sense, be set to a logical type or a style. It is not the learning of the *particular* style that you are playing at, but the fact of stylistic flexibility and the fact that the choice of style or role is related to the *frame* and *context* of behavior, and play itself is a category of behavior classified by context in some way. (Bateson 1956:149)

The messages exchanged in a play frame are "metacommunicative messages"—and the frame or context itself is established by a sequence of metacommunicative signals or symbols—that provide information about how another message should be interpreted (Bateson 1956). The play frame appears very often in the complex, protracted rituals of many pre-industrial hunting, agricultural, and religious ritual systems. Clowning, fooling, symbolic inversion, ritual transvestism, stylistic freedom in the manufacture of masks, costumes, body painting, and other disguises, wordplay, the telling and enacting of Trickster myths, riddling, folk dramas embedded in ritual performances, the invention of "wise words" (as among the Western Apache, described by Keith Basso)—all these provide means both for representing, in the privileged "subjunctive mood," the "latent system of potential alternatives from which novelty will arise when contingencies in the normative system require it," as discussed by Sutton-Smith, and also for constituting "the paradoxical metacommunicational messages" discussed by Bateson.

These are paradoxical, Bateson writes, in that the message "This is play" states, "These actions, in which we now engage, do *not* denote what would be denoted by those actions which these actions denote." Thus, in a play fight, "the playful nip denotes the bite, but it does not denote what would be denoted by the bite" (1972:180). It is simultaneously a bite and a not-bite. Helen Schwartzman (1978:218) endorses Bateson's comment that the word "denote" is used here in two senses, but they are treated as synonymous. This produces paradox and is inadmissible, says Bateson, if one rigorously follows the theory of logical types, because the terms are used at differing levels of abstraction.

Play, then, is part of liminality, including many types of ritual liminality. And since it involves metacommunication and metalanguages—verbal and nonverbal languages *about* the languages of every day, about its "natural" languages and messages communicated in such languages—play relates as much to the individual as to the person, and to relations among individuals. Paradox goes along with the individual, too, and without the "paradoxes of abstraction" in play, Bateson writes, "Life would be an endless interchange of stylized messages, a game with rigid rules, unrelieved by change or humor" (1972:193). Play would then be learning roles and rules, not learning *about* roles and rules. The latter is an operation which opens the way for critique, satire, irony with reference to the components of the social structure—for the player is no longer embedded in it but examines it from a liminal or antistructural distance. He can fill that interval, a metaliminal interval, with numerous tropes and other modalities of evaluation of the person and society which otherwise subsume experience. By creating metaphors he can learn to explain relations between known and named and unknown and unlabeled things and processes. The components of the moral system, which governs social-structural experience, can now be reflected upon, isolated, rearranged, assigned new meaning, rejected, approved, given new weight, depreciated, and attached to new symbols.

But in ritual the "individual," Burridge's "no one," is not only a liminal "player," with stress on his playful, critical, antistructural cognitive activities, leaving to the culturally embedded and defined person the burden of liminal seriousness. It is true also that the self, as the integrative energy of a human entity, experiences liminality as the successive disintegration of one state of the person, the emergence of the stateless individual, and the reintegration of the person in a new state. The person, the self shaped by social tradition, has his/her mysteries, too, wherein the self is unmade in order to be remade, dismembered in order to be remembered, in accord with the basal values of the given society and the central ethical, even salvation-offering, axioms of a structured religion—which may or may not support the postulates of the dominant politico-jural structure.

Universalizing religions may be in competition with civil religions, revitalizing movements with theocracies. The person who "plays" roles in secular life may be the reverse of playful in liminality while, as we have seen, the individual may "play" in liminality but be a nobody or "just anybody" in the social structure. There, like the comedian Rodney Dangerfield, he "gets no respect." The self, qua person, may confront deep problems if it is to acquiesce willingly in the roles defined for it by its society. Indeed, much of the discipline and ordeal found in many initiation rituals is directed to the forcible reshaping of the self in conformity with the moral order of society. Our Western veneration of individualism may partially blind us to the awesome thing that a perduring society is— a fact Durkheim never forgot—I mean society seen as a living tradition descending from a remote past, not society experienced as immediate, spontaneous communitas. Society "gathered to a greatness" in its quintessential liminal symbols is the reverse of banal daily experience of social life. Personhood, seen as a symbolic type, and social structure, its collective aspect, do, indeed, have their solemn place in liminality.

In an early article, "Betwixt and Between: The Liminal Period in *Rites de Passage*," in *The Forest of Symbols* (1967), I discussed "the heart of the liminal matter," the communication of *sacra* to initiands, divided, as Jane Harrison has indicated, into "exhibitions," "actions," and "instructions." The central cluster of nonlogical *sacra* might include, in cross-cultural perspective, evocatory instruments or sacred objects, such as relics of deities, heroes, ancestors or saints, aboriginal *churingas*, sacred drums or other musical instruments, the contents of Amerindian medicine bundles, and the fan, cist, and tympanum of ancient Greek and Near Eastern mystery cults. One example of a *sacrum* of "action" would be the ritual of the Lele pangolin sacrifice mentioned earlier.

Among the "instructions" received by initiands may be the main outlines of the theogony, cosmogony, and mystical history of their societies or cults, often with direct or veiled reference to the *sacra* exhibited. Great importance is attached to keeping secret from the uninitiated the nature of the *sacra* revealed, the formulas chanted, and instructions given about them. This esoteric knowledge or gnosis is the crux of liminality as it relates to the cultural engendering of personhood, and revitalization of the social structure. Once again a problem is posed, for while in such initiatory ritual processes instruction is usually given in ethical and social obligations, as well as in law and kinship rules, and in technological skills to fit neophytes for the duties of future office, the esoteric knowledge often seems to transgress the moral interdictions and commandments that are supposed to hold good in everyday life and are accepted there by the uninitiated as well as the initiated. Liminal gnosis, as presented in myths and other symbolic modes, abounds in direct or figurative transgressions of the moral order which rules secular life, such as human sacrifice, cannibalism, parricide, and incestuous unions of brother-sister, mother-son, or father-daughter deities.

Thus the hypothesis that myths are "paradigmatic" (models for human behavior) or afford precedents and sanctions for social status and moral rules requires some sort of qualification. Myths and liminal rites are not to be treated as direct and simple models for quotidian behavior. Nor, on the other hand, should they be treated as cautionary tales, as negative models which should *not* be followed. Rather, they are held to be, in the cultures that secrete them, high or deep mysteries which put the initiand temporarily into close rapport with the primary or primordial generative powers of the cosmos—Shiva, Tezcatlipoca, Kronos, Kali, Tonanzin, Demeter, the *Ungrund* or *Gottheit*—the acts and movements of which transcend rather than transgress the moral norms of human secular society. In myth is a limitless freedom, a symbolic freedom of action which is denied to the norm-bound incumbent of a social status in a social structure. What the initiand seeks through rite and myth is not so much a moral exemplum as the power to transcend even the moral limits of his previous status, although he knows that eventually he must accept the normative restraints inherent in his new status.

Liminality, seen from this angle, is pure potency, where anything can happen, as everything is stated to have happened to the primordial powers; where immoderacy is normal, even normative; and where the elements, the basic building blocks of culture, as I argued in *The Forest of Symbols* (1967), are released from their customary configurations and recombined in often bizarre and terrifying imagery. Monsters are unfamiliar combinations of familiar elements. Yet this potential boundlessness is in practice limited—though never without a sense of hazard—by the participants' knowledge that this is a unique situation, framed by the wisdom inherited by a group from its most creative predecessors as a bounded liminal space-time, and by a definition of the situation which states that the rites and myths must be enacted and told in a prescribed order and in an oblique symbolic form rather than as a literal reality.

The subjunctive mood is thus seen both as having and indicating power, and as ruling a domain of "as if," located in a past that is somehow not the historic past, and in a place where no one lives and works when the rites are done—and that is often burned, broken, dug up, or otherwise demolished or neutralized at ritual's end. Here there is all the ambiguity one finds later in art, which in more complex societies has often taken over many of the functions and attributes of preindustrial ritual systems. Often the *sparagmos*, the decomposition of ritual, has been the genesis of the arts. Music, dance, song, drama, painting, woodcarving, sculpture, narrative, and so forth are unified and orchestrated in preindustrial ritual. Each becomes specialized, professionalized, and in a measure secularized as societies pass certain thresholds of scale and complexity and development of the social division of labor.

So it is not merely a matter of dividing liminality into serious and ludic halves, the former concerned with transforming structural persons from members of one status role to another, the latter giving scope to the individual for subversion of the sociocultural status quo and the development of an individual moral style. Beyond the serious and the ludic lies the visionary or mystical, which transcends, perhaps even transgresses, both. Here we may be in the presence of our human ontological reality as an uncompleted being—or, rather, a community of beings still in process, still in evolution, still open-ended. In the deep cultural sincerity of the midliminal moment, we have an evanescent, fascinating, but fearful glimpse not merely of our nakedness when divested of manifest order but also of our still unformed clay, our radically unfinished state—a view of ourselves, indeed, all of us *frères et soeurs humains*, as liminal in the very nature of things: pedomorphic, infantile, rudimentary, more homologous with axolotls than with salamanders. Then we know it would be inauthentic to declare ourselves or any of our works perfect, whole, rounded off, anywhere near attaining closure.

Perhaps that is why our greatest artists—Homer, Murasaki, Dante, Shakespeare, Michelangelo, Beethoven, Bach, Dostoevsky—produce works full of futurity, of secrets which in some cases millennia of interpretation have hardly begun to bring to light. For such works are not just products of the creative process; they are creativity itself, flashes of the "fire that can," which can never be consummated or terminated because it is the sign of our species' most distinctive feature, its as-yet-unrealized evolutionary potential, its "meonic" freedom—to use Nicholas Berdyaev's term—its perennial hope, its unused cerebral potential. My lyricism here is a kind of *dennoch preisen*, in Rilke's phrase, literally "praising in spite of"—in my case, praising creativeness in our species in the teeth of our present gadarene or lemminglike drive to self-destructiveness. On the face of it, reading the disastrous daily news, despair seems a more appropriate stance than hope. But the face of things may be misleading, a social misconstruction of reality.

Rainer Maria Rilke caught this fitful creativity or poesis which propels humankind in great art and religion and, since it is human, should be taken into account by anthropologists. He caught it in his poem "Orpheus," the cornerstone of his sequence *Sonnets to Orpheus* (1922). Orpheus is more than poetic inspiration personified and fashionably assigned by a well-educated central European to a figure in classical mythology. The sixth-century B.C. Orphic cults with their emphasis on symbolic descent into the underworld, the movement of souls in transmigration from body to body, was perhaps the mystery cult which most stressed the generative character of midliminality. Rilke must have known this, and his poem has a ritual, *rite de passage*, character even as it escapes the frame of all ritual forms to declare creativeness in "song," that is, in celebration of becoming, as the liminal center of our human growth:

> Raise no commemorating stone. The roses
> shall blossom every summer for his sake.
> For this is Orpheus, his metamorphosis
> in this one and in that. We should not make
> searches for other names. Once and for all,
> it's Orpheus when there's song. He comes and goes.
> Is it not much if sometimes, by some small
> number of days, he shall outlive the rose?
>
> Could you but feel his passing's needfulness!
> Though he himself may dread the hour drawing nigher
> already, when his words pass earthliness,
>
> he passes with them far beyond your gaze.
> His hands unhindered by the trellised lyre,
> in all his over-steppings he obeys.
>
> (1977:95)

The last line, "in all his over-steppings he obeys," suggests that liminal creativity is obedient to what is coming into being rather than to what has been. It represents moral as well as aesthetic poesis, the "making" of new codes of conduct which may seem to transgress the morality of the structural order, that "morality" which implies conformity with generally accepted standards of goodness or rightness in conduct or character. Which is also the morality of the person, not of the individual.

A Surplus of Signifiers

I want to leave these deep waters where person and individual merge in the abyss of the presently unknowable—until it makes itself known as Orpheus—and focus on that upper level of liminality where the ordering of persons confronts the disordering and reordering potential of individuals, often in the guise of play but usually with serious moral intent. The triad of the Orphic (beyond play and order), the serious (including the liturgical), and the ludic (the world of play and the Trickster) occupies a good deal of liminal space/time—at least in its complex cultural aspect. The social aspect—simplified dyadic structures on the one hand, and communitas on the other—abandons itself to at least these three modes of cultural offering and dismembering.

In cultural history the structure/antistructure ratio in ritual shifts from preponderance of the former to that of the latter as societies gain in scale and complexity, as the division of labor becomes finer and more professionalized, and as the spheres of work and leisure become more clearly demarcated after industrialization has asserted the supremacy of clock time over the cycle of the seasons and the sundial and hourglass. These major sociocultural changes have radically influenced the types and styles of cultural performance.

During the 1970s, the authors I have discussed—Schoffeleers, Burridge, Zuesse, Sutton-Smith, Schwartzman, and others—created the possibility of extending the analysis of the properties of liminality to the study of morality in social and symbolic action. A further important contribution should be mentioned which throws new light on the semantics of ritual, particularly of its liminal symbolism, and hence on the cultural devices men and women use to discover meaning in or to ascribe meaning to the ways they develop or terminate their relations with one another, their patterns of mutual use and abuse, friendship and exploitation— their moral dynamics. This is the subject of a valuable essay by Barbara A. Babcock, "Too Many, Too Few: Ritual Modes of Signification" (1978). Drawing inspiration from the Prague school of linguistics, Lévi-Strauss's study of Cuna shamanism in "The Effectiveness of Symbols" (1963), and from Jacques Derrida's important paper, "Structure, Sign, and Play in the Discourse of the Human Sciences" (1970), Babcock criticizes those anthropologists and aestheticians who have identified art and ritual with order and unity, defining the latter for example, as Roy A. Rappaport did (1974:1), as "an attempt to impose logical necessity upon the vagrant affairs of the world." She cites Jameson, Morse Peckham, Roger Abrahams, and myself against this view, and notes that there is a confrontation of order and disorder, or structure and antistructure, in both religion and art.

The originality of Babcock's approach emerges in her discussion of the contrary processes of signification found in ritual and art. She examines my analyses of Ndembu ritual symbols, in which I stressed that some of these, at least the dominant or focal symbols, were multivocal or polysemous, that is, possessed multiple meanings and referents. Indeed, simple signifiers, like the white-sap-exuding "milk tree" used in puberty rituals among the matrilineal Ndembu, may have a wide fan of signifieds—to use Saussure's terminology for denotations—and an even wider polysemous aura of connotative meaning. Babcock suggests that this "surplus of signifieds" is only one mode of ritual signification. Ritual—even, indeed, the same performances in which multivocal symbols are employed—may also involve a "surplus of signifiers" and a "bracketing of signification." Every ritual process, she argues, "involves at least these three modes of signification in differing degrees of emphasis and combination" (1978:292). Put simply, "The relation between signifier and signified may be one to several; it may also be several to one, or one to one, or signification may be suspended altogether" (1978:294).

> Ritual events as well as distinct phases or sequences within a given event are initially marked or framed by a bracketing or ordinary signification. In one of two ways—by literally denying and stripping away *or* by multiplying to the point of indeterminate nonsense—we suspend customary meanings: by fasting or by feasting, by sexual abstinence or sexual license, by nakedness or by costumes of motley, by immobility or by excessive movement, by seclusion or public display, by silence or noise. . . . While bracketing through excess is more frequently the means of framing ludic or antistructural rituals or ritual phases, and denial more generally indicative of the serious and the structural, such is not always the case: priests wear costumes as well as clowns. (1978:297)

Here I would like to repeat that at the "Orphic" level of ritual, which transcends both structure and antistructure, the oppositions described by Babcock become irrelevant, a new arbitrariness appears in the relation between signifier and signified—things cease to signify other things, for everything *is*; the Saussurean significative dualism yields to a basal nondualism where signifier and signified dissolve into indiscriminable existence. Play and work, one and many, seen and unseen, and all other dichotomies become meaningless here, and reveal themselves as cognitive constructions for giving us a small woven shelter against the dark.

Babcock follows Derrida in arguing that

> A surplus of signifiers . . . creates a self-transgressive discourse which mocks and subverts the monological arrogance of "official" systems of signification. [She accepts Derrida's view that a surplus of signifiers calls into question the idea of a single privileged or transcendental signified implicit in serious and official discourse and in the interpretation thereof.] The bantering *anti*-signified of carnivalesque discourse is an insult both to the complementarity of ordinary speech and to the multi-signified of serious ritual communication. It is also a statement in praise and a demonstration of the creative potential of human signification as opposed to its instrumental and representative use. (1978:296)

Reverting to Zuesse's distinction between positive and negative liminality, the refutation of which led me into this long disquisition upon play and solemnity, we may see Babcock's distinction between multivocal symbols which express unity, continuity, and coherence, and symbols that possess "an excess of floating signifiers" (1978:297), as cleaving more closely to the data of liminality seen cross-culturally. She suggests that a dialectic is present in ritual, presumably in rites of separation and reaggregation as well as liminal rites. I quote her summary:

> In ritual, society takes cognizance of itself and communicates its major classifications and categories both through ordering them and through disordering them—by overdetermining *and* by rendering indeterminate customary processes of signification. (1978:296)

It is the individual who generates the multisignifier mode of signification—both of which, says Babcock, "differ from our daily, ordinary use of signs. In contrast to the complementarity between signifier and signified characteristic of normal discourse, ritual communication involves *both* an extremely economical *and* an extremely inflated relation of signifiers to signifieds" (1978:296).

How, then, should we relate these modes of signification to the modalities of human relationship which we have called communitas and social structure? Society, morality, and religion are bound up together as aspects of the Latin term *mores*, which contains the contradictory notions of custom and habit, based on group pressure, and the creative morality which may result from individual choice. Here, again, we should look at Durkheim's formulations, for they have strongly influenced anthropological thought. Durkheim, it is clear, views religion in terms which recall Henri Bergson's concept of "closed" morality and religion, as against "open" morality and religion. The type of religion bound up with closed morality he sees as a symbolic way of expressing socially approved attitudes so as to strengthen ties of mutual obligation. Bergson (in his *Les deux sources de la morale et de la religion*, 1932) argues that the pressure of social obligation combines with what he calls "la fonction fabulatrice," the mythmaking function, to counteract the possibly dissolvent or "deconstructive" effects of the growth of individual critical intelligence. Babcock would see the closed morality produced by obligatory pressures plus mythopoeic functions as being allied with the surplus of signifieds and support of the established tribal or national or civil politico-religious order. But surely something of the *fonction fabulatrice* also permeates the ludic capacity to generate a surplus of signifiers: Both the serious and the ludic can be put at the service of either communitas or social structure, of the individual or the person, and the mythmaking imagination can make both "interesting."

The "open" morality of the individual and the "closed" morality of the person everywhere interpenetrate in actual historical societies. There are not "open" societies (to use Popper's terms) with a pure morality of communitas, nor "closed" ones with a pure morality of roles and obligations. In the late 1960s many dropped out of the new closed societies created by bureaucracy and subtopias and sought to establish in communes and similar groups an open morality of direct individual-to-individual relationships. I wrote at the time (in *The Ritual Process* 1969:138–139), referring to the Haight-Ashbury community in San Francisco:

> For the hippies—as indeed for many millenarian [*sic*] and "enthusiastic" movements—the ecstasy of spontaneous communitas is seen as *the* end of human endeavor. But in the religion of pre-industrial societies, this state is regarded rather as a means to the end of becoming more fully involved in the rich manifold of structural role playing [since communitas is brief, as measured by objective time, though subjectively powerful and the seedbed of many subsequent thoughts, words, and deeds]. In this there is perhaps a greater wisdom, for human beings are responsible to one another in the supplying of humble needs, such as food, drink, clothing, and the careful teaching of material and social techniques. Such responsibilities imply the careful ordering of human relationships and of human knowledge of nature.

The central moral problem, then, is one of achieving a balance or right relation under given circumstances between the aspiration to communitas and the norms of an existing social structure. This balancing process, discussed by Barbara Myerhoff (1976) as an aspect of the power and style of an effective Huichol shaman, seems to have an affinity with Burridge's notion of individuality, which he described as the "opportunity and capacity to move from person to individual and/or vice versa." It is also reminiscent of Kierkegaard's image of the Knight of Faith, who looks like a person but is inwardly an individual, having overcome the contradiction between the Exception and the Mass.

The individual is alienated and anomic insofar as he/she has been extruded from the social-structural matrix; but insofar as he or she "formulates, or is the agent for the formulation of, new rationalizations and new moralities" (Burridge 1979:50), the individual may become a moral innovator. I do not discuss in this essay how the individual may participate in and demonstrate charismatic leadership. In any event the individual asserts his/her autonomy from the current cultural categories, whether they be those of premodern, modern, or postmodern cultural systems. Here the possibility of the amoral exists, as does the possibility that the innovator may substitute for the governing morality, for instance, a set of aesthetic criteria as the "art for art's sake" people do—the Gautiers, Mallarmés, and Wildes; also the possibility of the immoral or antimoral.

Here the liminal may become, for philosophical reasons, the criminal. Dostoevsky in particular worked out the dialectic of events following such philosophical crimes as that in *Crime and Punishment* of Raskolnikov, the alienated student who thought that he would liberate himself inwardly from bondage to the moral law and acquire charisma through the slaying of a miserly and exploitative old woman. As a result, through murder he transgressed not merely the state's law and the moral law, but also the deeper bond of communitas, thereby alienating himself not merely from the social structure but also from humanity itself, and putting himself deeper into bondage to the moral axioms of structure he had sought to annul.

We have seen how in religioritual systems of preindustrial societies, from hunting bands to feudal regimes, the Orphic, the serious, and the ludic, and the symbolic instruments conveying these styles of expressing transcendence and reflecting upon the immanent group's moral condition, were intimately related in unbroken sequences of liturgical events. With the emergence of the individual in complex industrial societies comes the emergence of a number of performative genres which I have called "liminoid" or "paraliminal," in an effort to convey the notion of something that is akin to the ritually liminal, like it but not identical with it. Such genres develop in industrial leisure and include theater, ballet, film, the novel, poetry, different types of music, modes of painting and sculpture, and many more, in both folk and elite culture. In many of them, works are created by individuals for individuals. Participation in them, whether as performer or audience, is voluntary—not obligatory, as in tribal rituals—and they are to a considerable degree deprived of direct transcendental reference.

Many genres have a greater affinity with the tribal ludic than with the tribal serious, with a surplus of signifiers than with a surplus of signifieds. Certain liminoid genres, despite their greater dependence on what Bateson might call "play frames" and the rhetoric of "deconstruction," have been placed in the position of bearing the weight of that moral or ethical reflexivity formerly "carried" in rituals which placed the actual conduct of persons into stark contrast with religious categories which guaranteed the truth of things. Some writers, for example, have called the theater of the absurd "profoundly theological." We may now

be seeing a reversal in the process of evaluation. Now the naked experience of the individual, stripped of categories, may generate artworks
which purport to reveal the venerated categories as illusory or irrelevant
for this age. Or those categories may be defended, as Martin Esslin has
argued that the theater of the absurd has attempted to do, by their apparent deconstruction as unliving words or concepts, the better to reinstate
the experiential truths which have long lain beneath them undetected and
in need of disturbance from long dormancy.

Whether the ludic, deconstructive, signifier-prolix frames within
which individual authors now work can ever be adequate substitutes for
the ritual frames whose symbolic contents and transcendental signifieds
reach beyond both the ludic and the serious to the paradoxes and ambiguities of the creative abyss—that is, in Blakean terms, "in love with the
productions of Time"—is, to say the least, problematic. Abysses are
dangerous because they are alluring. We may be tempted to fall endlessly
down in them from the responsibilities and obligations of the person and
the tasks of the individual—there is even, in Morse Peckham's phrase, "a
rage for chaos." An antinomian freedom may be hankered for, what
Jakob Boehme called "a lusting for the characteristics of the dark world."

This is more than literally incestuous, for it supposes a return to the
womb from which the cosmos itself came forth. But, as Yeats wrote, no
one can, save in self-delusion, "unwind the winding path." The "deep
ground" of the mystics must be sought forward, not backward. And one
suspects that the way forward is really quite simple. As simple as clowns.
My point about individual and person has perhaps best been made by
Federico Fellini, the peerless filmmaker and archindividual. The subtext
of this whole chapter, as the reader has probably guessed, is that life is,
among other things, a circus, where liminal folly may make deep sense,
Orpheus as clown. I will give Fellini's remarks on the famous Odd
Couple, the clown Auguste and the white clown. My only comment is
that its moral, if one call it that, is better than most sermons on forgiveness, that ultimate act of freedom.

> When I say clown, I think of the Auguste. The two types of clown are in
> fact the white clown and the Auguste. The white clown stands for ele-
> gance, grace, harmony, intelligence, lucidity, which are posited in a moral
> way as ideal, unique, indisputable divinities. Then comes the negative
> aspect, because in this way the white clown becomes Mother and Father,
> Schoolmaster, Artist, the Beautiful, in other words, *what should be* done.
> Then the Auguste, who *would* feel drawn to all these perfect attributes if
> only they were not so priggishly displayed, turns on them.

The Auguste is the child who dirties his pants, rebels against this perfection, gets drunk, rolls about on the floor and puts up an endless resis-
tance. [Parents, please note.]

This is the struggle between the proud cult of reason (which comes to
be a bullying form of estheticism) and the freedom of instinct. The
white clown and the Auguste are teacher and child, mother and small
son, even the angel with the flaming sword and the sinner. In other
words they are two psychological aspects of man: one which aims up-
wards, the other which aims downwards; two divided, separated
instincts.

My film *I Clowns*, ends with the two figures meeting and going off
together. Why is such a situation so moving? Because the two figures
embody a myth which lies in the depths of each one of us: the reconciliation of opposites, the unity of being.

Wasn't St. Francis known as God's clown? And didn't Lao-Tse say: "If
you make a thought (=the white clown), laugh at it (=the Auguste)"?

(1977:124–125)

Notes

CHAPTER I.   ENCOUNTER WITH FREUD

This chapter was first published in George Spindler and Louise Spindler, eds., *The Making of Psychological Anthropology*, pp. 558–583. Copyright © 1978 The Regents of the University of California.

CHAPTER 2.   DEATH AND THE DEAD IN THE PILGRIMAGE PROCESS

This chapter was first published in M. Whisson and M. West, eds., *Religion and Social Change in Southern Africa: Anthropological Essays in Honour of Monica Wilson* (Cape Town: David Philip, 1975), pp. 107–127.

CHAPTER 3.   VARIATIONS ON A THEME OF LIMINALITY

This chapter was first published in Sally F. Moore and Barbara Myerhoff, eds., *Secular Ritual* (Assen, Netherlands: Van Gorcum, 1977), pp. 36–52.

CHAPTER 4.   AFRICAN RITUAL AND WESTERN LITERATURE

This chapter was first published in Angus Fletcher, ed., *The Literature of Fact, Selected Papers from the English Institute* (New York: Columbia University Press, 1976), pp. 45–81.

CHAPTER 5.   SACRIFICE AS QUINTESSENTIAL PROCESS

This chapter was first published in *History of Religions* 16, no. 3 (1977): 198–215

1. I am employing the useful Latin term defined by Fowler as a "functional spirit with will-power," not quite a full-fledged deity in a "ripe polytheistic system" (Fowler 1911:119).

2. "Host" is a term which in Latin originally was *hostia*, "an animal sacrificed," before it became a consecrated wafer in the Eucharist—another example of a widespread tendency to switch from animal to vegetable sacrificial codes as the scale and complexity of religions increase.

3. Lienhardt divides Dinka "divinities" (*yeeth*) into two kinds: tutelary spirits, or genii, of descent groups, which he calls clan divinities, and free divinities, which are not in special relationships with descent groups but establish relationships with individuals and, through them, with their families (Lienhardt 1961:30).

4. Lienhardt writes, "The word for the speeches in a court case is the same as that for the speeches at a sacrifice and . . . we see that the 'statements' to which we have referred are in fact full delineations of a situation as it really is or (from our point of view) as the Dinka would wish it to be. 'You of my father, I did not neglect you in the past when my father died, it is not true that I caused confusion in the descent group of my father'" (1961:249).

5. To counteract this, rites were performed on 25 April, when the ear was beginning to be formed in the corn and was particularly liable to be attacked by this pest (see Fowler 1911:100). They took place in a grove or a clearing within it (*lucus*) (1911:146), and the sacrificial animal was a red dog (1911:179).

6. Well put by G. Van der Leeuw when he defined *dare* (to give) in the *do-ut-des* formula (I give that thou mayest give) as "to place oneself in relation to, and then to participate in, a second person, by means of an object, which is . . . a part of oneself (1938:351). Power here flows equally from receiver to giver and from giver to receiver, in a cycle of giving (the "dynamistic theory of sacrifice" of A. Bertholet in his *History of Hebrew Civilization* [1926: *passim*]).

7. These have been learnedly discussed by Irene Rosenzweig in her *Ritual and Cults of Pre-Roman Iguvium* (1937), which was originally her Ph.D. dissertation at Bryn Mawr College.

8. "With the instinct for order and organization that never failed them, the Romans . . . constructed a permanent power to take charge of their *ius divinum*, that is, all their relations to the deities with whom they must maintain a *pax*" (Fowler 1911:271–272). This was the college of pontifices under the pontifex maximus.

9. A *tribus* or district, among the Umbrians and Latins, was divided into *curiae* (*takvias* in Umbrian), or "tenths," and *gentes*, "patrilineal clans," subdivided in turn into "fives" or groups of five families (the Umbrian term is *pumperias*, five households joined in one group).

10. A system of beliefs centered on the notion that an animal or natural object is consanguineously related to a given family, clan, or moiety and taken as its emblem or symbol.

CHAPTER 6. THE KANNOKURA FESTIVAL

This chapter was first published in Peter Duerr, ed., *Sehnsucht nach dem Ursprung: Zu Mircea Eliade* (Frankfurt: Syndikat, 1983), pp. 467–491.

1. The headbands, I was told by Mr. Ueno, the chief priest at Hayatama on my 1981 visit, represent, by their tightness and "straightness," "concentration of mind and spirit."

2. Literally it means "entering the peak." It is used for pilgrimage in Kumano Shugendō.

3. The name Hayatama-no-Ō means "Quick Jewel Male." Spitting was essential in the purification ceremony (*Nihongi* 1972 vol. 1, sec. 26, p. 31).

4. Ichiro Hōri (1969:77) considers Shugendō to consist of a variety of elements, such as popular beliefs in mountains, the *dhûta* practices of Indian Buddhist asceticism, Chinese mythology, Taoist beliefs, the theology and practices of Japanese Tendai and Shingon Buddhism, and the magic and ritual of Shinto.

5. Susano-O-no-Mikoto was the younger brother of the sun goddess Amaterasu-O-Mikami. A god possessing fierce might, he was guilty of disturbing the peace because he was unable to control his own power. After being expelled from the Plain of High Heaven (*Takama no hara*) because of his violent behavior, he conquered a monster called Yamata-no-Orochi (Eight-Headed Dragon) and saved its victim, a young maiden. Thus he changed into a benevolent deity, performed many feats involving the rescue of others, and became a deity especially petitioned for salvation from disasters.

For the above material and throughout the chapter, much assistance was given by Masao Yamaguchi.

CHAPTER 7.   MORALITY AND LIMINALITY

This article, the 1980 Firestone Lecture at the University of Southern California, is published here for the first time.

References

APTER, DAVID
1963. "Political Religion in the New Nations." In C. Geertz, ed., *Old Societies and New States*, pp. 57–104. New York: Free Press.

ARINZE, FRANCIS A.
1970. *Sacrifice in Ibo Religion*. Ibadan: Ibadan University Press.

BABCOCK, A. BARBARA
1975. "The Novel and the Carnival World: An Essay in Memory of Joe Doherty." *Modern Language Notes* 89, Dec.:911–937.
1978. "Too Many, Too Few: Ritual Modes of Signification." *Semiotica* 23, 3/4:291–302.

BABCOCK, A. BARBARA, AND JOHN J. MACALOON
1987. "Victor W. Turner (1920–1983): Commemorative Essay." *Semiotica* 65, 1/2:1–27.

BAKHTIN, MIKHAIL
1968. *Rabelais and His World*. Cambridge, Mass.: M.I.T. Press.

BATESON, GREGORY
1956. "The Message, 'This Is Play.'" In Bertram Schaffner, ed., *Group Processes, Transactions of the Second Conference*, pp. 145–242. New York: Josiah Macy, Jr., Foundation.
1972. *Steps to an Ecology of Mind*. New York: Ballantine. First published 1955.

BELLAH, ROBERT
1973. *Emile Durkheim on Morality and Society*. Chicago: University of Chicago Press.

BERGSON, HENRI
1932. *Les deux sources de la morale et de la religion*. Paris: F. Alcan.

BERTHOLET, A.
1926. *History of Hebrew Civilization*, trans. A. K. Dallas. London: G. G. Harrap.

BLAKE, WILLIAM
1965. *Poetry and Prose*, ed. D. Erdman. New York: Doubleday. Written 1783–1822.

BOWLBY, R.
1969. *Attachment and Loss*, vol. 1, *Attachment*. London: Hogarth.

BRADLEY-SMITH, J.
1964. *Japan: A History in Art*. Garden City, N.Y.: Doubleday.

BURRIDGE, KENELM
1979. *Someone, No One: An Essay on Individuality*. Princeton, N.J.: Princeton University Press.

BURTON, SIR RICHARD
1964. *Personal Narrative of a Pilgrimage to Al-Medinah and Meccah*. 2 vols. New York: Dover. First published 1893.

CHRISTIAN, WILLIAM A., JR.
1972. *Person and God in a Spanish Valley*. New York and London: Seminar Press.

COHEN, ERIK
1982. *The Pacific Islands from Utopian Myth to Consumer Product: The Disenchantment of Paradise*. Aix-en-Provence: Centre des Hautes Études Touristiques.

COSMO, UMBERTO
1950. *A Handbook to Dante Studies*. Oxford: Blackwell.

CSIKSZENTMIHALYI, MIHALY
1975. *Beyond Boredom and Anxiety*. San Francisco: Jossey-Bass.

CURTIUS, ERNST R.
1953. *European Literature and the Latin Middle Ages*, trans. W. Trast. New York: Pantheon.

DANTE ALIGHIERI
1939. *Purgatorio*, Italian text with translation and comment by John D. Sinclair. New York: Oxford University Press.

DERRIDA, JACQUES
1970. "Structure, Sign, and Play in the Discourse of the Human Sciences." In Richard Macksay and Eugenio Donato, eds., *The Languages of Criticism and the Sciences of Man*, pp. 247–272. Baltimore: Johns Hopkins University Press.

DOUGLAS, MARY
1957. "Animals in Lele Religious Symbolism." *Africa* 27, 1:46–58.

DREVER, J.
1952. *A Dictionary of Psychology*. London: Penguin Books.

DURKHEIM, ÉMILE
   1915.   *The Elementary Forms of the Religious Life*, trans. J. W. Swain. London: Allen and Unwin.

FELLINI, FEDERICO
   1977.   *Fellini on Fellini*, Anna Keel and Christian Strich, eds., Isabel Quigley, trans. New York: Dell.

FARMER, LESLIE
   1944.   *We Saw the Holy City*. London: Epworth.

FERNANDEZ, JAMES
   1973.   "Analysis of Ritual: Metaphoric Correspondences as the Elementary Forms." *Science* 182, 4119:1366.

FORTES, MYER
   1961.   "Pietas in Ancestor Worship." *Journal of the Royal Anthropological Society* 91:166–191.

FOWLER, W. WARD
   1911.   *The Religious Experience of the Roman People*. London: Macmillan.

FREUD, SIGMUND
   1950.   *The Interpretation of Dreams*. New York: Random House.

FRIDELL, W. M.
   1973.   *Japanese Shrine Mergers, 1906–12*. Tokyo: Sophia University.

GEERTZ, CLIFFORD
   1972.   "Deep Play: Notes on the Balinese Cockfight." *Daedalus* 101 (Winter):1–37.

GENNEP, ARNOLD VAN
   1960.   *The Rites of Passage*. London: Routledge and Kegan Paul. First published 1909.

GIRARD, RÉNE
   1977.   *Violence and the Sacred*. Baltimore and London: University Press of America.
   1982.   *Le bouc émissaire*. Paris: Bernard Grasset.

GRANT, MICHAEL
   1971.   *Roman Myths*. New York: Scribner's.

HANDELMAN, DON
   1951.   "The Ritual Clown: Attributes and Affinities." *Anthropos* 76:321–370.

HANSON, ALLAN
   1975.   *Meaning in Culture*. London: Routledge and Kegan Paul.

HERTZ, ROBERT
   1973.   "The Preeminence of the Right Hand." In Rodney Needham, ed., *Right and Left*. Chicago: University of Chicago Press.

HŌRI, ICHIRO
   1969.   *Folk Religion in Japan*, ed. J. M. Kitagawa and A. L. Miller. Chicago: University of Chicago Press.

HUBERT, FR
  1962. *The Knock Apparition and Purgatory.* Knock Shrine Annual Pamphlet. Knock, Ireland: Knock Shrine Society.

HUBERT, HENRI, AND MARCEL MAUSS
  1964. *Essay on Sacrifice,* trans. W. D. Halls. Chicago: University of Chicago Press. First published 1899.

JUNG, CARL G.
  1963. *Memories, Dreams, Reflections,* trans. Richard Winston and Clara Winston. New York: Pantheon.

KEYES, CHARLES F.
  1976. "Notes on the Language of Processual Symbolic Analysis." Unpublished synopsis of a course of lectures, Department of Anthropology, University of Washington.

KING, GEORGIANA GODDARD
  1920. *The Way of St. James.* New York and London: Putnam's.

KITAGAWA, J. M.
  1967. "Three Types of Pilgrimage in Japan." In E. E. Urbach, R. J. Zwi Werblowsky, and Ch. Wriszubski, eds., *Studies in Mysticism and Religion: Essays Presented to Gershom G. Sholem.* Jerusalem.

KNOCK SHRINE ANNUAL
  1968. Knock, Ireland: Knock Shrine Society.

KOJIKI
  1969. Translated by Donald L. Philippi. Princeton, N.J.: Princeton University Press.

LAGRANGE, PÈRE
  1905. *Études sur les religions semitiques.* Paris: Lecoffre.

LÉVI-STRAUSS, CLAUDE
  1960. "On Manipulated Social Models." *Bijdragen tot de taal-, lande-, en volkenkunde* 116, 1:45–54.
  1963. "The Effectiveness of Symbols." In *Structural Anthropology,* pp. 186–205. New York: Basic Books.

LIENHARDT, GODFREY
  1961. *Divinity and Experience: The Religion of the Dinka.* Oxford: Clarendon Press.

LUKES, STEVEN
  1975. *Emile Durkheim: His Life and Works.* Harmondsworth: Penguin Books.

MALCOLM X.
  1966. *The Autobiography of Malcolm X.* New York: Grove Press.

MEAD, GEORGE HERBERT
  1934. *Mind, Self, and Society.* Chicago: University of Chicago Press.

MIYAKE, HITOSHI
  1978. "The Structure of Exorcism in Shugendo." English translation in manuscript of articles in *Henshin,* pp. 175–229. Kobundo: 1975.

MOORE, SALLY FALK
1976. "The Secret of the Men: A Fiction of Chagga Initiation and Its Relation to the Logic of Chagga Symbolism." *Africa* 46, 4:357–370.

MOORE, SALLY FALK, AND BARBARA MYERHOFF, eds.
1977 *Secular Ritual.* Amsterdam: Van Gorcum.

MYERHOFF, BARBARA
1976. "The Huichol and the Quest for Paradise." *Parabola: Myth and the Quest for Meaning* 1, 1 (Winter): 22–29.

NAGAI, SHINICHI
1970. *Gods of Kumano.* Tokyo: Kodansha.

NIHONGI: CHRONICLES OF JAPAN FROM THE EARLIEST TIMES TO A.D. 697
1972. Translated from the original Chinese and Japanese by W. A. Aston, 2 vols. Rutland, Vt., and Tokyo: Charles E. Tuttle.

OTTO, RUDOLF
1957. *The Idea of the Holy: An Inquiry into the Non-rational Factor in the Idea of the Divine and Its Relation to the Rational.* London: Oxford University Press. First published 1923.

PHILIPPI, DONALD L.
1969. Introduction and notes to *Kojiki.* Princeton, N.J.: Princeton University Press.

POMORSKA, KRYSTYNA
1968. Foreword to Mikhail Bakhtin, *Rabelais and His World.* Cambridge, Mass.: M.I.T. Press.

PONSONBY-FANE, R. A. B.
1962. *Studies in Shinto and Shrines.* Kamikamo and Kyoto: Ponsonby Memorial Society.

RADCLIFFE-BROWN, A. R.
1957. *A Natural Science of Society.* Glencoe, Ill.: Free Press.

RAPPAPORT, ROY A.
1974. "Obvious Aspects of Ritual." *Cambridge Anthropology* 2, 1:3–69.

RILKE, RAINER MARIA
1977. *Sonnets to Orpheus* in *Possibility of Being*, trans. J. B. Leishman. New York: New Directions.

ROSENZWEIG, IRENE
1937. *Ritual and Cults of Pre-Roman Iguvium.* London: Christophers; Baltimore: Waverley.

ROUSSEL, ROMAIN
1954. *Les pèlerinages à travers les siècles.* Paris: Payot.

SAPIR, EDWARD
1935. "Symbols." In *Encyclopedia of the Social Sciences*, vol. 14, pp. 9–15. New York: Macmillan.

SARTRE, JEAN-PAUL
1969. "Itinerary of a Thought." *New Left Review* 58:43–66.

SAYERS, DOROTHY
  1954. *Introductory Papers on Dante*. London: Methuen.

SCHOFFELEERS, MATTHEW, AND DANIEL MEIJERS
  1978. *Religion, Nationalism, and Economic Action*. Assen, Netherlands: Van
          Gorcum.

SCHWARTZMAN, HELEN B.
  1978. *Transformations: The Anthropology of Children's Play*. New York and
          London: Plenum Press.

SINGLETON, CHARLES S.
  1954. *Dante Studies 1: Commedia, Elements of Structure*. Cambridge, Mass.:
          Harvard University Press.
  1958. *Dante Studies 2: Journey to Beatrice*. Cambridge, Mass.: Harvard Uni-
          versity Press.

SMITH, BRADLEY
  1964. *Japan: A History in Art*. New York: Simon and Schuster.

SPERBER, DANIEL
  1975. *Rethinking Symbolism*. Cambridge: Cambridge University Press.

STARKIE, WALTER
  1965. *The Road to Santiago*. Berkeley and Los Angeles: University of Cali-
          fornia Press.

STONE, JAMES S.
  1927. *The Cult of Santiago*. Berkeley and Los Angeles: University of Califor-
          nia Press.

SUTTON-SMITH, BRIAN
  1976. *The Dialectics of Play*. Schorndoff, West Germany: Verlag Hoffman.
          Chapter "Games of Order and Disorder" was first presented at the
          Annual Meeting of the American Anthropological Association, To-
          ronto, in December 1972.

SWANSON, PAUL
  1978. "Shugendō and the Yoshino-Kumano *Nyubi*: An Example of Moun-
          tain Pilgrimage." Unpublished manuscript.

THOMPSON, R. J.
  1963. *Penitence and Sacrifice in Early Israel Outside the Levitical Law: An Ex-
          amination of the Fellowship Theory of Early Israelite Sacrifice*. Leiden:
          Brill.

TURNER, EDITH
  1985. Prologue to *On the Edge of the Bush* by Victor Turner, pp. 1–15. Tuc-
          son: University of Arizona Press.
  1992. "Rabbi Shimon Bar Yohai: The Creative Persona and His Pilgrim-
          age." In Smadar Lavie, Kirin Narayan, and Renato Rosaldo, eds., *Cre-
          ativity in Anthropology*. Ithaca, N.Y.: Cornell University Press.

TURNER, EDITH, AND VICTOR TURNER
  1978. *Image and Pilgrimage in Christian Culture: Anthropological Perspectives*.
          New York: Columbia University Press.

TURNER, VICTOR

1957. *Schism and Continuity in an African Society: A Study of Ndembu Village Life*. Manchester: Manchester University Press.

1961. "Ritual Symbolism, Morality, and Social Structure Among the Ndembu." *The Rhodes-Livingstone Journal* 30:1–10.

1962. *Chihamba the White Spirit: A Ritual Drama of the Ndembu*. Rhodes-Livingstone Papers no. 33. Manchester: Manchester University Press.

1964a. "Symbols in Ndembu Ritual." In Max Gluckman, ed., *Closed Systems and Open Minds: The Limits of Naivety in Social Science*, pp. 20–51. Edinburgh: Oliver and Boyd.

1964b. "Betwixt and Between: The Liminal Period in Rites of Passage." In June Helm, ed., *Symposium on New Approaches to the Study of Religion*, pp. 4–20. Seattle: American Ethnological Society.

1966. "Ritual Aspects of Conflict Control in African Micropolitics." In Marc Swartz, Victor Turner, and Arthur Tuden, eds., *Political Anthropology*, pp. 239–246. Chicago: Aldine.

1967. *The Forest of Symbols: Aspects of Ndembu Ritual*. Ithaca, N.Y.: Cornell University Press.

1968. *The Drums of Affliction*. Oxford: Clarendon.

1969. *The Ritual Process: Structure and Anti-Structure*. Chicago: Aldine.

1975a. *Revelation and Divination in Ndembu Ritual*. Ithaca, N.Y.: Cornell University Press.

1975b. "Ritual as Communication and Potency." In Irma Honigmann, ed., *Symbols and Society: Essays on Belief Systems in Action*, pp. 58–81. Athens: University of Georgia Press for the Southern Anthropological Society.

1985. *On the Edge of the Bush*. Tucson: University of Arizona Press.

VAN DER LEEUW, G.

1938. *Religion in Essence and Manifestation*. New York: Macmillan.

WALSH, MICHAEL

1967. *Knock: The Shrine of the Pilgrim People of God*. Tuam, Ireland: St. Jarlath's College.

WILSON, MONICA

1957. *Rituals of Kinship Among the Nyakyusa*. London: Oxford University Press.

WITHERS, C.

1947. "Current Events in New York Children's Folklore." *New York Folklore Quarterly* 3:213–222.

YAMAGUCHI, MASAO

1973. "Kingship, Theatricality, and Marginal Reality in Japan." Paper presented at A.S.A. Conference, Oxford, July.

ZUESSE, EVAN M.

1979. *Ritual Cosmos*. Athens: Ohio University Press.

Index

About the Author

Victor Turner (1920–1983) is recognized worldwide for his work as an anthropologist and comparative symbologist. His research on ritual and symbolism took him initially to Africa, where he studied amongst the Ndembu, and then to India, Israel, Mexico, Ireland, and Japan as well. In 1963 he left a post at the University of Manchester to come to the United States, where he joined the faculty of Cornell University. During the next years he published *The Forest of Symbols, The Drums of Affliction*, and *The Ritual Process*. In 1977 he moved to the University of Virginia, where until his death he was William R. Kenan Professor of Anthropology and Religion. In these last half dozen years, his interest shifted increasingly from ritual to theatre, from social processes to cultural performances, and from the "liminal" phase of tribal ritual to the "liminoid" of complex, postindustrial society. An earlier collection of essays, *On the Edge of the Bush: Anthropology as Experience*, was published by the University of Arizona Press in 1985.

About the Editor

Edith L. B. Turner, anthropologist author, and poet, edited this volume of her late husband's essays from the perspective of a co-fieldworker. From the time of their first research venture to Northern Rhodesia, she worked alongside Victor Turner, pursuing her own special interest in the women of the various cultures in which they lived. Since 1983 she has been director of Comparative Symbology, Inc., and a lecturer in anthropology at the University of Virginia since 1984.